FURNITURE

FURNITURE

MODERN + POSTMODERN

DESIGN + TECHNOLOGY

SECOND EDITION
JOHN PILE

A Wiley-Interscience Publication
John Wiley & Sons, Inc.
New York / Chichester / Brisbane / Toronto / Singapore

Library of Congress Cataloging-in-Publication Data:

Pile, John F.
    Furniture, modern and postmodern / John F. Pile.—2nd ed.
        p.   cm.
    Rev. ed. of: Modern furniture. 1979.
    "A Wiley-Interscience publication."
    Includes bibliographical references.
    ISBN 0-471-85438-7
    1. Furniture design.   I. Pile, John F. Modern furniture.
II. Title.
TT196.P54   1990
684.1—dc20   90-31000
                                                                CIP

ISBN 0-471-85438-7

Printed in the United States of America

10   9   8   7   6   5   4   3   2   1

CONTENTS

PREFACE TO THE SECOND EDITION

In the 10 years since *Modern Furniture* appeared in 1979, a variety of important changes has taken place in the worlds of architecture and design leading to an explosion of developments in furniture design. The supremacy of the modernism of the 1920–1970 era has been challenged by critics and detractors whose opinions vary from the mischievousness of Tom Wolfe's *From Bauhaus to Our House* (1981) to the serious and thoughtful commentary of Robert Venturi's *Complexity and Contradiction in Architecture* (1966). Whether from serious motives or foolish, many designers have struck out in new directions that have developed in directions so remote from the main line of modernism as to require a new name. The confusing term *"post-modernism"* has come into general use even as some of its major practitioners deny its applicability. In this book, it will have to serve for the revisionist efforts that seek to escape from the restraints of order, logic, and simplicity that doctrinaire modernism imposed.

Efforts to break away from a strong tradition have inevitably spurred counter-reformation efforts to maintain the modernist tradition by developing it with new strengths and new flexibility. While not yet so clearly recognizable as a style, these efforts deserve their own identification with a term—*"late modernism"* will have to do until a better phrase is coined. In the chaos of new terminology, "high-tech" has come into wide use to suggest design that grows out of the mechanistic vocabulary of modern science and technology, particularly in those advanced forms associated with the aerospace industry and with the growing importance of computers and the techniques associated with them. An attempt to generate a parallel counter direction to be called "high-touch" seems to have faltered, perhaps because it was never clear what it meant.

Outside of the terminology of criticism and commercial promotion, the recent decade has brought some major changes in the realities that furniture design serves. Most striking has been the change in offices as they have become an increasingly significant work environment. More than 50% of all employed people are now office workers according to various statistical studies. The earlier office with its many small rooms each furnished with isolated desks, chairs, and cabinets has increasingly given way to the "open office", a work space more like a factory floor with many workers arranged more or less according to the theories of "office landscape" planning. Too much openness has developed new demands for privacy leading to a proliferation of office systems that deal with both visual and acoustical privacy in various ways with varied levels of success. A new understanding of the impact of the workplace and its furniture on health and longevity has brought the concepts of ergonomics into an important role in furniture design. The domination of the computer and its associated wiring and other needs has generated the "electronic office" leading to furniture to suit those needs.

In the world of domestic furniture, the dominance of historicism has slipped away to such an extent that consumer magazines and retail outlets now offer modern furniture in a greater variety (albeit often of poor design and constructional quality) and specialized outlets exist that offer *only* modern design, much of it quite excellent. Supermarket-like retail distribution makes more modern furniture more accessible to consumers than ever before.

Taken together, these developments mean that the settled, even boring status quo of only 10 years ago has turned into something of a ferment with an amazing outpouring of new design constantly surfacing representing various shadings of viewpoint within the design community. Modernism is by no means dead, but its varied forms now require complex and confusing terminology to distinguish directions that are too diverse to be covered by any one term. In this book, the response has been to add many new illustrations and new supporting text to bring the content up to the date of publication. The accelerating pace of change suggests that a third edition may be called for in less than 10 years.

JOHN F. PILE

New York, New York
April 1990

PREFACE TO THE FIRST EDITION

The furniture that appears in my earliest memories, the furniture of my childhood home, came mainly from my grandparents' generation. Several Morris chairs and some massive, sturdy examples of the "mission style" in golden oak were intermingled with the nondescript "traditional" furniture of the 1900s to 1920s and an occasional "reproduction" loaded with medieval carving that related to my father's intermittent Gothic enthusiasms. When, in response to some boxes of German toy building blocks (the marvelous modular *Anchor* or *Union* blocks, now unfortunately no longer made), my interests turned to architecture, my parents entered a subscription in my name to the *Architectural Forum*, making me perhaps the youngest subscriber in that magazine's long history. In 1935, there was not much truly modern architecture visible in that magazine, but what I saw there immediately caught me up in an excitement that I had previously reserved for steam locomotives and aircraft.

Surprisingly, the modern buildings that appeared in that *Forum* often had furnishings totally different from anything in my family's house or any other house I had ever been in. The furniture floors of Philadelphia's John Wanamaker store exhibited nothing like these items, although a few tubular chairs could be seen in the housewares department. It was not until the 1939 New York World's Fair that I was finally able to see, in Aalto's Finnish Pavilion, actual examples of the kind of modern furniture that this book is concerned with. Those bent plywood chairs and tables captured my interest and remained in my memory more strongly than the Trylon and Perisphere. Enrolled in architectural school, my doctrinal enthusiasms for modern furniture became strong enough to lead me to buy my first modern chair, an early Risom design for Knoll using canvas webbing to form a seating surface on a simple birch frame. John Wanamaker was at last carrying this item, yet placed it discretely with outdoor furniture.

My fellow architectural students and I shared a desire to design modern furniture—it seemed almost more important than building as we became aware of the Bauhaus, Mies, and Le Corbusier. I can remember long discussions of the mystery of furniture: how it was put together, what was inside its sealed overstuffed masses, and even how it could be represented in drawings. I made several attempts at drawings, but could find no one with the courage to attempt the construction of a prototype.

Once out of school, my first serious job was with an industrial designer whose practice included interior design work—offices, showrooms and even an ocean liner—and my work began to involve the selection of furniture for these projects. There was not much to select from. Hans Knoll was producing a handful of Risom designs (including my tape-seated chair) and Herman Miller was just introducing the 1946 group of George Nelson designs. Otherwise there was little more than the Artek plywood furniture designed by Aalto and imported. Occasionally, when nothing was commercially available to solve a particular problem, I was drafted into designing something special, perhaps because I was the only one available who showed enough interest (or ignorance) to be willing to try. My first commercially produced piece of furniture was a solitary, small round table with metal legs, which would still be a respectable item in any current product line.

When I left that office to teach, I found a way to fill my idle hours by doing some drafting for Paul McCobb, a designer who was about to become briefly famous for the first decent modern furniture to achieve success as a department store staple. McCobb designed by producing a tiny (but precise) perspective sketch, which he passed to me with verbal instructions about dimensions to the eighth of an inch. My job was to produce detailed (usually full-size) drawings for the factory. My initial fear that my lack of knowledge would be exposed was dispelled when my drawings proved to be far more complete and detailed than anyone in the factory had ever seen (or had any desire to see).

Later, a friend told me that George Nelson had lost his best furniture designer and had an eye out for a replacement. This led to an 11-year association with the Nelson office, constantly involved with Herman Miller furniture. I was often a designer, sometimes my own draftsman and model-builder, occasionally an expediter of others' design production, a liaison between client and factory and, finally, even the firm's treasurer. At least in the earlier years, Nelson's office had a very free, atelier-like atmosphere and was an ideal place to learn from one's own and others' mistakes and successes. My co-workers included a number of people who have subsequently become well known (Irving Harper, William Katavelos, Charles Pollack, Don Petit), and there was a constant flow of visitors whose stays ranged from hours to years, and who seemed to conduct an endless seminar. Buckminster Fuller, Ettore Sottsass, Alexander Girard, Isamu Noguchi, and Charles Eames were there regularly for one reason or another, usually concerned with furniture. My own designs (always discreetly cloaked under the firm's identity) appeared regularly and had lives lasting from one brief showing to many years. The experience of seeing them through the steps from concept to production and distribution, and the same experience in processing other designers' work kept me on a regular schedule of factory visits and meant endless meetings with sales, managerial, and production people at Herman Miller. Probably no other education in the possibilities and problems of modern furniture could have been as complete.

While all of this was happening, I was also usually teaching a course called "furniture design" in one or more design schools as one of my assignments. It is a difficult subject to teach. A furniture designer needs to have some creative ideas about what furniture can and should be, of course; but he also needs instant mental access to a very diverse and miscellaneous mix of information about materials, processes, body mechanics, available gadgetry, and the history of successful and unsuccessful efforts of all the designers who have struggled with furniture problems over the last four or five thousand years.

Compared to the design of large buildings (or even small ones), ships, aircraft, or highway systems, furniture design may seem simple—in a way it is, because each project is of comprehensible and manageable magnitude. A design is usually the work of an individual or a collaboration of two people; it is never the product of the large team typical of major architectural projects or in the "styling studios" of automobile manufacturers. Yet this simplicity is somewhat deceptive. The long history of furniture development and the extensive and personally intimate experience every user has had with familiar furniture generate an extraordinary sensitivity that makes everyone a demanding critic of any new furniture design. Certainly bad furniture is designed and manufactured constantly, but the serious designer does not measure his proposals against commercial and shoddy production. Instead, he is aware of the remarkable successes that are part of furniture history (e.g., Georgian cabinetwork, a simple Windsor chair, the products of the American Shaker societies) and the modern designs that have come to be called "classic."

With these standards in mind, the student of furniture design discovers how difficult it is to propose a new product that offers any real advance over what already exists. He also discovers, with a rough proposal in hand, how hard it is to assemble the dimensional data, information about materials and the ways they can best be worked, and to synthesize all of this in a way that will transform the rough idea into a viable design, ready for production and use. This book is intended to bring together, in one place, as much of the information that the modern designer might need as will fit into a reasonably sized, single volume. In choosing examples to cite and selecting information to include, I have inevitably incorporated my own preferences and opinions. Yet I have tried (in Chapter 3) to explain the basis for these opinions so that it will be possible for the reader to decide rationally whether to agree with me or to disagree totally or in part. In the latter case, aware of the viewpoint that this book represents, the reader can make his or her own mental allowances and may seek other references in compensation.

I would like to express my appreciation to the various employers, co-workers, and students who have helped me learn about furniture and have shaped my point of view. I am also obligated to the manufacturers, designers, publications, and museums that have supplied the illustrative material for this book. Credit is given as completely and accurately as possible, but some material from my own collections of drawings, clippings, brochures, and slides has been difficult to identify fully. A general apology is offered for any errors or omissions of credit that may have arisen from this source.

JOHN F. PILE

New York, New York
September 1978

FURNITURE

1

INTRODUCTION

The Scope and Purpose of This Book

The term "modern furniture" can mean simply recently made or recently designed furniture, or it can designate a special kind of furniture, designed and made recently or currently, but having a particular character that makes it special and different from furniture made in the past. This book is concerned with the latter meaning. Most modern furniture in the first sense is not truly modern at all in the second sense. Occasional surveys made by various magazines concerned with the manufacture and distribution of home furnishings give the percentages of furniture of various "styles" that are being made and sold in a particular recent time period. For many years in the recent past "modern" has always appeared as a minority category, and only within the last few years has it begun to be an important contender compared to other styles such as "colonial" or "French provincial." Most recent surveys show modern furniture still represents less than 50% of that currently made and sold in the United States. In other words, half or more of the modern furniture made is only modern in its date of manufacture.

In every historic period and in each geographical area where furniture has been made to any significant extent, that furniture has been uniquely characteristic of its own time and place. Ancient Egyptian furniture is different from ancient Greek or Roman furniture. Medieval furniture is not easily confused with the furniture of the Renaissance. The well-known styles of the 18th century are readily recognizable and express a point of view typical of that time. Even Victorian furniture, although it sometimes attempts to borrow from earlier times, has its own qualities for better or for worse—often, in our present view, for worse. As the consistency of Victorian attitudes began to fade around the beginning of the 20th century, however, we saw the beginning of attitudes that persist to the present—attitudes suggesting that efficient factory production and remarkable technological developments in materials can be put to use to make objects that imitate those of past periods more or less accurately. The making of furniture rapidly became a field in which design creativity came to be feared. Quality furniture became "antique reproductions" carefully faking the appearance of designs of the past, down to inclusion of "aged" finishes and even newly manufactured wormholes to add a look of "authenticity." Inexpensive furniture followed along with imitative designs that hardly can be said to "reproduce" anything from the past, but which try to suggest past styles with enough imitative detail to justify application of stylistic name tags. "Provincial" or "colonial" are terms that modern American families think of as the normal descriptions for the look of a dining table or a television set.

The modern furniture that this book is concerned with is actually the truly "historic" furniture of our own time because it is designed in a way that is uniquely characteristic of the present time. It is the work of designers who are original and creative and have no interest in the making of reproductions, accurate or otherwise. It is not necessarily "recent" in terms of years, since there are designs that are truly "modern" in character that have been in production for as long as 80 or 90 years. Even long ago these designs showed that the modern era of industrial technology was totally different from the Renaissance or the 18th century and started design development in ways that would both exploit and express the differences.

Modern furniture is usually thought of as having certain stylistic characteristics, but any attempt to list those features must be undertaken with caution. It is possible to think of excellent examples that are exceptions to almost any specific characteristic which might be named. Most modern furniture is mechanistic in character, but there are designs which depend on hand craftsmanship and show that fact very clearly. Chrome-plated steel and glass are favorite materials, but woods that have been in use for thousands of years are even more common. Most modern furniture uses smooth surfaces and is free of decoration, but individualistic decoration is typical of the work of certain noted modern designers. Industrial quantity production is often a stated ideal, but some famous designs, including some that are most "industrial" in appearance, are still made by hand one unit at a time.

With the limited time perspective available to us at present, it is not possible to name visual details that identify a "modern style" in the way that Chippendale or Louis XVI can be identified. Instead, it seems easier to use negative identifying traits. Modern furniture never imitates a past style and is never based on past style in any narrow sense. This does not preclude modern designers' learning from and being inspired by historic examples; it only indicates a refusal to recall appearance for the sake of nostalgia or ostentation. In contrast, the "traditional pieces" produced by many mass manufacturers deliberately try to suggest that they come from some romantic and luxurious past time however absurd this suggestion may be. A Spanish Renaissance television cabinet, a Gothic radio, a French provincial piano, and Early American upholstered living room furniture are all commonplace in the "modern" home. The modern furniture that this book discusses has no relation to this nonsense. Whatever its good and bad points may be, it is always designed in terms of its own time and place.

It is a curious reality that the habit of imitation is so strong in the design of commercial furniture that "modern" is sometimes thought to be one more style that can be readily imitated. As a result, some manufacturers have asked their staff designers to produce designs that imitate "genuine modern" furniture. Just as historic styles are distorted, cheapened and misimitated for commercial production, modern designs can be "knocked-off"* through imitation that almost always misses the point of the original, copies its least significant aspects, and introduces modifications that distort its real values. Such synthetic "modern" furniture is often given stylistic names such as "Moderne", "modernistic," or "contemporary" that seem to recognize its superficial and imitative character. Unfortunately, a large proportion of the "modern" furniture seen and bought by the consumer public is of this sort. In this book, we are not concerned with such furniture except to the limited degree that its method of production may be of interest.

The modern furniture that is worthy of serious interest is almost invariably the work of an individual or, occasionally, the result of a collaboration. It does not come from anonymous groups or from corporate departmental organizations. The people developing it are sometimes craftsmen, sometimes design professionals (very often architects), occasionally engineers or inventors, but whatever their background, they are invariably concerned with the serious possibilities of furniture in both a utilitarian and an artistic sense.

We are accustomed to viewing historic furniture displayed in art museums—not merely because it sometimes carries painted or carved decoration but also because it often can be considered as serious creative art in its totality. It is not only the elaborate and luxurious furniture that was made in the past for aristocratic use

---

* The term "knock-off" is trade jargon for an unauthorized copy.

and display that deserves this attention; a simple Windsor chair can be as worthy of museum display as its contemporary carved and decorated Chippendale or Hepplewhite counterpart. In furniture design, as in architecture, the intelligent solution of practical problems can combine with an expressive development of form to produce a useful and visually meaningful result. As industrialization pushed aside the developed crafts of the 18th century, the possibilities of intelligent design seem to have been largely neglected, so that an effort toward reform was necessary to rediscover what furniture design could be. The details of this reform and the various "movements" involved are reviewed in a later chapter. The end results have emerged as a point of view, a "school," or even a "style" (if we can use that word without implying superficial fashion and change introduced for its own sake) that is as representative of the present era as any of the great historic periods were characteristic of their own times. Thus, in studying modern furniture we are examining an art form as well as a type of utilitarian product.

The art of furniture is, in conventional classifications, a minor art, not to be ranked with the fine arts in importance because utilitarian considerations dominate it so strongly. A comparable utilitarian domination has not prevented architecture from admission to the "fine arts" category, and the relation of furniture to architecture is in many cases so close as to make furniture design seem almost a branch of architecture. Whether minor or not, however, the art of furniture design makes it possible for every user, every householder, to own and use contemporary works of high quality and great interest. Oddly, most householders, most users or "consumers" of furniture, have no interest in this aspect of the things they buy, own, and use. There is an awareness of the appearance of furniture, but that awareness is focused on furniture as a vehicle for display of "taste" in terms of fashion as understood by the consumer magazines and the manufacturers who support them through their advertisements. Furniture becomes an element in household "decor" viewed like fashion apparel as a transient medium for ostentation and whim. Because of its long life, the up-to-date furniture of recent years becomes the dreary burden of ugliness that characterizes the average room interior of the 20th century.

To understand that furniture design is (at its best) an art form, and to view needed furniture as an opportunity to collect objects of aesthetic taste, intellectual quality, and of lasting, almost permanent value, requires a view that the average modern consumer has not had occasion to develop. This view requires some thought, some knowledge, and a degree of lively interest—the kind of interest that the automobile enthusiast brings to his car, the music lover focuses on concerts and records, or the gourmet cook devotes to food.

An effort has been made here to collect in one place a cross section of the information necessary to value, understand, and enjoy the best modern furniture. Also, if the reader has a more technical interest in furniture, the book includes information on the technical aspects of furniture design and construction, data on dimensional standards, and various other bits of knowledge about furniture that have previously been available only in a diverse jumble of catalogs, manuals, and "how-to" books.

This book is not intended to be a how-to text for the furniture craftsperson. Anyone interested in making furniture needs to develop the appropriate skills from specialized manuals and through direct experience in shopwork. It is to be hoped, however, this book will be helpful to craftspeople in designing the projects that they plan to undertake. Skilled craftsmanship can only produce good modern furniture when it is coupled with thoughtful design that may precede shopwork or develop as shopwork progresses. But, however design and craft are combined, only a blending of the two can lead to results of genuine excellence.

Professional designers with background and training in architecture, interior design, or industrial design will also find it useful to have information on the special problems of furniture design gathered together in one place when the time comes to undertake a furniture project. This may occur when a special need surfaces in connection with some other project that cannot be filled readily with any furniture product in current production. It can also arise when an idea for a new and different solution to some furniture problem comes to mind spontaneously—as often happens to designers—possibly as a result of dissatisfaction with some familiar product.

First efforts in furniture design, even when undertaken by designers trained and experienced in other fields, can use all available aids. Possibly because it comes into such intimate contact with the body of the user, or perhaps because it relates to such long traditions, furniture design is very sensitive to tiny variations in size and proportion. It is very easy to design (on paper or in a model) something that seems quite reasonable, and then to discover, on seeing a full-size sample that an ungainly, uncomfortable, or fatally fragile product has been produced. There is no way of guaranteeing that such unpleasant surprises may not occur, but many suggestions are given here that will at least reduce the likelihood of such disaster.

The reader with a serious interest in modern furniture is urged to consider this book as a starting point in building up a library of other furniture related references. Most books on the subject of furniture that have appeared in the past are unfortunately, for the purposes of the modern reader-designer, oriented toward the concerns of antiquarians and collectors. While antique furniture offers certain kinds of hints and suggestions, its value as a collector's item or investment, the focus of so many books on the subject, is of little concern to the modern designer. Frequently, books dealing solely with modern furniture seem to be not much more than scrapbooks of photographs of the designs that appealed to a particular author or editor. The most useful source of more exact data on modern furniture probably lies in the catalogs and brochures that the manufacturers of good modern furniture make available to their customers. In addition to photographs, such literature usually provides dimensions, technical specifications, and in many cases even scale line drawings. A small shelf of this type of literature from the handful of companies that produce a range of good modern furniture can be an invaluable reference.

Literature from the suppliers of materials and parts that go into furniture and from the makers of the machinery used in furniture production can also be very useful. Materials, particularly plastics and finishing materials, are undergoing constant change and development. New manufacturing techniques appear constantly, so that anyone interested in designing for factory production faces a continuing problem in keeping up to date on what is possible and practical. Both design and technical magazines attempt to keep readers current on such matters, but manufacturers' literature is usually more complete and less inclined to the questionable claims of press-agentry. A catalog and brochure library from this source is also a necessary part of a furniture design reference library. Although a short bibliography is provided at the end of this book, new material appears constantly; therefore the reader must make an effort to update the reference shelf at regular intervals.

Perhaps the most useful references are actual pieces of furniture. It is worthwhile to own a few key examples of the best modern furniture that will be readily available for examination of details, measurement of dimensions, tests of strength or balance, and similar kinds of investigation. For those who live in major cities, the manufacturers' showrooms act as virtual museums of furniture design, where it is always possible to study and note how others have solved (or failed to solve) certain problems. Away from commercial showrooms, furniture in use in public places (e.g., airport waiting rooms, college common rooms, office reception areas) or on display in the few retail shops that offer good furniture may be available for first-hand examination. A pocket tape and notebook are always useful for recording key dimensions, sizes of parts, and angles of surfaces. Because of the scarcity of published data, it is worthwhile to collect observed information and any clippings, photostats of book or magazine illustrations, or other similar bits of information in a file for ready reference. This book is illustrated mainly with material that the author has collected in this way over a number of years, but it is impossible ever to have enough information about the specifics of furniture that has been in production at various times.

Objects as commonplace as articles of furniture are little documented and known only in a vague and general way to the general population of users and yet, this pattern is common enough for most everyday objects. The typical householder has no idea of how dishes and glassware are made, and the motorist is not ordinarily able to explain how a car operates, so it may not be surprising that the internal organs of an upholstered sofa are mysterious, that the differences between a comfortable and an uncomfortable chair are inexplicable, or that the best uses of veneered versus solid wood parts are rarely understood.

Knowledge of such matters is essential in designing furniture and useful in making selections among standard products in regular production. With furniture, as with any other artifact of everyday life, more knowledge—especially "rare" and "behind-the-scenes" information—is a source of interest and even entertainment. Using an object without understanding it can never be more than a convenience; using and understanding puts the user into a kind of remote communication with maker and designer, and an interaction results that makes the utilitarian stimulating and, occasionally, exciting.

2

DESIGN BASICS

The modern, technologically developed world that we live in has not developed a clear and widely accepted point of view about how the physical objects with which it is equipped should be designed. The most advanced technological objects do not seem to present much of a problem. We take it for granted that aircraft and submarines, power stations and radio towers, satellites and moonlanders will be properly designed, and, we find that the soundness of their design is manifested in their appearance. We do not always think of the term "beauty" when we look at such things, but that is probably only because that term is too much associated with museums and "fine art." It is not unusual to say that these technically developed objects "look right" or are "handsome." They are, we feel confident, "well designed."

When we turn our attention to the generally simpler objects of everyday life, houses and household objects that fill them, we find far less consistency and assurance. Houses are trimmed with meaningless mass-produced "colonial" doorways and shutters. Kitchens are lined with steel cabinets fronted in plastic imitation knotty pine. Carpets and wallpaper are covered with flowers; linoleum and vinyl tile imitate brick or flagstone. New furniture pretends to have been made in the 18th century with decorative turnings and homespun cushion covers. Electric lights are disguised as oil lamps or candle holders. The television set is housed in a giant "credenza" of plastic on a metal frame complete with false wood grain and imitation wormholes. These are the things shown in the furniture or department store or to be ordered from the mail-order catalog.

Radio and high-tension electric towers take forms developed on the basis of logical engineering. (Photograph by the author.)

The householder makes choices among "styles" on the basis of taste formed by viewing illustrations in magazines, images visible on film and television, and displays in dealers' shops.

Although arrangements are sometimes more rational in offices, schools, hospitals, and other public buildings, we note that the astronauts, freshly returned from the moon, were housed in quarters furnished in "colonial maple" from a mail-order house. If we compare the norms of contemporary household equipment and furnishings with scenes from the 18th century, the Renaissance, or the Middle Ages, we are forced to conclude that we live in a period that has lost its way in design terms. Technological progress and the "high standard of living" that make it possible for so many to have such a variety of conveniences and comforts have also pemitted the production of goods designed in an infinite variety of ways, most of them disastrously ill-considered and foolish.

A modern jet airplane. (Photograph courtesy Cessna Aircraft Co.)

In past eras the problems of making well-designed objects seem to have been technical and economic rather than intellectual. In the Middle Ages or the 18th century, there was no difficulty in developing ideas for admirable houses and household equipment. The sole difficulty was in solving practical problems (heat, light, sanitation) and in making things widely enough available so that most people could benefit from what was possible. In contrast, we live in a time when everyone feels free to develop and express individual taste but when objects of reasonable, not to say excellent, design have become rarities made only by a few specialized makers and distributed only through special channels to a relatively small public that has developed an unusual (in our time) concern for design.

Television cabinet with "historic" details thermoformed in plastic.

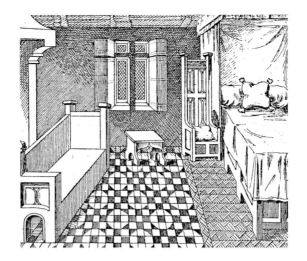

Medieval room interior. (From a 15th-century miniature.)

Renaissance (Elizabethan English) Interior.

The library at Kenwood House, London; by the Adam Brothers, 1767–1768. (Photograph by the author.)

A point of view that makes such a broad condemnation of the preferences and practices of a major portion of the population probably needs some detailed explanation and defense. The view that tells us design matters are "all a matter of taste," that there can be no better or worse in such things, and that every person should choose individually is very widely held and has a certain attractiveness in its analogy with democratic freedom of choice in other areas. It even has a certain attractiveness to designers who enjoy feeling free to produce anything they fancy, secure in a confidence that no one can offer any criticism in a field in which there are no standards.

Actually, there are clear and rational standards of design excellence just as there are standards for musical composition or performance, for literary excellence, or even for good cookery. This is not to suggest that only one right answer to any given problem exists in any of these areas. There can be innummerable good sonatas, good poems, and good roasts just as there can be any number of excellent chair or table designs. The point is simply that badly designed chairs and tables, like bad music, poetry, or cooking are very different from good quality counterparts and that the difference is both important and identifiable. Many people, perhaps a large majority, are content with bad music, bad cooking, and bad furniture. In music and cooking, there is probably less tendency to think that what is popular must be good than in furniture design. Even when we may be at a loss to spell out what makes for excellence in these other areas, we are usually ready to admit that such standards must exist. In the case of furniture (and many other everyday products of modern life) it seems to have become almost routine to believe that there are no standards, no directions that separate better from worse. As a result, it probably is necessary to examine some of the standards that have been recognized and discussed over a long period to see if these are not almost self-evident bases for intelligent evaluation, criticism, and creativity.

The American architect, Louis Sullivan, is usually credited with having said "form follows function," a concept that he actually borrowed from the earlier sculptor and writer Horatio Greenough.* It is a much quoted statement that surfaces in every discussion of what the goals of good design should be. Whether Sullivan (or Greenough) meant that form inevitably *will* follow function, or that form *should* follow function is not certain, but the quotation is used most often in support of the latter view. In its most extreme form this concept leads to a somewhat doctrinal view of "functionalism," which suggests function is the *only* issue that can properly influence design. This view has a certain appeal in its simplicity, and describes with some accuracy how many strictly utilitarian objects are designed, often with excellent results. Military equipment, industrial plants, and many engineering structures (e.g., bridges, electrical transmission towers, or water tanks) might be considered strictly functional designs.

In many everyday objects, houses, automobiles, and most types of furniture, a study of function fails to lead to clearly defined design approaches. A house is used for many different things by different people at different times. An automobile, similarly, can carry

* Horatio Greenough, *Travels, Observations and Experiences of a Yankee Stonecutter*, New York, 1852.

The Salginatobel bridge in Switzerland by Robert Maillart. (Photograph by the author.)

a wide variety of things and people at different speeds on differing roads in differing climates. A chair can hold people of differing sizes and shapes for different lengths of time and for different activities (resting, reading, eating, conversing, napping), and a table will hold whatever is placed on it. In many cases of this kind form determines function, or at least influences it. Our choice of house, car, chair, or table reflects our intended use; but once chosen, the object suggests use.

Intended function and appropriate form have a close relationship. One does not try to drive down a road in a house, eat dinner from a bed, or sleep in a bookcase. Most simple functions (and most furniture functions are relatively simple) can be well served by a wide variety of forms. One can sit on a rock, on a keg, or on the floor. Sleeping is possible on the ground or floor, on an air mattress, in a hammock, or in a bed. Objects can be stored in innummerable kinds of boxes or on open shelves. Thus evaluation of design success on the basis of function turns out to be somewhat limited. It is easier to recognize failures in functional performance than to evaluate relative success. A chair on which it is impossible to sit at all, for any period or for any purpose, would clearly be a functional failure, but is hardly imaginable. To look for maximization of function in objects as simple as chairs is difficult. Are we to try for maximum comfort? In what posture, for what size and shape person, for how long, and at what cost? A large overstuffed chair may offer maximal comfort in some situations, but it will not serve for work at an office desk, or for the passengers in a bus or airplane, nor will it offer much portability or economy. We most often examine such objects to determine if they will serve *some* function, usually a common one, reasonably well. The objects that pass this test of functional merit will be of very varied design merit. In fact, it is not uncommon to find that something which is very badly designed is quite successful in terms of basic function. Almost everyone has some acquaintance with a wonderfully comfortable chair which has nothing to recommend it except its comfort. Anyone who can say "that chair is very comfortable, but hideous" is admitting that function is not, in itself, a complete guide to design excellence.

What other considerations are involved in design excellence? What of the useful chair that breaks in ordinary use and is in the repair shop many times until it is discarded, broken again, in the attic or garage? What of the desk that shakes and rattles when one writes (or types) on it? The strict functionalist theorist might argue that these problems spoil the object's functioning, as they do, and that they are merely another aspect of functional problems. Still, we note that a different choice of material, a better joint or an extra brace could deal with problems of this sort with no basic changes in overall form or dimensions. These are technical prob-

The typical "ugly but comfortable" overstuffed chair and sofa. (From a Larkin Bros. catalog of 1925, author's collection.)

lems relating to structure, manufacturing techniques, and craftsmanship in relation to materials. In analysis of any design, it usually seems logical to separate considerations of function from those of structure while admitting that these two values interact very closely. Poor materials, bad craftsmanship, and shoddy manufacture are not necessarily indications of bad design if they are simply problems that need correction. A design cannot assure quality control in manufacture, but certain kinds of design error can defeat all efforts at quality in production. Even if it is perfectly made, a desk with legs that are too thin for their material and without appropriate bracing will be inclined to shake in use. Shelves of certain plastics will, if heavily loaded, be subject to "cold flow" and develop a permanent sag that will inevitably be unsightly. We are led then to add to our list of design criteria the need for wise and appropriate choices of materials and manufacturing techniques. No one word sums up these considerations as neatly as "function" covers all aspects of utility, but "structure" serves fairly well if we understand the term to include material specification as well as its deployment.

It is still possible to visualize an object that serves a function adequately and is well made of suitable materials but is nonetheless unsatisfactory as an example of design excellence. Think again of that comfortable but monstrous chair that we have all encountered. It is perfectly possible that it is well made, sturdy, and lasting, but that it is still undeniably objectionable in some other way. We say that it is ugly, monstrous, ungainly, or hideous to suggest that, in spite of its comfort and sturdiness, we find the chair lacking in some other way. What do we mean when we use these other terms that seem to mean only "I do not like it"? How can we recognize ugliness, ungainliness, or monstrosity if we have no defined index of what these terms mean?

It is, of course, possible that such terms are being used in an illogical and arbitrary way. We may dislike the looks of our ugly chair only because we have been educated to like or dislike certain kinds of appearance for no clear reason. Perhaps our parents, teachers, or the magazines we have read have conveyed to us certain arbitrary points of view that we hold out of habit. Such "tastes" explain in part the real liking that many people feel for badly designed objects, and the deep suspicion that frequently greets new concepts. The systems of preferences that are called "taste" vary with time and place, and it is not unusual to discover that one's own taste has changed with time and experience. The Victorian era tended to favor elaborate decoration, dark and gloomy coloring, and tall, narrow shapes. The resulting overstuffed interior now strikes us as heavy, stodgy, and a bit depressing. Modern preferences for smooth surfaces, open spaces, and clear, bright colors may eventually seem similarly dated.

It is, nevertheless, a mistake to brush aside all of these matters as merely whims and to suggest that all design decisions are equally good (assuming that functional and structural requirements are met) as long as they please some audience. Within the vocabu-

A characteristically cluttered Victorian interior.

lary of Victorian taste there were better and worse designs, and there are better and worse designs being developed and produced now. The elements of difference that we are discussing here are usually called matters of "aesthetics," questions of what seems better or inferior to the visual sense and the other senses insofar as they are involved. "Feel" is often important in relation to furniture, while hearing, smell, and taste usually have little significance. Are the sensory reactions that we have to the objects around us really only matters of arbitrary likes and dislikes, preferences based only on learned "tastes" or randomly determined preferences? If so, all discussions of aesthetic values become pointless and have no more meaning than the discussion of the merits of various flavors of candy or ice cream. Any design becomes acceptable if it is attractive to a public, however large or small, that finds it desirable.

This is the point of view on which modern industrial production is based, the point of view that has made objects of any real design quality so rare in the modern world. The difficulty with all efforts toward a more serious attempt to raise aesthetic qualities, to make things truly "beautiful," is that we lack any clear standards and well-accepted directions to pursue in seeking these objectives. Philosophical discussions of aesthetic values rarely seem to relate effectively to the real activities of the working designer. The branch of psychology called "experimental aesthetics" has not produced working guidelines that are any more effective than some simple rules of thumb that have been known for thousands of years. Even those rules (e.g., color harmony, systems of proportion, need for "balances") are of surprisingly limited use in practice. It is too easy to find examples that violate all such rules and are striking successes, or that observe the rules and are totally without interest. Thus the temptation is strong to throw up one's hands and revert to the attitude that says, "I will do what pleases me and call it 'aesthetic' because I like it." Before we surrender and accept this viewpoint, however, it is worthwhile to examine the familiar analysis of design purpose that we have been paraphrasing.

Vitruvius, the Roman architectural writer (known through his translator Sir Henry Wotton, 1568–1639*) is usually credited with the statement that good architecture (and by extension, good design) results from the qualities "commodity, firmness and delight." These terms closely match the modern concepts of function, structure, and aesthetics and continue to serve as a well-stated summary of the values which, although interrelated in practice, have enough independence to be recognizable separately as characteristics of any object. Excellence in function and in structure are easily identifiable qualities. There may be some disagreement about whether a

* From *The Elements of Architecture*, 1624.

certain object is fully or ideally functional (the comfort of a certain chair, for example). There can be similar disagreement as to what material and structure will do a particular job best, but whatever the disagreements, there is ready consensus about what these objectives are and that they are desirable objectives.

It is the third value of "delight," or aesthetic success that leads us away from consensus and into the confusions of variable taste. The chair exhibited in a museum of modern art as an example of aesthetic success may strike a typical museum visitor as laughable or repulsive. Yet the chairs in that visitor's home will never find their way into the museum, much as they may please their owner. Even the "authorities" who direct museums, edit magazines, and teach in design schools encounter such drastic disagreements about the merits of different designs that it is impossible to rely on an established body of accepted authoritative opinion.

Perhaps Vitruvius, Wotton, and those critics who have accepted their analysis have led us into a trap by misidentifying that third value of "delight." Delight is not an attribute of an object; it is a human reaction that results as much or more from the makeup of the human viewer as from any characteristics of an object. To attempt to build into a design qualities that will reliably delight everyone, or even a large majority of viewers and users in unknown places on into an infinitely extending unknown future, is to attempt an impossible and an absurd task. This does not mean that there is no "third quality" beyond function and structure. Rather, the third quality has been misidentified, or at least mislabeled. We must look for a better identification for that quality by considering what it may be in more basic terms. The qualities that we are discussing are those that present themselves to the viewer-user's senses. A chest of drawers may hold its contents satisfactorily (function) and be sturdy (structure) without offering anything constructive to the user's vision (and to his other senses when they are involved). To ask what an object can offer to human senses, let us first consider the functions of the senses.

This question may seem too obvious to merit discussion, yet the answers are not always instantly forthcoming. It may be helpful to ask first what the basic usefulness of the human senses (and the senses of the other "higher" animals) may be. They are clearly parts of the biological organism developed by the evolutionary process as aspects of the species' (and so of the individual's) biological equipment to aid survival. The survival and success of the human species cannot be explained on the basis of size or strength, or as a matter of numbers. The dinosaurs were larger; lions, tigers, and horses are stronger; ants and roaches are more numerous (and probably better organized), and yet humanity appears to be more powerful and more successful. The usual explanation notes the larger size and better performance of the human brain with its ability to favor adaptation through superior problem-solving ability.

The brain is an information-processing unit. It depends on a supply of information to be stored for future reference and also as the raw material for the problem-solving function. The primary source of information (probably the only source) is the intake of data through the use of the senses. We know what our world is like, what we are like ourselves, and how we relate to our world as a result of what we see, feel, hear, and so on. Even the knowledge that comes to us secondhand through reading, pictures, and similar means is only internalized and made available to our thought processes through the senses.

Over the tremendous span of time during which the brain and senses of animals and of the human species developed, the realities that existed to be dealt with were what we now call "natural"—the earth and the living things that inhabit it. Human beings began to alter that natural environment in any important way, to invent and to make things in such recent time (in biological terms) as to be insignificant. Our minds and our senses are equipment for dealing with our natural environment through knowledge, understanding, and appropriate adaptation. Although invention, technology, and all the developments that make up "civilization" have transformed the world we live in, our senses, brains, and adaptive abilities have not had time to change significantly. We use our senses to learn about and understand the humanly modified world in exactly the same way that earlier generations used them to deal with the natural world.

When human beings invent and make objects, those things become subjects for sensory exploration and for understanding in the same way that natural circumstances always have been. We know about the earth, plants, animals, and the phenomena associated with them as a result of looking and thinking about what we have seen. We learn about human activity in the same way. We know our way around our home, our town, and our country, and we understand roads, buildings, automobiles, tables, and chairs mainly because we see them, feel them, and can remember and think about the data that our senses have collected.

Man-made objects differ from objects in nature only in that the human maker has an active part in the aspects of the things made that will be sensed by observers and users. A tree grows as it does for its own species survival-related reasons, and we bring our observation and understanding to it in a one-way process of information intake. When we consider our awareness of table or chair, we realize that a two-way process is involved. The inventor/designer/maker has given it a form that makes it useful, but which will also be seen and thought about by the viewer/user. As viewer and user, we are learning about the object in question, and are also aware that its form is not the consequence of an inevitable evolution, but is the result of conscious, human decisions. We are in touch not only with the object but also with its human creator. Designed objects are thus a channel of communication between people quite as much as language, writing, or the arts. Our knowledge about people and situations in remote times and places stems largely from our ability to inspect the physical objects made in those times and places. This form of communication is very effective. One can understand the middle ages better by visiting a cathedral, a castle, and a preserved village than by reading a book. Our understanding of our own time is derived chiefiy from our daily relationship with the innumerable things that make up our largely artificial environment.

Every designer, in attempting to solve practical problems by inventing new forms for useful artifacts, is inevitably creating forms that other people will see, interpret, and try to understand. He or she is thus communicating personal ideas about the object being developed and also, to some degree his ideas about what human life and human civilization is or should be. This aspect of design is its "third dimension," beyond utilitarian function and satisfactory structure. It is an aspect that can be considered "aesthetic" if we understand that term to mean more than superficial liking. As in the fine arts, likability is only an incidental quality of a work while the communication of meaning, thought, and point of view is the essential element of worth.

The elements that we think of as making up form, shape, color, texture, and so on are able to convey meaning in a direct way that is more immediate, effective, and reliable than verbal communication. We can truly know an object, a building, a town, city, or countryside best by direct, sensory experience. As we use things, we come to know and understand them, establish a relationship to them and, in an indirect way to their designer/maker, although that person may be remote in place and time. An old chair, table, or cabinet is a source of understanding of its time of origin and of the thinking of its designer. If we enjoy it in some way, we are in touch with the skill, intelligence, and effectiveness of the person who created it. In our own time we can note the objects around us that relate similar skill, intelligence, and sound intentions. Unfortunately we can also observe how objects may put us in touch with the ineptness, stupidity, greed, and mistaken intentions of their designers and makers. This becomes the basis for reasonable criticism of design and establishes guideposts and directions for the working designer in the search for problem solutions that go beyond simple utility and become artistically creative as well.

Evaluation of any design may thus be structured in ways similar to the following pattern.

Functional Issues

Will the object serve its purpose well? Even if the primary answer to this question is "yes," are there secondary practical problems that make its success less than total? Under this heading one may also investigate such matters as safety considerations (what is currently called "environmental impact"), side effects of use that may be disadvantageous. Does the object consume materials, burn a fuel, or use energy; if so, does it do this efficiently and with a minimum of objectionable waste products? Can it be cleaned, maintained, and repaired easily? All of these questions comprise a first evaluation, a screening to discover if the design in question satisfies the most obvious criteria by doing the things that called it into being with a minimum of troublesome effects. Many objects, even utilitarian ones, are more difficult to evaluate in these terms than might be expected because intended uses are not always sharply defined. A building erected as a rental speculation is intended to serve any tenant who chooses to rent space in it, and the needs of the tenants may vary greatly. Similarly a drawer chest is intended, in most cases, to contain anything that the owner may put into it. One can evaluate a special purpose object more precisely than a general purpose design. A file cabinet must hold filed papers of specific sizes, but a residential storage cabinet or shelf unit must be suited to a wide range of uses.

In both of the above mentioned cases a spurious function is often discussed, the desire of the owner of the building or the manufacturer of the furniture to see the design "make money." This kind of verbal play gives rise to some confused thinking. No utilitarian object makes money in the sense of this being its real function, unless the object is a coining press or a bank-note printing press—either of which, while literally making money, might or might not "make money" for their owners by generating profit. Generation of profits is not a true function; it is a side effect that may result from the sale or rental of an object in our economic system according to complex relationships between the utility of the object, the need of users for it, its scarcity, and other similar economically determined values. An object of excellent functional utility may not "make money," yet objects that are worthless in these terms can be profitable to someone. This is not to suggest that someone's desire to make money may not be a motivating force in the production of objects, including items of excellent design—it often is—but that is a different aim from the desire to produce functional or any other design excellence. The two may work in parallel to produce excellence and profits, but excellence can also appear in a nonprofit context just as profits can be generated by foolish, worthless, and destructive plans of action.

It is a reasonable functional criterion, with economic connections, to expect that the cost of using an object falls within a range that the anticipated user will find acceptable. First cost, the cost of making and distributing an object, falls between functional considerations and the next set of values, as discussed below.

Issues of Structure and Material

If a design has passed our first test of functional usefulness, we may then ask if it is well made. The separation of this issue from functional criteria often becomes unclear when it is pointed out that things must be well made in order to work well. Yet this separation is a useful one conceptually, in critical analysis and possibly even more in the creative process of design. The invention of a problem solution, or of a form that will serve a purpose, often comes before selection of materials and structure and can be quite apart from it. One can imagine, for example, thinking of a new and better way to arrange elements to make up a folding chair without thinking specifically about whether it would be made of wood, metal, or plastic. Perhaps the same concept could be used in any or all of those materials. The specifics of the realized object would, however, have to consider materials and processes and use them well. A different choice of materials will lead to a different object, even if the same concept in functional terms is used in both. An aluminum rowboat is conceptually similar to a wooden rowboat, but is specifically different and must use different details to be successful. Choice of material can effect function in important ways, but unlike materials can often serve the same functions or functions that differ only in slight degree. The wooden and aluminum rowboats can be used for the same purposes, but one's choice of which to own might be influenced by intended use. A wooden and a metal version of similar chairs are often produced with the choice left to the purchaser or user on the basis of his or her understanding of the relation of the material to the intended function.

We have an intuitive grasp of what quality means in terms of materials, workmanship, and structure, and tend to value excellence even beyond what is required for utility. Often, precise workmanship and neat exterior finishes are not strictly necessary to make an object useful. An automobile would still do its job if its exterior were made of crudely assembled scrap materials rather than of smooth polished paint and chrome, but we tend to prefer the latter as evidence of competence in manufacture. We also accept the idea that there is a reasonable limit to the quality needed for a given purpose. We do not expect the precision craftsmanship of a watchmaker in the building of a barn or shed. Obviously, an airplane requires more care in construction than a wheelbarrow.

Materials and structure also have economic impact. Rare and expensive materials lead to high first cost and may have no particular functional advantage. We still accept the idea that a gold watch, a marble building, or a stainless steel and leather chair have their place even though cheaper materials can perform in similar ways. We tend to be interested in economy to the extent of appropriateness for intended use rather than as an absolute virtue. Yet first cost is only one aspect of economy. Better materials and workmanship, even if more costly during manufacture, can reduce repair and maintenance costs and increase durability and useful life so that more expensive approaches are often economic in long-range terms.

We have assessed a design in terms of basic function, structure, materials, and workmanship and are ready to approach the last phase of evaluation.

Communication of Meaning Through Form

Communication of meaning through form or (if we can avoid being misled about the meaning of the word) "aesthetics"—these two sets of criteria discussed above are part of the accepted working vocabulary of a wide range of designers outside the fields that consider design to be an art-related activity. Engineers design bridges, ships, aircraft, and satellites on the basis of intended function and the technicalities of materials, structure, and mechanism. The resulting forms are often successful in aesthetic terms, but only as an incidental (although highly probable) by-product of technically motivated decisions. Furniture can be designed in this way too; stockroom shelving, drafting tables and stools, army cots, and similar furniture products are developed without thought for visual character. The results are erratic in aesthetic terms—occasionally excellent, but often indifferent. If we assume equal success in functionaland structural terms, how can we evaluate design excellence in this third way in engineering works, in utilitarian furniture, or in the more thoughtfully designed furniture that this book is primarily concerned with? It becomes a matter of observing whether the forms that the object presents to our senses puts us in direct and clear touch with the functional and structural intentions of the designer and whether his or her way of organizing these forms makes individual communication strong and forceful.

We are accustomed to deriving pleasure from seeing and understanding natural things—skies, rocks, flowers, insects; we are moved by the realization that everything about these natural situations has significance even when we do not fully understand what that meaning is. We find the same kinds of meaning in the best painting, sculpture, and music. It also exists for us in architecture and other utilitarian design where the relationship between utility and expressive meaning is, at best, similar to that relationship as we recognize it in nature.

The bridge, ship, bench, or stool of technically successful design but less successful form is usually unclear, ambiguous, confused, and noncommunicative. It does not seem to symbolize itself in a way that is easy to retain in memory and to explore for levels of meaning. Design excellence in aesthetic terms is a matter of clarity and precision, of expression of reality and intent so that a utilitarian thing stands for more than its everyday self. Evaluation in these terms cannot be any more precise than assessment in terms of function and structure, but it is by no means merely a matter of expression of whim or taste influenced by the chances of changing fashions. There is never *one* right answer to a problem in any of these terms, but the difference between better and less good proposals becomes very clear as soon as the general direction of objectives is recognized.

In the hope that it may make this analysis clearer, several examples of historic and recent furniture designs are presented here with a discussion of design evaluation attempted in terms of the criteria discussed above. The reader may find it interesting to collect other examples and attempt a similar analysis to test the usefulness of the concepts suggested here.

1 Windsor Chair

This term refers to the generic type, but the specific example illustrated here is the one under discussion.

FUNCTION

Extraordinary comfort, despite the hard materials used, is characteristic of Windsor chairs. The shaping of the seat tends to reduce concentrations of pressure on the body, and the typically short seat reduces the likelihood of constriction at the back of the knees. The back structure permits body conformity, while the lines of the individual spindles are not felt under the lesser pressure that the body exerts on the back.

STRUCTURE

Structural ingenuity is at the heart of the success of the Windsor chair. The widely splayed legs tend to spread outward under load, but this spreading action locks in the ends of the stretchers as they come under tension. Both legs and stretchers are turned with increased thickness where they are to receive other members, re-

A Windsor chair from Washington's Mt. Vernon.

duced thickness where they are to meet and enter other members. The back is a cantilever structure in which triangulation is subtly used—visible only in true side elevation. The spindles are placed in compression and the curved outer member in tension as pressure is placed on the back. Simple techniques of turning, carving, and assembly generate a light structure of extraordinary strength and durability.

VISUAL EXPRESSION

The unique appearance of the Windsor chair is entirely generated by the problem solution outlined above, particularly by the structural approach that makes a small amount of light material remarkably effective. It is hard to imagine that the form would ever have come to mind as an abstract visual fantasy. Generated by mainly technical and craftsmanly considerations, the expressiveness of its performance and constructional origins are memorable and, for most users and viewers, extremely likable. Although the basic type of Windsor chair was made by many chairmakers, the simplest ones usually share a visually impressive directness. Efforts to make Windsor chairs in quantity in factory production, although quite common, never seem to produce chairs of good visual quality. When the direct contact of the craftsman-maker with the problem and its solution through the direct working of material is eliminated, the product loses some element of expression that turns it into a crude copy of some handmade original.

2   Victorian Reed Organ

This organ was exhibited at Centennial Exhibition of 1876 in Philadelphia; a much-illustrated example of the extremes of Victorian taste.

FUNCTION
The working parts of the reed organ, like those of the modern electronic organ are small, internal and easily absorbed into the unit needed to give the player control. The control parts, keyboard, stop knobs, pump pedals, and music stand must be of certain sizes and placed in specific relationships to make playing possible. These functional requirements are easily met in this and virtually all other designs for similar instruments.

Mason and Hamlin organ exhibited at the Philadelphia Centennial of 1876.

STRUCTURE

Wood box construction houses the parts and holds the elements used by the player in a proper relationship. The simplicity of the problem offers no particular challenge and the solution is adequate here.

VISUAL EXPRESSION

Our amazement at this design, easy to acknowledge with the wisdom of hindsight, arises from the fact that the external design is rich in elaboration that has no relationship to the modest realities of the object. The complex, almost architectural forms suggesting windows, galleries, gables, and crockets are totally arbitrary clothing wrapped around the basics of the instrument inside. The strong impact of the complete object is undeniable, but it diverts our thinking from what the object really is. The Victorians, we must assume, enjoyed being coaxed into fantasies of Gothic mystery, religiosity and, perhaps, horror. Respect for music and the contribution that this modest and homely instrument could make to musical performance is pushed aside by the designer's demand that we admire his or her (spurious) historical knowledge and virtuosity in adapting the vocabulary of medieval stonecutting to the woodwork of his instrument case. It is difficult to imagine that the carved external forms would ever have occurred to the inventor or maker of the musical mechanism inside. It is even hard to believe that these forms would have been developed by a craftsperson with a real knowledge of and respect for his material. Instead, we are confronted by forms that must have been produced in drawings on paper, isolated from the work of production. We suspect that the efficiency of some newly developed woodworking machinery, powered carving machines working automatically to reproduce stock patterns, stimulated such design. The purpose was to offer to the newly expanding and newly wealthy middle class access to what they supposed was a reproduction of the richness that had only been available to royalty (and the ecclesiastic equivalents of royalty) in the past. The intention of this design is to create or further a certain kind of mythic thinking, an attempt to make dreams real.

3 Tubular Armchair of 1925 by Marcel Breuer (Often called the Wassily chair in homage to Breuer's friend, Wassily Kandinsky).

FUNCTION

The body-contact surfaces of seat, back, and arms are planes of stretched canvas or leather that provide a limited amount of stretch to give body conformity and a degree of spring or "bounce" in response to movement. Heights and angles are planned to accom-

Breuer's Wassily chair of 1925. (Photograph courtesy of Stendig Inc., New York.)

modate modern postures of relaxed seating. The comfort of the chair is excellent, surprisingly so to anyone who assumes that only massive cushions and springing can provide ease for lounge seating.

STRUCTURE

The seating surfaces are stretched, and tension in the material provides the springiness needed. The support structure is of bent chrome-plated steel tubing, positioned as required to hold the membranes under tension at the appropriate heights and angles. The form reduces the number of parts, bends, and connections to minimize production cost, while ingeniously positioning the support tubes so they will not make body contact. Except for touching the fronts of the arms with the hands (an optional contact), the user does not make contact with metal at all. The chair weighs only 35 lb—a comparable armchair with conventional upholstery may weigh three or four times as much. Cost is about half that of a comparable conventional chair produced in similar quantity and marketed through the same distribution channels. Theoretically, greater economy is possible if the design were produced in sufficient quantity to justify highly efficient mass manufacturing techniques.

VISUAL EXPRESSION

Although the design is now more than 50 years old, it continues to surprise anyone seeing it for the first time. Expectations based on the familiar mass of upholstered armchairs generate skepticism about the possibility of comfort. Experience with the chair's good functional performance converts the initial shock to admiration. The clarity of concept, using only two materials with each assigned a distinct function—membrane for body support and linear tube for structure—makes the form a direct outgrowth, a kind of visual diagram, of the approach used as problem solution. Color and texture contrast between the two materials emphasizes the characteristics of each and leads to a deeper appreciation of the strengths, textures, and other dramatically contrasting qualities. Interestingly, this was the first (or one of the first) tubular metal frame chairs ever attempted and it remains an outstanding example of the type.

4 Molded Plywood Chair by Charles Eames

FUNCTION

Heights and angle of seat and back surfaces are positioned in two versions, one for upright seating for dining or desk use (illustrated), the other for low lounge seating. The hard seating surfaces are given improved comfort by curvatures that approach body contours and so distribute pressure. In addition, wood parts are connected to the frame with rubber shock mounts that permit a limited amount of movement and adjustment to changes in body position. Easy maintenance and good durability result from the wear-resistant materials.

STRUCTURE

Like the Breuer chair discussed above, this chair separates the body support parts from the structural frame and uses materials chosen as optimum in each role. Similar designs were also developed using molded plywood for the support parts as well as seat and back, but they lack the clarity of separation of the two-material chair. The seat and back are of molded plywood, layers of veneer stacked and molded to shape under heat and pressure in a press.

Molded plywood chair by Charles Eames, 1946. (Photograph courtesy of Herman Miller, Inc.)

The steel frame uses four simple pieces held together by three welds. The difficult problem of connecting the thin plywood parts to the frames was dealt with by bonding to each plywood part several rubber shock mounts (two for the back, three for the seat) which contain an embedded, threaded insert. Screws run through holes in the frame into these inserts. Seat and back can be removed easily for stock storage, shipping, or repair. One structural problem remains unsolved: because of the in-line position of the two mounts holding the back, it is possible (by pushing back and down on the top edge of the back) to tear off the rubber mounts from the plywood. Although normal use will not cause this to happen, it is not an uncommon occurrence. A third mount or some other means of restraining the possibility of rotation of the back would eliminate this hazard.

VISUAL EXPRESSION

The clarity in the separation of functions and assignment of materials (as with the Breuer chair) makes this chair highly expressive. The fact that the body support parts have rounded, "organic" shapes heightens the clarity of articulation. Various woods are used for face veneers, including some that are deeply grained (e.g., ash). The random variation in grain patterns means that no two chairs are identical and gives each an element of uniqueness.

5 "Steelframe" Storage System

This system was developed by the author for George Nelson and Company, technical development by George Mulhauser.

FUNCTION

General storage for household use is provided in drawers, sliding door compartments, and on open shelves. The system includes various combinations of these three types of enclosure so that the user may make a selection to suit individual needs within an overall pattern extending through all units. Tops are either plastic or (where the top compartment is open) glass for easy maintenance.

STRUCTURE

The key concept behind the development of this system is the elimination of the conventional wood box into which other boxes (the drawers) slide with the resulting weight and cost of double walls. Here the structure is a cage of steel angles welded together in a way that suggests the steel structures of modern building construction reduced to the scale of furniture. The drawers and shelves are wood, since production in this material is economical

Steelframe *furniture group. (Photograph courtesy of Herman Miller, Inc.)*

and wood surfaces seem more suitable for household applications (as compared to the metal components used in office furniture). The steel cage structure is sufficiently stiff not to require any bracing with panels of diagonal members, and permits unusually open access where drawers and doors are not required.

VISUAL EXPRESSION

The cage structure is entirely visible externally and appears linear compared to the solid elements of drawers, doors, and back panels. To emphasize the clear separation of structural support in one material as distinguished from enclosure, the frames are either black or white. These "noncolor" colors show up as "serious" and technological by implication. In contrast, the drawers and doors are painted in bright, clear, primary or near primary colors. This tends to lighten the "serious" or "industrial" implications of the exposed cage structure and makes the units easier to relate to residential interiors. The variety of colors makes it possible to generate groupings with many different kinds of visual character (a black frame with all blue drawers, for example, is very different from a white frame holding a red-orange drawer and yellow sliding doors). The colors are also related and can be used together successfully. It is interesting that later versions with natural walnut drawers appear heavy and clumsy.

The drawer pull is the only mildly playful element in this design (developed by Gerald Gulotta as a simple metal sculpture). Its value to the whole can be tested by imagining the substitution of a stock round knob, an alternative that would certainly not be objectionable but would tend to make the total impact "ordinary" and banal.

6 Desk and Storage System by Warren Platner

FUNCTION

This system was developed for use in the executive offices of a corporation housed in an outstanding modern building. It provides the work and conference surfaces for normal office use, and storage through a system of supports, shelves, and case units that can be assembled in a variety of ways. This makes it possible for each user to have a unique storage assembly suited to particular needs and simultaneously establishes a consistency between various offices in the same group. It also permits future rearrangements as users' needs (or users) change. A special telephone unit is a part of the system, so that the phone and related buttons are neatly housed without cluttering a desk or storage unit and without visible dangling wires.

Office furniture developed by Warren Platner for use in the MGIC Plaza building in Milwaukee. (Photograph courtesy of Knoll International, New York.)

STRUCTURE

Cast steel feet and steel tubular supports reduce the structural parts to minimum size. The off-center desk support allows maximum clearance for feet and legs. The desk top is wood-edged to provide a sturdy surface with a pleasant feel; the actual desk top and case fronts are leather, since that softer material can be expected to hold up satisfactorily in these locations.

VISUAL EXPRESSION

There is a clear intention to harmonize the desire for lightness and delicacy that the designers associated with the character of the building with the traditional desire for a sense of luxury in executive working areas. These units are meant to appear impressive without being massive or unduly ostentatious. Their large scale and the fine materials used convey a sense of luxury, while the lightness of the forms avoids an oppressive feeling. The unit construction of this storage system is clearly expressed so that it is immediately recognized as adjustable, but the modular relationship of the parts is sensed so that there is no suspicion of makeshift or temporary character. The natural colors of the wood, metal, and leather surfaces relate to each other and establish a quiet, unobtrusive background. Thus one expects stronger color to come from other objects, plants, works of art, or the occupants of the room rather than from the furniture.

7 "Jefferson" Chair and Ottoman by Niels Diffrient

FUNCTION

A lounge or reclining chair provided with various accessories that make it adaptable for relaxation and rest, for television watching, but, unlike most similar chairs, for reading and serious work as well. The range of adjustability of the chair permits semi-reclined positions, but also supports a more nearly upright posture relating to the accessory elements available to carry the keyboard and CRT

The "Jefferson" armchair. (Photograph courtesy SunarHauserman)

screen components of a computer. Any computer-related work becomes possible while seated in a chair of luxurious, ergonomically planned comfort. Other accessories provide for task light and extra table surfaces for reference materials, ash tray, coffee cup, pencils, note pad, and other incidentals.

STRUCTURE

The chair uses cast aluminum side frames with tubular steel cross members and a formed steel spine. Armrest and headrest supports are die castings. Plastic shells for the seating elements support foam filled, removable cushions. The tilt mechanism uses a gas-filled pressure cylinder, the head rest a spring-loaded cylinder, both operated by controls mounted on the arm. The auxiliary units are supported by cast aluminum bases with tubular steel support columns holding fiberglass tablet surfaces.

VISUAL EXPRESSION

The design expresses the complexity of its varied functions through the marked separation and articulation of the many elements. The chair looks as functional and complex as it really is, but the relationships of the elements in form and position holds the totality together in a way that is comprehensible and not so overly mechanistic as to be forbidding. The "soft" forms of the cushions, arms, and headrest are immediately understandable as suggestive of comfort so that most viewers are attracted and curious to try the promised functional benefits, not repelled by a sense of a forbidding "machine for sitting."

8 Hannah Office System by Bruce Hannah

FUNCTION

A complex modular office work station system designed to make special provision for intensive "electronic office" functions relating to computer use and other electronic communication devices and their associated wiring. Work stations can be planned to accommodate almost any conceivable variety of electronic and conventional office equipment and panels can be arranged to provide varied levels of screening ranging from full openness to fairly complete privacy screening. Task lighting and many accessories for varied types of storage and display are part of the system. The unique functional provision of this system is the very large wireway spaces that are provided within a box-like wiring raceway in the lower portion of the lengthwise "spine" combining units. Wireways branch from this spine within the panels of individual work stations to serve equipment wherever it may be located.

A Hannah office system installation. (Photograph courtesy Knoll International, New York.)

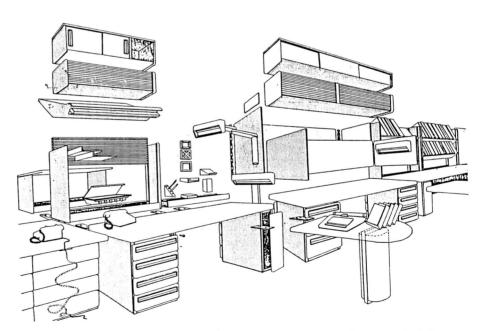

The Hannah office system—a group of components shown in an exploded diagram. (Illustration courtesy Knoll International, New York.)

STRUCTURE

The basic material is sheet steel formed into boxes and structural profiles. Drawers are of a tough fiberboard with a black vinyl plastic surface. Drawer fronts and cover panels are a glass filled, molded plastic. Worktops are particleboard cores with veneer or plastic laminate surfaces. All of the elements are prepared for on-site assembly with simple tools.

VISUAL EXPRESSION

The system has a strong and unique visual character, more apparent in actuality than in photographs. As compared to other office systems, the Hannah System suggests the strength and efficiency of industrial equipment while the plastic surfaces and softened corners avoid any sense of excessive harshness. Complexity is present, at least in installations that exploit the system's electronic capabilities, but confusion is under control. The materials and certain components, the ribbed cover panels in particular, hint at the design direction often called "high-tech" with its recall of the laboratory or other technical facility. An office using this system develops a visual character that conforms to the realities of the modern "electronic office" facility.

9 Chairs by Robert Venturi

FUNCTION

These are "side" or dining chairs providing usual upright seating position for dining or writing at a table.

Robert Venturi molded plywood chairs; "Art Deco," left and "Sheraton," right. (Photograph courtesy Knoll International, New York.)

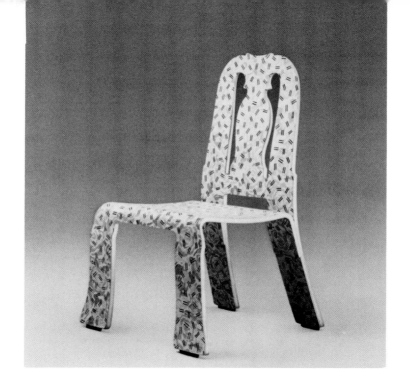

Venturi "Queen Anne" chair with "Grandmother pattern" floral surface decoration. (Photograph courtesy Knoll International, New York.)

CONSTRUCTION

Molded plywood is used to produce the two pieces which form the simple structure of these chairs. The molding is, in both cases, a simple one-way curvature bend with one piece forming the seat and two front legs, the other piece the back and back legs. The two pieces are assembled with a broad adhesive joint below the rear of the seat on either side. Each piece is cut out to form a strong silhouette and the back surfaces are perforated to further modify the basically simple forms. Surfaces are variously veneer and laminates with decorative color patterns as options. An optional cushion pad is available covered in a wide variety of fabrics and leathers.

VISUAL EXPRESSION

These chairs present a strong, startling, even shocking image generated by their cut-out forms and colorful surfaces. Each forms a kind of full size, three dimensional cartoon-like reference to a historical precedent—not a particular design that is imitated, but a sketchy recreation of the spirit of a Queen Anne, Chippendale, Empire, Sheraton, or Art Deco ancestor. The intention is playful, a bit humorous, and clearly intended more to create visual (and, perhaps, mental) stimulation than to provide utilitarian seating. The stylistic term "post modern" seems to apply although the designer does not favor it.

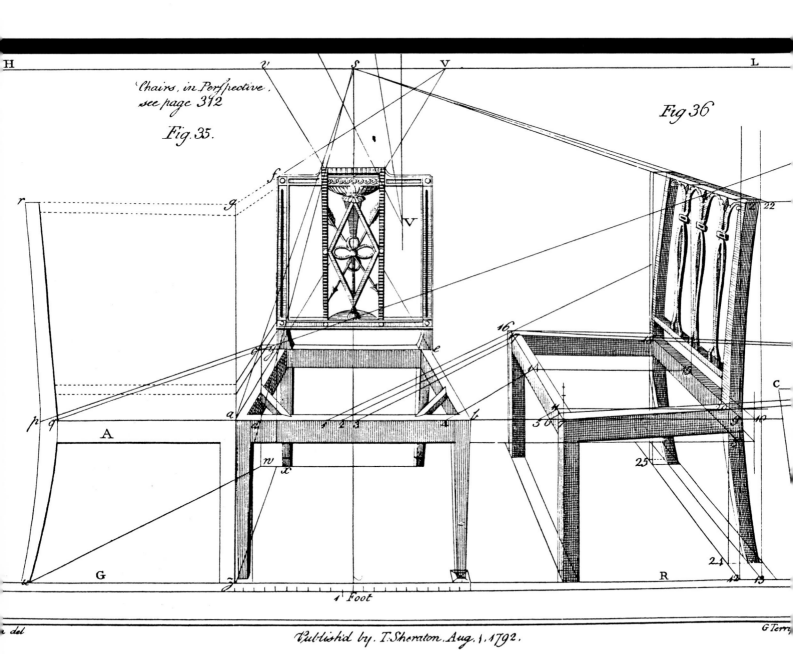

H · · · v′ · · s · · V · · L

Chairs, in Perspective.
see page 312

Fig. 35.

Fig 36

Published by T. Sheraton, Aug. 1, 1792.

1 Foot

del

G Terry

3

HISTORICAL BACKGROUND

Before searching out the origins of modern furniture, it may be helpful to consider briefly the origins of *all* furniture. Insect and animal architects and builders are not unknown (wasps, many birds, beavers build nests or houses), but furniture seems to be a human invention. The upright human posture may have been a stimulus. Walking and standing lead to tired feet and the desire to sit or lie down. The ground surface is a longer trip down and up again for humans than for other animals, and the hands are several feet above the ground, making a raised surface helpful for many kinds of manual work. Despite these realities, human beings seem to have lived without furniture, at least in the current sense, until only a few thousand years ago and a fair proportion of the world's population still functions with little or no such equipment. Even such complex and highly developed societies as that of Japan have avoided or minimized the dependence on furniture that Western civilizations take for granted.

It is quite possible and probably more desirable physiologically to sit or squat on the ground or floor and to use simple bedding on the same surface. However, once furniture is introduced into a society, it seems destined to become widely accepted. In recent years even Japanese culture has adopted "Western style" furniture to a large degree, to the detriment of the aesthetic quality of the Japanese interior and, probably, of health in that country.

Three different determinants encourage development of furniture, and usually tend to act in consort, as follows:

1. A desire to seek improved comfort through the use of inventions rather than through bodily training. When walking in the woods, one sits on a log or a stone to avoid the dust and damp of the ground and to make getting down and up easier. This is surely the beginning of the endless inventions that have the same aim in more and more elaborately developed forms. Beds and bedding may be assumed to have the same point of origin.

2. Other technological inventions can often be better used on raised surfaces than on the ground. Tools suggest a work-bench. Writing and its implements suggest the desk. Complex food preparation and service in dishes suggest the table. Accumulation of tools and implements and the materials that they process suggest the need for storage. Shelves and boxes in various combinations become essential to "civilized" humanity with its astonishing collection of gadgetry.

3. Although these practical issues are certainly real, they do not totally explain the fact that some developed cultures operate with a minimum of furniture while others focus strongly on furniture as a key possession. Everyone knows it is possible to live successfully on a camping trip with only the objects that will fit in a backpack, yet watching the loading of the van (or vans)

Traditional Japanese interior without furniture. (Drawing from Edward S. Morse: Japanese Homes and their Surroundings, *courtesy Dover Publications, New York.)*

when a modern family moves suggests an astonishing dependence on a vast collection of complex and bulky furniture items. This dependence may be mainly symbolic or ceremonial. We know that a throne is a king's vital symbolic possession. The word "cathedral" derives from "cathedra," the bishop's *chair* which it was built to house. An important element of many governments is the "cabinet." Simple civilizations where furniture serves only practical needs get along with a few stools, baskets, and boards on horses. Our furniture serves to bolster egos and demonstrate "taste" (for better or for worse) with its implications about social and economic ranking.

It is not surprising that ancient Egyptian civilization created complex and thoughtfully designed furniture. It was a bureaucratic and rigidly ranked civilization, one that developed and used a great variety of complex objects and sought elaborate comfort for its upper classes. It also was a civilization that, through its funerary customs, arranged to preserve a vast collection of its everyday objects in a remarkable way that makes them available for modern study. Egyptian chairs, beds, and even cosmetic cases are all available for our inspection in museums even though they were made from materials that could hardly have been expected to last for thousands of years under normal conditions of use or storage.

By contrast, ancient Greek furniture is best known to us from illustrations, most often vase paintings, which often conventionalize or omit realistic detail. Similarly, ancient Roman furniture is known to us through paintings rather than examples, although the availa-

A grouping of ancient Egyptian furniture. (Courtesy of the Metropolitan Museum of Art, New York.)

ble information makes fairly clear reconstruction possible and reminds us that our own ideas about posture are not the only and inevitable ones for a developed civilization. To eat, we sit upright on chairs while the Romans preferred to recline.

Although these civilizations (and others, such as that of ancient China) developed complex furniture, modern European furniture is not derived from these beginnings. After the collapse of Rome, furniture reverted to its minimal and primitive beginnings and only reappeared in complex, developed forms as the medieval era moved into its own kind of complicated and rich civilization. Sigfried Giedion, in *Mechanization Takes Command,** begins his account of the modern chair with a discussion of the medieval developments that head the succession of events leading to modern furniture.

Medieval furniture of a functional sort was restricted to simple stools and benches, boards on trestles ("the groaning board"), storage boxes, and beds. The last were often built into alcoves because of the severe winters in northern Europe. Trunklike box chests were the universal storage device and were also often used as a place to sit. The chair, at first mainly a ceremonial seat of honor, emerged as a special form of box or chest modified with back and arms to make a setting for formal, upright sitting. Most medieval furniture that has been preserved was part of aristocratic or religious settings and often shows elaborate carved decoration. Everyday furniture has largely disappeared, but painted and drawn

* Oxford University Press, 1948 (also available in reprint by W. W. Norton 1969).

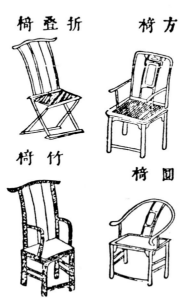

Examples of traditional Chinese furniture types.

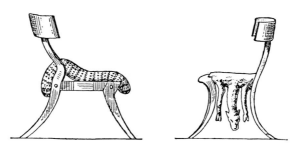

Ancient Greek chairs. (Drawings developed from vase paintings.)

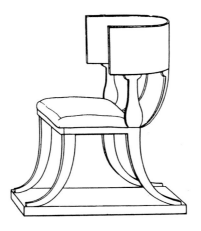

Chair from ancient Rome.

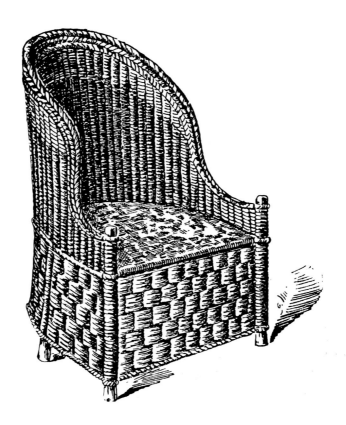

An ancient Roman chair of wicker.

*Medieval chair clearly derived from a storage chest.
(Photograph courtesy of the Metropolitan Museum of Art,
New York.)*

*A simple storage box made elaborate
by the rich overlay of Renaissance
carved decoration. (Photograph
courtesy of the Metropolitan Museum
of Art, New York.)*

illustrations of that time suggest it was not only simple, but that there was very little of it. Even the castle or palace was very empty by modern standards, with only a few pieces of furniture used to augment built-in benches, window seats, and storage niches.

The Renaissance added to this pattern of medieval austerity a few ingenious furniture types (e.g., folding stools and chairs), but was otherwise known for increasing the quantity and elaboration of furniture rather than for any other striking innovation. However elaborate the decoration of chairs and "credenzas" might become, the basics of comfort and convenience remained relatively primitive. Only as the Renaissance ended, particularly in the 18th century, was there a beginning along the line of development that sought physical comfort and practical convenience in improved and, in many cases, complex furniture. More varied seating types began to appear, sofas with arms and chaises, upholstery was improved and cabinet furniture began to develop toward more functional specialization with the appearance of many kinds of drawer chests, desks, and "secretaries."

Concurrent with the appearance of these technical developments, external embellishment turned toward the idea of "style" as something imitative of past or distant times and places. Elements of classical architecture entered the furniture world to be joined by various exotic elements, particularly the "chinoiserie" that reflected increased knowledge of the Orient derived from increasing travel and trade. The famous furniture "periods," of such great interest to antique collectors thus combine extraordinary development in

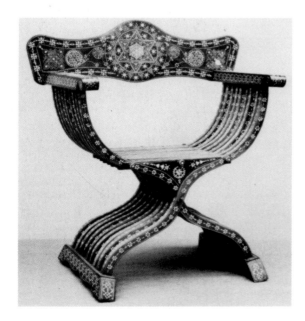

An elaborately decorated example of the Italian Renaissance folding chair. (Photograph courtesy of the Metropolitan Museum of Art, New York.)

Louis XV era comfort combined with aristocratic ostentation. (Photograph courtesy of the Metropolitan Museum of Art, New York.)

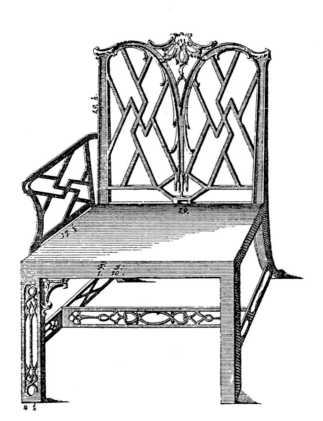

Thomas Chippendale in Chinese mode. From the 3rd Edition of The Gentleman and Cabinet-Maker's Director *of 1762.*

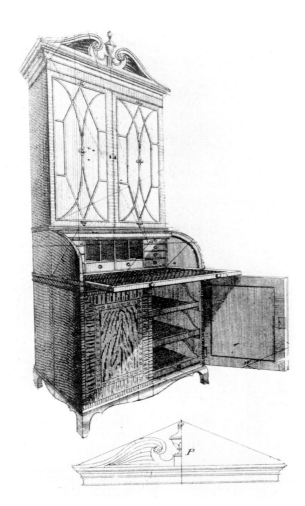

18th Century elegance and practicality: A "Cylinder Desk and Bookcase" from Thomas Sheraton's Cabinet-Maker's and Upholsterer's Drawing-Book *of 1791–1794.*

craftsmanship and inventiveness with ideas about visual design that have come to seem archaic. However admirable they may be in their own ways, the forms of elaborate furniture developed for European aristocratic classes seem remote from the ideas that have led to modern furniture. On the other hand, with an increasingly affluent middle class, simpler kinds of furniture combining the ideas of comfort and convenience with a less pretentious visual expression began to appear.

American beginnings coincide with this time period and were often closer to this burger tradition than to the "high styles" of the French and English aristocracy. The Windsor chair, developed in England and widely made in America, and the practical pine furniture of New England were often truly functional as well as handsome. Unfortunately, the vogue for "Colonial" imitation tended to mimic the more aristocratic styles that became common in America when an aristocratic class emerged (whatever the intentions for a "classless society" may have been), frequently with a dismal lack of success.

An early American chair which converts into a table. (Photograph courtesy of the Metropolitan Museum of Art, New York.)

American Windsor chair of 1750–1775. (Photograph courtesy of Metropolitan Museum of Art, New York. Gift of Mrs. Russell Sage, 1909.)

The modern furniture discussed in this book is not the result of a smooth evolutionary development from these origins, but is rather the product of a kind of revolution—a new beginning in design attitudes. The reasons for this break in developmental continuity lie in the developments of the 19th century, which made modern furniture possible but were used to generate a chaos of historic imitation. The term "industrial revolution" describes the rapid acceleration in science, invention, and technology that had its beginnings during the Renaissance, but which came to full fruition in the mid-19th century. Availability of iron and steel, the development of the steam engine, and the rapid advances of industrial production brought about a tremendous change within a very short time. Objects of all sorts could be made cheaply in vast quantities, and a "consumer public" emerged ready to acquire and take advantage of the new products of industry. The craftsman cabinetmaker and upholsterer began to be replaced by the furniture factory. The desire of the average man to own as much and as elaborate furniture as only royalty could have afforded in the Middle Ages could now be satisfied. In the Victorian era, furniture manufacturers developed a vast variety of elaborately decorated designs that challenge historians to find appropriate stylistic designations. "Rococo revival," "Italianate," and various other styles, more or less based on earlier historic precedents were produced along with designs that

A Victorian chair of characteristically ornate design as illustrated in a magazine advertisement. The frame was black walnut, the upholstery fabric crimson and gold damask according to the accompanying text.

An upright piano manufactured by the English firm of Collard & Collard in "Rococo" style as exhibited at the 1851 Crystal Palace exhibition in London and illustrated in the exhibition catalogue.

were quite original but invariably heavily decorated in styles that may be called "General Grant" or merely, when other words give out, "Victorian." Technological advances led to the introduction of springs in upholstery and mattresses, the use of brass and iron tubing for bed frames, and clever mechanical inventions for reclining chairs, convertible sofa-beds and even, in one instance, a piano convertible into a bed. Designer–manufacturers, such as John Henry Belter (1844–1863), introduced techniques of production using laminated veneer which was pressed and carved to generate the ornate forms that the increasingly affluent middle-class demanded. New functional needs led to the development of such new furniture types as the office desk (typically a roll-top with complex storage provisions) and swivel chairs for office workers and managers.

The Victorian interior stuffed and overstuffed with comfort, elaboration, and useless detail became the setting of middle-class life while the wealthy turned to increasingly accurate and elaborate imitation of past styles. Gothic castles, French chateaus, and Georgian manor houses, reproduced with some accuracy had to be filled with furniture of the appropriate imitative style, and furniture factories became adept at producing "periods" in quantity at department store prices.

Invention and industrialization provided the potentialities for a new kind of furniture; disgust with the absurdities of stylistic imitation provided the motivation for the revolutionary break that led to its development.

A number of "premodern" developments in the 19th century gave some advance notice of what modernism was to be. In America the religious sect called "Shakers" developed (out of religious belief) communities in which buildings, furniture, and equipment were all conceived for practical efficiency and entirely without decoration. Although the movement was small and closely contained, some furniture was manufactured and sold to nonmembers and

Functional simplicity in American Shaker work of the 19th century. (Photograph courtesy of the Metropolitan Museum of Art, New York. Purchase 1966. Friends of the American Wing Fund.)

became known as a special example of how directness and simplicity could generate its own kind of beauty. In recent years Shaker furniture has been widely admired as a surprising example of a modern design concept that appeared long before any "modern movement" had even been thought of.

In England, William Morris (1834–1896) and the Arts and Crafts movement that he led, proposed an abandonment of the Victorian absorption in decoration and imitation through factory production. Morris urged a return to medieval craftsmanship as a basis for making all sorts of goods, including furniture, which, while not necessarily totally simple in style, would have the advantage of expressing the skill and directness of good workmanship. "Arts and crafts" tended to become a style per se and, in its rejection of any relationship to industrial production, was doomed to a limited role. Society was not about to give up the economy of factory made production in exchange for Morris's ideals of aesthetics and quality. The movement, however, had a strong intellectual influence among later designers, and became a kind of ancestor of modernism. The term "Morris chair" for the armchair with an adjustable back tilt that became a common household object of the Victorian era remains a reminder of Morris's role.

Another reformer, Charles Locke Eastlake (1836–1906) who followed after Morris encouraged a more ornamental direction with what he called the Art Furniture Movement. Eastlake's book *Hints on Household Taste* (1868) urged a "tasteful" style that would be less ornamental than the typical production of the Victorian era, although his ideas of simplicity now seem elaborate and clumsy to modern view. In America, the Eastlake style was taken up by a number of manufacturers, such as the Herter Brothers in New York, and became one more variant on the prevailing ornamentalism of the Victorian period.

In Europe a different kind of movement emerged as a pioneering effort to escape from historic imitation as the only approach to design. The name *art nouveau* is used to identify an approach to architecture and every other kind of design, including furniture, that turned to nature for inspiration rather than to craftsmanship. The Belgian Henri van de Velde (1863–1957) was the most vocal theorist of this movement, and was joined by another Belgian, Victor Horta (1861–1947), and the Frenchman Hector Guimard (1867–1942) in work of similar originality. Art nouveau was a style of flowing curved forms based on plant shapes of stems and leaves. Although the major work was architectural, art nouveau designers typically completed their buildings with interiors outfitted down to the smallest details with objects of consistent design. If door handles and light fixtures were all to be specially made, it is not surprising that a new vocabulary of furniture was also developed. The ideas behind art nouveau were based in the fine arts, and its ac-

Desk and chair of c. 1900–1903 by Hector Guimard.
(Collection, The Museum of Modern Art, New York, Gift of
Mme. Guimard.)

ceptance was always limited both geographically (it was primarily a
Belgian and French movement) and to an audience of cultivated
and rather special taste. Later, art nouveau was understood as being
simply another style, a fashionable alternative to the older historic
styles. This view seems to have been accepted by the originators,
some of whom lived on and practiced design in less original ways
for many years after art nouveau had been forgotten.

Several other 19th century designers who worked in original and
innovative ways are now often spoken of as exponents of art nou-

Chair of 1895–1896 by Henry van de
Velde. (Collection, the Museum of
Modern Art, New York.)

Chairs and umbrella stand, c. 1900–1905, by Hector Guimard. (Collection, The Museum of Modern Art, New York, Gift of Mme. Guimard. Photograph by George Barrows.)

veau although this historical classification can be questioned on the basis of their isolation from the Belgian-French movement and the character of their work. In Scotland, Charles Rennie Mackintosh (1868–1928) was an architect who also approached the interiors of his buildings (and projects that were strictly interior renovations) with great ingenuity and developed unique furniture that must have seemed eccentric and curious in its own time. In the United States, H. H. Richardson (1838–1886) occasionally designed furniture for his own architectural projects and also represented an independent point of view that was taken up by Louis Sullivan (1856–1924) and his disciple, Frank Lloyd Wright (1869–1959). Wright's importance and influence as an architect is unquestioned, but his furniture design remains a subject for debate. Like the other architects mentioned above, Wright recognized that his innovative buildings could not reasonably accept the kind of furniture that was available through regular sources and was therefore led to design furniture according to his own intentions. He seems to have been aware of Morris and the Arts and Crafts approach, and also to have had

Three chairs by Charles Rennie Mackintosh, 1897–1904. (Photograph courtesy of Atelier International, Ltd., New York.)

H. H. Richardson's design for a chair for the Converse Memorial Library at Malden, Mass.

A "Craftsman" armchair as illustrated in an L. & J. G. Stickley Onondago Shops catalogue of 1905.

Pine chair with plush upholstery by Frank Lloyd Wright, 1904. (Collection of the Museum of Modern Art, New York. Gift of Frank Lloyd Wright. Photograph by George Barrows.)

some sympathy for the commercial "Mission style" furniture developed in America by Gustav Stickley (1857–1942), but his own direction was more individualistic and personal and somewhat forbidding to many observers. Wright used massive wood members in sternly geometric ways and often added his own kind of carved geometric decoration. This furniture was conceived as part of a total architectural interior and can be puzzling and strange when viewed out of context. Wright's work in architecture continued up to his death and was characterized by a continuing development always paralleled by related designs for furniture. His 20th century work is not "premodern", but is an integral part of the modern movement.

It has become customary to speak of all the late 19th and early 20th century work that avoids historicism as part of the art nouveau movement despite the fact that the variety of expression fails to suggest any one common direction. The work of Antoni Gaudi (1852–1926) in Barcelona often includes furniture of fantastic curvilinear form that can readily be related to other art nouveau work. On the other hand, the work of Josef Hoffmann (1870–1955) and the other members of the Vienna-based movement called the Sezession, including Josef Olbrich (1867–1908), Otto Wagner (1841–1918), and Kolo Moser (1868–1918), are so geometric and rectilinear in character as to make the art nouveau label inappropriate. Hoffmann's furniture suggests Wright's designs in some ways, but Wright's work did not become known in Europe until 1910–1911, when an elaborate presentation of his work was published in Holland. Before that date it must be assumed that similarities between his work and that of European designers was entirely a mar-

Chair in carved oak by Antonio Gaudi. (Photograph courtesy of the Museum of Modern Art, New York; Gaudi Exhibition Funds.)

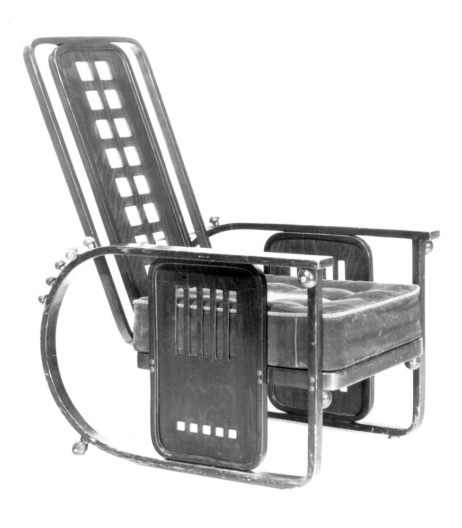

An armchair with adjustable back (of the type often called a "Morris" chair), a 1905 design of Josef Hoffman made by the Viennese firm of J. & J. Kohn.

ter of independent but parallel development. After 1910 direct influence is at least a possibility.

Despite their various efforts to escape from the bonds of historic imitation, none of the designers or movements described so far had any significant relation to the growing domination of industrial technology which was the primary event of the times. Truly industrial furniture appeared without much connection to art and design "movements" in the inventive production of Michael Thonet (1796–1871) and his brothers, whose firm developed the technique of steam-bending wood into curved shapes that could then be screw-assembled into frames for chairs and other furniture products. This technique economized on material and was suited to "production line" factory manufacture. By its nature, it precluded imitation of historic prototypes and forced the Thonet firm to develop truly original designs having a relationship to modern industrial techniques. Bentwood furniture stood outside the world of "artistic"

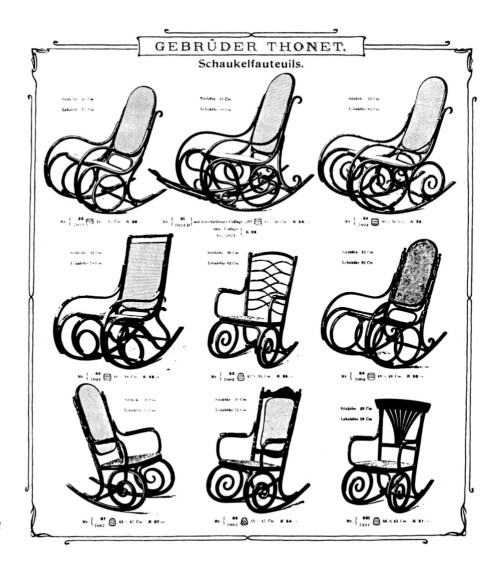

GEBRÜDER THONET.

Schaukelfauteuils.

Page from a Thonet Brothers catalog of 1904.

taste and was regarded as strictly utilitarian. Its acceptance on the basis of practicality and economy was overwhelming. Thonet chairs became commonplace everywhere and remain so today. Recognition that many Thonet designs were also marvelously successful creative achievements had to await the emergence of modern architecture and modern design in the developed sense that those terms now imply.

In 1923 Le Corbusier (the universally accepted pen name of Charles-Edouard Jeanneret, 1887–1965), in his *Vers une Architecture,** set forth in powerfully stated prose the logic that forms the basis for modern architecture and design. At about the same time

* Le Corbusier, *Vers une Architecture,* Editions Crés, Paris, 1923; English translation by Frederick Etchells, The Architectural Press, London, 1927.

Thonet bentwood armchair of 1870; frequently used by Le Corbusier and named for him in recent years. (Photograph courtesy of Stendig, Inc., New York.)

he began to build the handful of early buildings, mostly houses, that illustrate his ideas. Frequently, the furniture that he found appropriate for these buildings was the unpretentious bentwood of Thonet. Indeed, Corbusier's name has become attached to a particular Thonet armchair that was one of his favorites, so it is often supposed that it is Corbusier's design. That design, Thonet's model B-9, was actually developed in 1870, 17 years before Corbusier's birth. Eventually, with increasing practice, Le Corbusier felt the need for additional furniture appropriate to his building and, with Pierre Jeanneret and Charlotte Perriand, he developed a number of designs that use "modern materials," such as chrome-plated steel in a way that generates excellent utility and also demonstrates an ideological preference for expression related to industrial production. Upholstery is turned into cushions held in metal cage structures. Chairs rotate or have movable backs, and a chaise is adjustable through a large arc for any desired seating angle. Springs are replaced by stretched elastic bands that do not require enclosure of massive space; tables are slabs of material (often glass) supported on cage structures of welded oval aircraft tubing or, sometimes, on simple standard pedestals based on the type used for restaurant tables.

Le Corbusier was concerned with storage arrangements that

Cushioned armchair by Le Corbusier, 1929. (Photograph courtesy of Atelier International, Inc., New York.)

would avoid the clutter of conventional chests and cabinets by built-in provisions or large storage units that could act as space dividers—the original "storage walls." Later (in 1935) he demonstrated what has become known as "modular storage" in a model apartment shown at the Brussels exhibition. In this display large cases of standard dimension were placed side by side on an understructure that used standard restaurant table bases. Inside the cases were special storage arrangements for records and papers and a radiophonograph with its parts exposed to view rather than hidden behind panels.

Before starting his professional career, Le Corbusier had worked briefly (for five months in 1910) in the Berlin office of Peter Behrens, an influential, pioneer premodern German architect. While

Adjustable position chaise by Le Corbusier 1929. (Photograph courtesy of Atelier International, Inc. New York.)

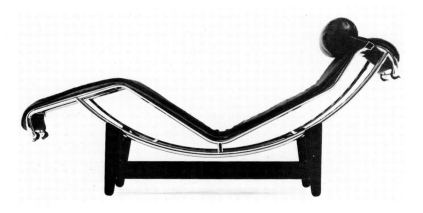

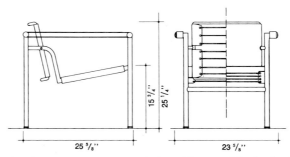

(Top) Le Corbusier armchair with movable back, 1928. (Photograph courtesy of Atelier International, Inc., New York.) (Above) Elevations of the armchair shown.

there, he met and knew Walter Gropius (1883–1970) and Ludwig Mies van der Rohe (1886–1969), two young German architects destined to become together with Corbusier the three most important figures in the development of modern architecture in Europe, and each destined to exert an important influence on the development of modern furniture.

Gropius designed some standardized modern furniture for retail distribution in 1927, but his influence is more significant as the director and intellectual leader of the famous school of design called The Bauhaus, founded at Weimar in 1919. This institution brought about a new synthesis of the craft-oriented ideas that had characterized the Deutsche Werkbund, an organization devoted to the reform of design, the constructivist ideas of the Dutch movement called De Stijl, and the industrially oriented approach toward architecture that Gropius himself represented.

The Bauhaus facilities (particularly at the new building at Dessau designed by Walter Gropius from 1925 onward) included fully equipped shops, and students were expected to work in wood and metal, among other materials, to develop designs in terms of real materials and production techniques rather than in drawings alone. Furniture, with its strong connections to architecture, was an important subject for study and a number of highly influential designs were produced by Bauhaus students and instructors. The designer best known for work in furniture at the Bauhaus was Marcel Breuer (b. 1902). His early work in wood uses thin strips and flat planes organized into structures that are often quite complex, clearly influenced by the work of De Stijl design, particularly that of Gerrit Rietveld (1888–1964).

Rietveld's designs were developed as sculptural forms intended for aesthetic impact as much as for comfort or utility (although they are not as uncomfortable or inconvenient as is sometimes supposed), and his use of bright primary colors in some designs accentuates a sense of abstract or diagramatic qualities. Breuer's wood armchair of 1922 might almost be mistaken for a Rietveld design, but his work began to change in character as he turned toward the use of metal frames. While riding a bicycle, Breuer thought of using the strong chrome-plated steel tubing of which that vehicle is made as a material for chair frames. Today, his first tubular steel armchair of 1925 (discussed on p. 000) remains a highly useful and much admired design. The use of chrome tube quickly became a widely accepted basis for development of modern furniture. It is suitable for efficient factory production techniques, requires little or no costly tooling, and is used in furniture that is both strong and light in appearance and actuality. The use of chrome tube has come to represent a "Bauhaus style" to modern consumers and

Wood side chair by Gerrit Rietveld 1934. (Photograph courtesy of Atelier International, Inc., New York.)

Probably the most famous of Rietveld chairs with parts in bright red, blue, and yellow; black painted frame. 1917–1918. (Photograph courtesy of Atelier International, Inc., New York.)

commentators. Probably the most widely known and used of Breuer designs is the simple cantilever chair, made with or without arms, in which the absence of rear legs allows the tubing to flex slightly and give the chair a gentle springiness. This concept had been developed by the Dutch architect Mart Stam (b. 1899) in designs using straight tube joined with standard fittings, but the Breuer design with continuous bent tubing found its way into production with the same Thonet firm that had developed bentwood furniture. Breuer has continued to design furniture from time to time, often using other materials such as aluminum and bent plywood, but the

Marcel Breuer armchair of 1924, with oak frame and handwoven wool seat and back straps. (Collection, the Museum of Modern Art, New York; Phyllis B. Lambert Fund.)

Breuer cantilever ("Cesca") chair in arm and armless versions. (Photograph courtesy of Knoll International, New York.)

Bauhaus designs of the 1920s have remained his most influential work.

The third architect in Behrens office in 1910, Mies van der Rohe, was also destined to produce furniture of wide influence. Like Le Corbusier, he realized that there was no available furniture suitable for use in the buildings that he was designing and he was led to solve this problem by generating his own solutions to furniture problems. His tubular cantilever chairs date from 1926, but have been over-shadowed in reputation by the chairs and table of steel bar frame construction that he designed in 1929 for use in the German pavilion at the Barcelona exhibition of that year. The chair in particular, with its X-frame of steel bars supporting tufted leather cushions on leather straps has taken on a special status as the most admired of all furniture designs of the 1920s. Actually the chair is difficult to manufacture, requiring hand craft techniques despite its "industrial" appearance, correspondingly costly, and offers no unusual features of comfort or utility. Nevertheless, this design seems to possess some special aesthetic quality that has made it a symbol of modern design ideals. Mies' work in furniture included several other cantilever chairs, tables, a lounge couch, and some massive upholstery of conventional construction, all distinguished by a certain sense of classic proportion that was characteristic of all his work. Mies became director of the Bauhaus in 1930 and remained

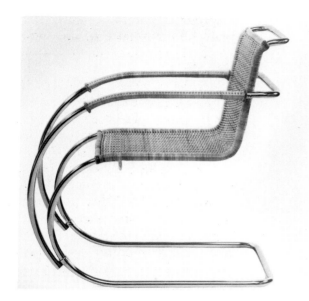

Mies van der Robe armchair with steel frame, cane seat and back. (Photograph courtesy of Stendig, Inc., New York.)

in that post until the school was disbanded under political pressure from the Nazi regime. This historic fact, along with the character of his work, make it a part of the particular German contribution to the development of modern design that is invariably associated with the Bauhaus name.

In the United States in the 1920s and early 1930s, there was virtually no awareness of the design developments taking place in Europe, and a general rejection of the directions that had been suggested by Wright. Instead, the "traditional reproduction" became the commercial norm of Grand Rapids (where most American furniture factories were located) until well into the 1930s. In those

Mies van der Robe's Barcelona Pavilion furniture, chair, table, and ottoman. (Photograph by George Barrows.)

Depression years a few flickers of originality surfaced, connected with the emergence of the "new profession" of industrial design. American industrial designers were less theoretical and idealistic than the European modern architects. They tended to see modern design as a "style," connected with the new, aerodynamically generated idea of "streamlining"; a style that could aid stagnating industry by promoting a desire for a new set of forms that would make existing products seem outmoded. The Chicago Fair of 1933 became a showcase for "streamlined modern" approaches, sometimes mechanistic in their origin and other times more related to the strictly decorative directions that have come to be known by the stylistic term "art deco," a reference to their origin in the French Arts Decorative movement of the 1920s—a movement concerned with the rounded corners and zigzag lightning motifs that were often called "modernistic." Bauhaus-generated elements, such as the bent chrome tube vocabulary joined with automotive streamlining to produce a modern style in products such as the furniture designed by Gilbert Rohde (1894–1944) for several American companies.

Modern furniture of more genuinely serious quality first became known in the United States when the tiny Finnish exhibit at the New York World's Fair in 1939 included some plywood furniture manufactured in Finland and distributed by a firm called Artek. This furniture was the work of Alvar Aalto (1898–1976), a Finnish architect who had explored ideas that closely paralleled those of the Bauhaus, but used the birch of his native country's forests rather than metal tube as a primary structural material. The wood became a fully industrial material in these products because it was not traditional solid stock but plywood made up in curved (molded) strips and sheets. Aalto's furniture has the same qualities

An "art deco" bureau with typical "waterfall veneer" details.

Molded plywood of ca. 1934 by Alvar Aalto. (Photograph courtesy of ICF Inc., New York.)

of directness and logic as that of the other three European pioneer architect-furniture designers, but seemed a trifle less forbidding in the America of the 1930s, probably because natural wood seemed a more comfortable material than polished chrome tubing to the generally conservative taste of that time. By this time some modern architecture was beginning to appear in the United States, and Artek established a showroom in New York to make Aalto furniture available in this country.

Except for steel office furniture with its plane surfaces and rounded corners (another contribution of the industrial designers urge to "streamline"), no other modern furniture was available in the United States until World War II. During the war, when furniture production was generally greatly curtailed, the firm of H. G. Knoll began production of a small group of designs developed for that firm by Jens Risom (b. 1916), a Dane who had learned furniture design and craftsmanship in Copenhagen. Risom's designs used simple frames of solid birch to support canvas webbing for seating. Simple and direct tables and storage units completed a small group that could be produced in spite of wartime shortages and fitted the increasing need for modern furniture that would relate to the rapidly growing body of seriously conceived modern architecture in America. The Knoll firm has since become one of the principal manufacturers and importers of outstanding modern furniture in the United States and abroad.

At the end of World War II the Michigan firm of Herman Miller, a prewar maker of Gilbert Rohde designs, was led to George Nelson (b. 1907), an American architect and architectural writer who had published (1944) a proposal for a modern storage system developed together with Henry Wright under the name "Storagewall." Although this design was only briefly in limited production, interest in it convinced the Herman Miller management to appoint Nelson their director of design. The first postwar Miller furniture appeared in 1946 under the Nelson name—an extensive group of seating and storage furniture incorporating many of the ideas of pioneer European modernism in forms that began to find some acceptance in the United States. A system called BSC (Basic Storage Components), which appeared in 1949, was a production version of the Nelson storage-wall concept. Nelson's atelierlike office harbored many creative furniture designers in the years that followed and produced a wide variety of distinguished modern furniture, including some of the first office furniture of serious design excellence.

One of Nelson's major contributions to the development of modern furniture resulted from his introduction of the Herman Miller firm to the designs of Charles Eames (b. 1907). Eames had achieved recognition in the design field when he and Eero Saarinen (1910–1961) won two first prizes in a competition organized by the Museum of Modern Art in 1940, entitled "Organic Design in Home Furnishings." The Eames-Saarinen submissions included a system of modular storage cases and chairs of molded plywood using sculptural shell forms supported on steel legs. The

BSC system by George Nelson, 1949. (Illustration from Herman Miller catalog, author's collection.)

CONVERSATION

Prizewinning chair design by Eames and Saarinen from the Museum of Modern Art's competition "Organic Design in Home Furnishings." (Photograph courtesy of the Museum of Modern Art, New York.)

difficulty of molding the complex curves of the chair shells prevented their production, but Eames and his wife Ray continued to work on related chair designs and finally developed forms practical for quantity production in 1946.* When these chairs (and related tables and storage units) were exhibited at the Museum of Modern Art, Nelson urged their addition to the Herman Miller product line, thus beginning a long and productive association of the Eames' with that firm. Forms similar to those of the original molded chairs were produced in 1949, when developing plastics technology finally made it possible to mold chair shells with complex curves in fiber glass, a plastic reinforced with embedded strands of spun glass.

Saarinen, whose primary work was in architecture, also occasionally returned to the furniture concepts of the Museum competition and eventually developed shell-form chairs of his own which have been manufactured and distributed by Knoll. This firm also became the manufacturer of chairs of wire frame construction developed by

---

* Work in molded plywood commissioned by the U.S. Navy (splints and other parts usually made of aluminum) helped the Eames' toward solutions to furniture problems. The chairs that resulted were manufactured briefly by the Evans Products Co. before they were taken over by Herman Miller.

Modular storage system developed by Charles Eames as exhibited at the Museum of Modern Art in New York in 1941. (Photograph courtesy of Charles and Ray Eames.)

Saarinen pedestal-based chairs with Fiberglas plastic shells shown with a related table of Saarinen design. (Photograph courtesy of Knoll International, New York.)

Saarinen's pedestal-based chairs with Fiberglas plastic shells; a derivation from the competition-winning design. (Photograph courtesy of Knoll International, New York.)

Wire chair by Harry Bertoia. (Photograph courtesy of Knoll International, New York.)

Harry Bertoia (b. 1915), a sculptor and designer who had worked with Eames on a similar group of designs that appeared in 1951.

With the success of the Knoll and Herman Miller firms, a gradually increasing number of modern furniture designs have become available in the United States. Imports from Europe, particularly Denmark and Italy, have become widely accepted along with a constantly expanding body of work by American designers. The general acceptance of modernism in every phase of professional design had, by the late 1950s made of it something of an academy imposing its dogmas with such success that some form of rebellion became inevitable. Grumbling about the monotony of glass tower skyscrapers and the claimed "coldness" of modern furniture became common among the general public and showed up in critical essays and books. The publication of Robert Venturi's book *Complexity and Contradiction in Architecture* by the Museum of Modern Art in 1966 signaled recognition by a respected institution that a serious challenge to the ideas of modernism could be respectable. The book deals only with architecture, but its view that simplicity, logic, and order are not the only or best criteria for design is readily applicable to furniture. The response in the design community has been the development of a new strain of modernism called, paradoxically, "post-modernism."

If modernism is viewed as a style belonging to a period that began early in the 20th century, whatever might follow that style

A teak-framed armchair from Denmark designed by Hans Wegner. (Photograph courtesy of Knoll International, New York.)

Chairs and sofa designed by Robert Venturi. (Photograph courtesy of Knoll International, New York.)

can, logically, be called post-modern. In practice, the term has been attached to a particular stylistic development characterized by a turn away from the logic of functionalism toward a more open acceptance of references to past history, toward use of ornamentation, and to movement toward whimsical, playful, and sometimes eccentric directions. Toward the end of the 1970s, post-modern furniture began to appear incorporating ornament and using forms that are often unrelated to functional logic along with rich materials, unexpected colors and suggestions of traditional stylistic mannerisms. The furniture designs of Michael Graves (b. 1934), an architect whose work has become well known for its post-modernist character, are striking examples of the new style. The work in furniture of Robert Venturi often refers to the aspects of the recent past that were, not long ago, regarded with contempt—as in the bulging overstuffed sofas that suggest the excesses of Victorian and 1920s Art Deco designs. A chair group (described in Chapter 2) uses the modern, technologically sophisticated production technique of molded plywood, but uses cut-out forms to suggest historic styles (Chippendale, Queen Anne, or Art Deco) and painted surface decoration with strong colors and patterns.

Venturi chair of molded plywood with cut-out "Chippendale" design. (Photograph courtesy of Knoll International, New York.)

*Venturi chair in "Empire" pattern.
(Photograph courtesy of Knoll International, New York.)*

In Italy, the appearance in 1980 of a loose-knit design group with the name of *Memphis* with Ettore Sottsass (b. 1917) as a leader began its own challenge to the norms of modernism with designs of curious, eccentric, and playful form using bright colors and strong patterns in ways that were clearly intended to disturb, shock, and generally upset critics and theorists whose support of modernism had become routine. Whether Memphis design is an aspect of post-modernism, or a separate but parallel development has not become altogether clear. Indeed, debate is still under way as to whether the post-modernist direction will become the dominant style of the latter years of the 20th century or turn out to be no more than a minor deviation in a more consistent line of historical development. Those who favor the latter view are continuing to work in ways that can be understood as evolutionary developments within the main line of modernism rather than as rebellion against it. In an effort to give such work its own identification, the term "late modern" has appeared in architectural criticism. Late modern work continues in the direction of modernism with a search for simple and logical forms having a strong base in func-

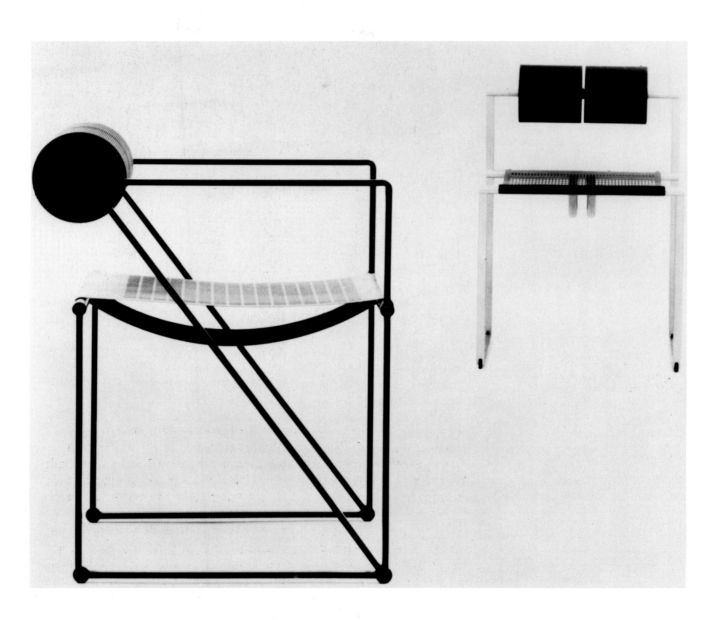

"Seconda" chair, a 1982 design by Mario Botta. (Photograph courtesy of ICF, New York.)

One-piece injection-molded plastic chair designed by Verner Panton. (Photograph courtesy of Herman Miller, Inc.)

tional ideals. Aside from its date, the identifying characteristics of *late* modernism are willingness to explore more adventurous forms, use of varied materials (including fine woods, stone, and materials associated more with hand craft than with industrial production) and inclusion of details that may be complex, even luxurious rather than strictly utilitarian. The designs of Richard Meier (b. 1934), Charles Gwathmy (b. 1938), or Massimo Vignelli (b. 1931) in the United States or of Mario Botta (b. 1943) in Switzerland, can be viewed as late modern works, although the term has not achieved as much currency in furniture design as in current architecture.

Further complication of terminology for recent design arises when the popular term "high-tech" is applied to work that follows the line of development of modernism with strong emphasis on the use of materials, constructional techniques and details suggestive of modern technology as it appears in science, industry and such advanced fields as aero-space technology. Perhaps this kind of work might best be viewed as a sub-category of late modernism

Rocker lounge chairs made up of two fiberglass moldings. Designed by Eero Aarnio. (Photograph courtesy of Stendig, Inc., New York.)

embracing the furniture of such designers as Mario Botta (mentioned above) or Joseph Paul D'Urso (b. 1943) whose work emphasizes the use of technological materials and details along with the simple forms associated with minimalist art.

Today modern, post-modern and late modern furniture is most readily accepted for use in offices, commercial and institutional interiors where professional interior designers and architects are usually involved in furniture selection. In residential situations, a certain nostalgic conservatism tends to survive and leads the typical consumer to choose furniture that attempts to reproduce or recall some historic period or distant place ("Colonial", "Mediterranean" or "Oriental"). Modern design ideas are making increasing inroads in this area, but there are still only a few manufacturers who attempt to produce the serious work of skilled designers. Too much of the "modern" furniture offered to consumers is imitative, anonymous, and developed to meet an annual style change cycle. The time when the typical householder will own and use furniture comparable in design quality to that of past historic periods is still somewhere in the future.

4

THE TECHNOLOGY
OF FURNITURE

The designers and makers of historic furniture did not confront many serious technical problems. They worked within a tradition that had developed answers to most of the problems that were likely to arise; they used familiar materials and the processes of designing and making were so closely interwoven that experience and common sense provided answers to problems as rapidly as they arose. As a result most historic furniture is, in modern terminology, "well-engineered"; it is strong and sturdy, well constructed from well-chosen materials. If cared for and not misused, it does not tip over, come apart, or break. The legend that fine antiques are very delicate and fragile is largely a myth, encouraged by the fact that the modern American practice of overheating interiors in winter causes wood to shrink and warp and glue to dry out. Given reasonable environmental treatment, most old furniture, including designs that may look fragile, will prove to be structurally well conceived, although often "overstructured" with parts larger than needed so as to provide a generous margin for error.

The modern designer cannot safely rely on tradition, common sense, and instinct. Inspection of the trash put out in any modern community will reveal innumerable pieces of fairly new and supposedly good quality furniture discarded, broken in some irreparable way as a result of design that embodies some engineering error. The modern designer often uses recently developed or unfamiliar materials and constructional techniques, frequently experiments with new forms that have not been tested with long use, and often develops designs on paper without any immediate reference to shop practice with real materials and real techniques of manufacture. Modern life is hard on furniture; we ship it in trucks, sprawl or climb on it, clean and wax under and around it with machines, and generally do not treat it with the care that was probably characteristic of the conditions of use in the past.

Clearly, furniture design in the modern context must include some careful thought about the technical problems involved. Although the term "engineering" usually suggests large structures and may seem pretentious in relation to furniture, it actually describes the level of consideration that technical furniture problems deserve. In many ways engineering large structures is simpler—buildings and highways are not usually moved around and are used in ways that are more consistent and predictable than is the case with furniture. In truly complex and difficult problems of ships or aircraft, engineering becomes a specialty and teams often work for long periods on a single project. Testing, frequently over long periods, is also part of such design projects. Most furniture is the work of one individual (or at most a few), who must design in terms of form and engineer as well. While testing is often undertaken to check out a completed design, the expectation is that if the designer has done his job, the tests will simply offer assurance that all is well. To have any hope of success in engineering terms, the designer needs to think through the nature of the problems involving any piece of furniture more carefully and more systematically than might seem necessary. It is extremely easy to conceive, model, and draw a piece of furniture that may seem practical and logical only to find, in prototype or production, that some problem surfaces which makes the design impractical. Such errors are costly, embarrassing, and add to the consumers' all too well-founded suspicion of the unfamiliar.

Furniture is so diverse in its uses and its materials that it may seem difficult to make any general points about its engineering. Actually engineering approaches that are well known in architectural and other structural engineering serve the furniture designer well, although some changes in emphasis are generated by the special problems of furniture. It is convenient to separate these problems into two headings that describe two different and, in most cases, unrelated expectations we bring to furniture. These expectations involve *stability* and *strength*. Although these terms as used here must be narrowly defined to make distinctions clear, they will serve as a basis for sorting out the problems that the furniture designer must face.

Stability. Refers to the properties of an object that cause it to remain in the position in which it has been placed; normally, in the case of furniture, in an upright position.

Strength. Refers to the properties of an object that resist whatever forces might tend to break it, make it come apart, or cause it to sag or vibrate excessively.

Stability is only a matter of remaining in place, not tipping over, while strength is concerned with the internal integrity of an object; a piece of furniture can be strong but unstable, so that it may fall over while still remaining intact. An object that is weak may break, or deflect, or shake in use even though it remains upright. Some confusion can arise in identifying a cause of failure since, in falling over an object may break, or, the collapse following a failure of strength may be seen as falling over. A user confronted with either problem may employ either term, but the distinction must be clear if we are to analyze what each of the two problems require of us. The engineering of buildings and other large structures tends to emphasize strength considerations, since any forces that might tend to cause instability would almost certainly create strength problems long before actual overturning would occur, especially since buildings are normally anchored to the ground. Wind pressures against the side of a tall building, for example, are absorbed by internal strengthening to prevent deflections that might be disturbing. One can hardly imagine an entire building rolled over on its side by wind (although this does happen to small structures in hurricane force storms). In contrast, most pieces of furniture have ample strength to hold together and can be turned over on a side or on end quite easily with deliberate effort. This possibility is used in moving and shipping furniture every day. However, unless there is deliberate intent otherwise, a piece of furniture should remain upright with its feet or base on the floor in the position that the designer and user intend. In most historical furniture the problem is simply dealt with by positioning legs or base to provide support at the outermost corners of the object. Common sense suggests that this almost guarantees stability, although there can be problems when objects are tall and thin. It is possible to imagine overturning a grandfather's clock, for example, by leaning against it too heavily. The more adventurous forms of modern furniture with upper parts cantilevered out from a small base and with light construction used for tall units are far more likely to generate stability problems.

Strength in any object is a matter of choosing materials and sizing parts so that anticipated loads will not cause any part to break, of designing ways to make joints between parts strong enough to resist any forces that might break them, and of establishing an overall configuration of the object that will aid in limiting stresses in parts and joints to levels that stay within the intended limits. Although actual breakage is often a threat in furniture, strength problems may also arise at stress levels far less than would threaten breakage. Thus a shelf that sags visibly or a desk or table that vibrates excessively may seem unsatisfactory even when there is no threat of actual collapse.

Sound engineering design of furniture requires consideration of stability and strength in a systematic way and a careful effort to ensure that no problems will arise. In terms of strength, it is often worthwhile to make sure that the design structure is not *too* strong—parts that are larger than necessary by more that a reasonable safety factor represent excess material and therefore excess weight and cost that could be reduced advantageously.

Analysis of both stability and strength problems must begin with awareness of the forces that an object must resist. The architectural engineer begins his calculations by noting these forces known in the field as "loads." Most of the loads that effect buildings are called "static," meaning motionless. The force that makes static loads effective is, of course, gravity. Every object is being pulled downward toward the center of the earth by a force that we call the weight of the object. The static loads in a building are classified as "dead loads," the weights of the building's own parts, and "live loads," the weights of snow on the roof and of people and objects that may occupy the building. Although people may move about, it is customary to provide an estimated static live load figure that makes sufficient allowance for this movement without trying to consider its exact patterns. "Dynamic loads" are the result of movable, changing forces. Wind is the only important dynamic loading that is usually taken into account in the engineering design of buildings, but dynamic loads can be very significant in machinery, vehicles, and similar moving objects.

The loads that must be considered in furniture design are of the same types and can be dealt with in much the same way, with certain important exceptions. In most cases the dead loads present in furniture are relatively small—it is hard to visualize an article of furniture collapsing of its own weight—but, in situations where overturning may be a problem, the weight of the object itself and the way that weight is distributed are often important issues. Arriving at the weights of the parts of a piece of furniture during the process of design can be undertaken in two ways or any combination of two ways. Weights can be calculated by multiplying the volume of each material present by the weight of that material or, if this is difficult, an existing object or part of similar material can be weighed on a scale and calculation used to allow for the relative size. Tables of weights of materials by volume are provided in most engineering handbooks and manufacturers of unusual materials can supply weights of their products. Table 1 gives weights of some frequently used furniture materials. Where weight is given by vol-

TABLE 1
WEIGHTS OF MATERIALS—DEAD LOADS

Note: Weights are given in pounds per cubic foot. To convert to the weight of a particular part, multiply the three dimensions of the part in inches by the given weight, and divide by the cubic inches in a cubic foot, (12 × 12 × 12 = 1728). Thus, a solid oak top 36 in. × 72 in. × 1½ in. will weigh:

$$\frac{36 \times 72 \times 1.5 \times 50}{1728} = 112.5 \text{ lb}$$

A slide rule or electronic calculator will expedite such calculations.

Weights of plastics of a particular type will vary considerably with different formulations, nature, and quantity of added fillers and other variables. Foamed plastics have weights determined more by the nature of the foaming process than by the basic material used. Weighing a specimen of the material is the only certain indication of the weight of a particular formulation.

Weights of a few unlikely furniture materials (e.g., water, gold) are given for comparison.

Material		Weight per Cubic Foot (lb)
Woods, soft	Red cedar	23
	Redwood	28
	Spruce	28
	Hemlock	33
	Fir, Douglas	34
	Pine	38
Woods, hard	Walnut	37
	Maple, soft	38
	Maple, hard	44
	Birch	44
	Hickory	50
	Oak	50
	Ebony	76
Plywood	Fir	34
Metals	Magnesium	100
	Aluminum	166
	Cast iron	448
	Wrought iron	480
	Steel (mild)	489
	Bronze	524
	Copper	558
	Lead	710
	Gold	1215
Plastics	Polyethylene	56–59
	Polystyrene	64–66
	Melamine	64–124
	Nylon	66–70
	Polyurethane	68–93
	Acrylic	69–79
	Polyester	74–85

TABLE 1
WEIGHTS OF MATERIALS—DEAD LOADS (CONTINUED)

Material		Weight per Cubic Foot (lb)
Miscellaneous	Polyurethane foam, rigid	1.5–16
	Polyurethane foam, soft	2.5–6
	Glass-reinforced polyester (Fiberglass)	105–143
	Particle board	27–55
	Hardboard	55–70
	Water (7½ gal per cu ft)	62
	Concrete	110–155
	Brickwork	120
	Glass	156
	Marble	160
	Granite	165

ume, it is necessary to calculate the volume of the part in question in order to multiply by the weight per volume unit. Thus, a table-top 30 in. × 66 in. × 1½ in. of solid oak will weigh

$$\frac{30 \times 66 \times 1.5}{12 \times 12 \times 12} \times 50 \text{ lb} = 85.94 \text{ (say, 86) lb}$$

50 lb is the weight of oak per cubic foot (Table 1) and the number of cubic inches in a cubic foot is 12 × 12 × 12. Obviously, it is necessary to keep all calculations consistently in either feet, inches, or (in modern practice) metric units. Weights of parts made of bar or tubing can usually be calculated more easily by using the weight per lineal foot and multiplying by the measured length of material used. It is often easiest to estimate the weight of a complex or irregular part (e.g., a steel file drawer or a plastic chair body) by simply weighing a similar unit on a scale. An ordinary bathroom scale serves well for this purpose. Calculation allows for differences in size.

Live loads imposed on furniture are mainly gravity loads, the weights of people and objects placed on the furniture. In architectural engineering average weights are usually used, but in furniture it is often wisest to use a reasonable maximum. A sofa designed on the basis of the average weight of a person might collapse when used by several excessively overweight users. A bookcase may be packed with heavy magazines or records rather than with an average mixture of books. The normal uses of furniture will impose loads so much less than the reasonable maximums, that they need hardly be considered. Table 2 lists some typical live load weights.

In addition to gravity live loads, it is often necessary to consider

TABLE 2
WEIGHTS OF APPLIED (LIVE) LOADS

Note: In most cases, when considering loads that may be applied to furniture, maximums are more important than averages. The heaviest person who may sit in a chair is most likely to overstress its structure. A sofa may be used by three overweight persons at one time. A storage unit may be totally packed with 12-in. phonograph records. Averages are significant only when the number of units in question is large enough to ensure that an averaging effect can be counted on.

Applied Loading		Weight (lb)
Persons	Child (4 yr)	38
	Adult (average)	172
	Adult (maximum)	300 (or more)
	97.5 percentile	231 (or less)
Stored materials	Books	36 per cubic ft
	Books 8 in. ht per ft	12
	Books 10 in. ht per ft	22
	Books 12 in. ht per ft	40
	Records (12″)	40 per running ft
	Files (letter, per ft)	20
	Files (legal, per ft)	24
	Dishes, glassware, etc.	12 (average)
Objects	Typewriter (portable)	10–20
	Typewriter (office)	25–35
	Typewriter (electric)	30–45
	Projector (8 mm)	24
	Projector (16 mm)	40
	Tape recorder	40
	Mattress (54″ × 76″)	50
	Bedspring (54″ × 76″)	40–85
	Attaché case (filled)	10–15
	Suitcase (filled)	20–40

dynamic loads and loads imposed as side thrusts. When a person literally "drops into a chair," the impact loads the supporting parts by a factor of two or three times the equivalent weight after it has come to rest. The carriage return of a typewriter on a desk, or the act of cutting a tough roast on a table imposes loads that are both dynamic and in a sideways direction. Also, furniture is most often damaged by forces other than those involved in its normal use. Furniture may be dropped from the tailgate of a truck on delivery, or it may be dragged over a carpet or some obstacle when being moved or during cleaning. People stand on tables or chairs to reach high objects and perhaps sometimes dance on pianos. Children bounce on beds and use chairs and tables as playground equipment. It is not possible to design furniture to be stable and indestructible under every circumstance, but some consideration should be given to a reasonable range of such unusual loadings.

This requires thinking through possible hazards and providing a "factor of safety" margin of extra stability and strength to allow for unpredictable problems.

Loads that take the form of side thrusts are not usually very significant in designing furniture, with the possible exception of objects that are tall and thin. Such objects may be tipped over if a person leans heavily against only one side—a tall bookcase, a grandfather clock, or a tall flat screen might cause this problem. Very light objects used outdoors may be subject to tumbling or sliding from wind pressures. These are usually the only situations in which side thrusts are significant.

In practice, the intended function of a piece of furniture usually makes it possible to estimate appropriate live load before design is undertaken. Dead loads can only be estimated after a proposed design has been developed and a choice of materials made. It then becomes possible to consider questions of stability and strength and to continue to monitor these issues as design progresses.

Many furniture configurations are inherently stable and require no particular investigation of this issue. Common sense will indicate to most observers that an object that is not particularly tall and thin and touches the floor or ground at points along its outermost perimeter will not be inclined to turn over under any gravity loads that can be applied to it. Even side thrusts will cause it to slide along the floor rather than to overturn, so that only a special effort (as might be made in moving or shipping) will upend it. Most traditional furniture is of this sort. When the body, or any upper part of an object overhangs its base (cantilevers, in engineering terminology), it becomes theoretically possible for a gravity load applied on the cantilever to overturn the object. Whether this will happen depends on the length of the cantilever and the magnitude of the load applied. Resistance to overturning comes from the weight of the object.

The concept of a "center of gravity" (CG) is useful in dealing with these matters. Although the force of gravity pulls downward on all parts of any object, it is possible to locate a particular point in an object around which it will balance in any position. The object behaves as if all of the gravity pull affecting it were concentrated at this point. In an object that is symmetrical in plan (top) view, this point will be at its physical center. Since most furniture is symmetrical, it is usually possible to find a CG on the centerline. When a piece of furniture is not symmetrical (a desk with a drawer pedestal on one side, for example), the desk and the pedestal may be considered as separate units, each with its own center of gravity at its respective center. Similarly the loads applied, people and objects, are generally symmetrical and can be considered as acting along a vertical line through their respective centers of gravity. If the CG of an object and the gravity loads imposed on it all are located at points above the area of the object's base,* the object is stable and can only be overturned by the application of side thrusts. If the CG of an object is located at a point not above the area of its base, it must overturn (rotate) into a new position. The most common stability problems in furniture arise where an object is designed so that it is stable in itself but is shaped so that loads can be imposed in a way that will upset its stability. A sofa may cantilever beyond its leg base at each end. When a person sits alone at one end, will the unit tip? A desk with a long overhang may tip if someone sits or leans heavily at the outermost edge.

Whenever such a possibility exists, stability may be checked by calculation through an equation of moments. The engineering concept of a "moment" makes it possible to take into account the familiar mechanical principle of leverage in a systematic way. Any force will be multiplied if it works "through a level," and a moment is simply a means of expressing that multiplication. A force (in pounds) times the length of the lever arm through which it works (in inches) gives a moment of force in inch-pounds. This concept makes it possible to see the stability of an object in terms of a contest between moments of forces. If the moments tending to cause overturning exceed those resisting overturning, the object will tip over. In the sofa mentioned the possibility of overturning is centered about the leg base at the left. The weight of the sofa can be thought of as acting at its CG, at its center. If the weight of the sofa is 180 lb, and the distance of the CG from the leg is 30 inches (in horizontal dimension), the moment resisting overturning is 180 × 30 or 5400 in.-lb. If the person seated at the left end weighs 260 lb, the CG is 15 inches from the same leg. The moment tending to overturn is 260 × 15 = 3900 in.-lb, considerably less than the moment resisting overturning, so that in this situation there will be no problem.

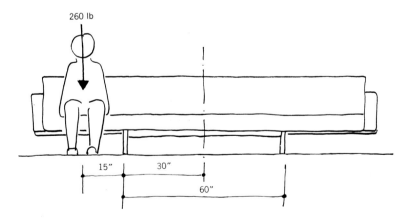

* The base area may be a polygon defined by the points at which legs, glides, or casters touch the floor or ground.

In investigating this problem, an "equation of moments" was used in which we noted that stability will be lost if the overturning moment(s) more than equal the resisting moment(s). That is,

$$WR \times lr = WO \times lo$$

(where WR is the weight resisting overturning and lr is its lever arm; WO is the weight tending to produce overturning and lo is its lever arm)

describes the condition at exactly the loading that will cause overturning to begin. This same equation can be used, according to which variable is made the unknown, to find out how heavy the sofa must be made to be safe, to find the weight of the heaviest load that can be placed at its end or, with a bit more complication, to locate the leg at a point that will give a satisfactory degree of stability.

Moments on either side of such an equation can be added together to deal with nonsymmetrical objects or with multiple loads. For example, in the desk diagram, if the desk without pedestal weighs 170 lb, and the loaded pedestal weighs 125 lb, will the desk tip if a 180 lb person sits or leans on the right edge? The resisting moment is the weight of the desk times its lever arm of 19 inches, while two moments tend toward overturning—the 125 lb pedestal times the 9 inch lever from its CG to the leg, plus the 180 lb person times an 18 inch lever arm. Thus:

Is 170×19 more or less than $(125 \times 9) + (180 \times 18)$?
3230 is less than $1125 + 3240$
3230 is less than 4365

Therefore the desk will tilt. Could the desk be made safe by adding weight to it symmetrically (e.g., by making the top of a heavier

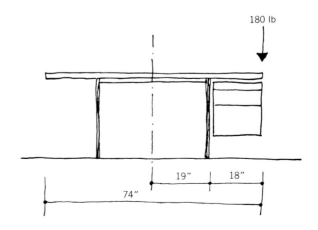

material)? We can see that it could be, but how much weight would be needed?

$$W \text{ (unknown)} \times 19 = 4365$$

$W = 229.7$ (say 230) lb, so it would be necessary to add an extra 60 lb to make it stable in this situation. One can investigate other possibilities, such as adding weight at the extreme left, making the desk longer, or locating the right leg under the pedestal in similar ways.

The location of the CG in height dimension is immaterial in these problems since gravity loads work in a vertical direction in all cases. Common sense suggests that a tall object is less stable than a low one, but they are actually no different in terms of the gravity loads that cause tipping. Once tipping begins, however, a low object or one with a low CG will require more rotation before the CG moves to a location that is not above the base than will a tall object or one with a high CG (see diagram). If the force that is causing tipping is removed before the CG has moved beyond the extent of the base, the object will recover. Once the CG passes beyond that point, rotation will continue even if the force is removed. These situations are familiar when we consider the side thrust that can be applied to a tall piece of furniture by leaning on it. The magnitude of thrust that can be applied in this way can be measured (with a scale) as falling in a range of about 40 to 50 pounds; 60 pounds would include some factor of safety. To evaluate its effect, it is necessary to note the height at which the thrust is applied. The vertical location of the CG of the object being tipped is still of no importance in predicting whether tipping will occur. It is a factor in determining how much rotation must occur before the object will fail to recover when the side thrust is removed. In practice, when an object begins to tip, this will be noticed and the side thrust will be removed. If this is done before the CG passes a "point of no return," the object will recover its normal position. If a slight displacement of the CG passes this point, it is possible that

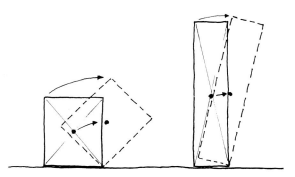

Low object on left must be tipped through a much larger angle than tall object on right before its center of gravity moves to a point outside the area of the base, with overturning resulting.

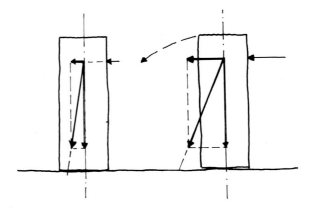

Small side thrust (left diagram) will not cause tipping, larger thrust (right diagram) will. Vector diagram produces "resultant" arrow, which indicates if tipping will occur.

the object will fall over because the side thrust cannot be removed quickly enough to permit recovery. Whether tipping will occur at all can be investigated through diagrams such as a "parallelogram of forces." A diagram is made that shows a scale elevation of the object in question. The weight of the object is shown by a downward directed force arrow passing through the CG drawn to a convenient scale. A force arrow with a length drawn to the same scale is drawn at the level where the side thrust would be applied, with its end at the intersection with the downward (gravity force) arrow. These two arrows now form two sides of a rectangle. If this rectangle is completed, its diagonal will be a "resultant" of the two forces, a single force and direction indicating how the two forces will interact. If this arrow, when extended, falls outside the base of the object, tipping will occur. If it falls within the base of the object, no movement is to be expected. If tipping does occur, recovery will follow removal of the side thrust unless the CG has been moved far enough to pass beyond the space above the original base. In that case the object will roll over even after the side thrust has been removed. (See diagrams).

One can visualize, for example, leaning against a heavy refrigerator. If it does not slide, it may tip. On noticing the tipping, one tends to pull back and the refrigerator moves back into a vertical position. If one continues to push, the refrigerator reaches a tilt beyond which it overbalances and falls. Concentration of weight in the bottom lowers the CG and makes overturning difficult while a concentration of weight in the top makes the "point of no return" easy to reach and overturning is more likely. The force needed to begin the tipping is the same in either case.

If a 6 ft 0 in. high by 12 in. deep bookshelf unit is symmetrically loaded and weighs 480 lb, is there any possibility that it will tip when a person leaning against it applies a side thrust of 80 lb at a point 5 ft 0 in. above the base? In the diagram, the parallelogram of forces shows a resultant arrow R which, when extended,

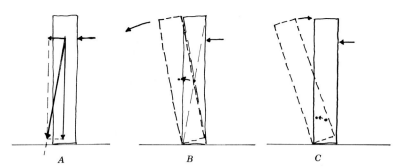

Vector diagram A shows that tall unit will be tipped by side thrust shown. If tilted as far as shown at B, it will fall over as the center of gravity passes beyond a vertical line from the edge of the base. At C, the same size unit with a low center of gravity can be tipped to a greater angle, but will recover when side thrust is released.

falls far outside the base. The unit will tip easily. It will recover until tipped far enough to move its CG beyond the edge of the base and will then fall (see diagram). The first diagram can be used to explore possibilities for reducing this problem by increasing the weight of the unit or by widening its base. Redistributing weight to lower its CG will have no effect on the ease with which it can be tipped, but will improve the chances of its recovering an upright position if the side thrust is removed.

In considering questions of stability, the issue will be most critical in relation to the axis along which least stability can be anticipated. A table may appear fully stable when viewed in lengthwise elevation, but still be unstable with respect to its short dimension. Objects with three legs or triangular bases are always problematic because neither of the two usual elevations (front and side) as normally drawn reveal the axis in which overturning is most probable. Thus it is necessary to diagram the object in the orientation in

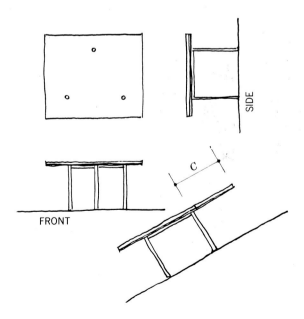

Front and side view suggest good stability, but third view taken perpendicular to the direction of longest cantilever C, shows that a stability problem may exist.

which maximum cantilever beyond the base is visible, and to test its stability in this plane in order to have confidence in its stability characteristics. Objects on rollers or casters also need special attention because the line of the base in contact with the floor may shift by rolling once tipping begins. This makes overturning more likely.

Scale models built with materials having weights in correct proportion are often useful in investigating stability questions and are very helpful in visualizing the actions defined in the equations and diagrams outlined above.

The problems of adequate strength in furniture are more obvious than problems of stability and, perhaps for that reason, seem less difficult to define and analyze. We expect any well-made piece of furniture not to break or come apart and not to sag, vibrate, or "wiggle" to any excessive degree in all ordinary and reasonable uses. Almost all traditional furniture was made overstrong, with members larger than needed and with well-designed joints to ensure that no strength problems would arise. Modern furniture designers can follow this practice and so, on a simple "common sense" basis, ensure that their designs are fully adequate in strength. Although engineering calculation is rarely used to check strength in furniture (as it almost always is in architectural and structural engineering), it is useful to have some understanding of the kinds of stress that furniture must withstand and the means of ensuring needed strength. Strength means provision of adequate structure to absorb the stresses that will be generated by the same dead and live loads that influence stability. These are: the weights of the object itself, of the "live" loads of people and objects, and the dynamic and side loads that may appear in addition to gravity loads. These loads generate stresses in the parts of an object that fall into several specific classifications:

> **Compressive** stresses appear where materials are pressed or "squeezed," most often by gravity loads applied from above. Legs

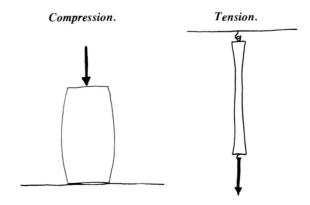

Compression.   *Tension.*

of chairs and tables, ends of shelf units, any elements that are like posts or columns will usually be primary carriers of compressive loads. In most cases the vertical parts of furniture that are natural and convenient to provide are adequately strong enough to carry the compressive stress that develops. It is unusual to see breakage or collapse of a leg or upright as a result of simple compression.

Tensile stresses are the opposite of compressive stresses; they appear where material is pulled or stretched. Objects that are suspended from above generate tensile stresses in the hanging members, and certain materials (such as wire or cable) are very efficient when used in tension. Tension members are uncommon in furniture, however, except in certain kinds of bracing that will be discussed below.

Bending stresses combine compression and tension and are common in furniture parts. Shelves, the structures of beds and sofas, the tops of tables and desks are typically designed to carry loads in a bridgelike pattern, supported at each end but loaded in between supports. Parts in bending stress tend to sag between supports, developing compressive stresses in their tops and tensile stresses in their bottoms. If carried over a support continuously, these stresses will reverse position with the tensile stresses moving to the top and the compressives stresses to the bottom. Failure in bending is not unknown—a shelf may buckle or break if overloaded, but problems short of failure are much more common. A shelf may sag so that it is unsightly when heavily loaded. A bed, table, or desk may deflect and vibrate to an uncomfortable degree. Dealing with bending stresses involves limiting unsupported spans and designing parts in bending stress with sufficient material and with suitable cross-sectional forms to deal with anticipated stresses. Structural engineering texts and handbooks provide the basis for calculating members

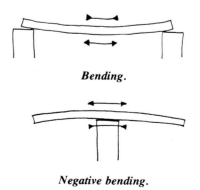

Bending.

Negative bending.

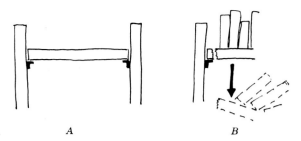

Situation A, in which shear might lead to failure B.

to deal with bending stresses, but in most furniture applications simple experimentation will serve more conveniently to ensure that adequate structure has been provided.

Shear stresses are seldom critical in furniture applications. They arise when opposite forces act on a piece of material close together in a way that can cut or "shear" it. Heavy loads on short spans can sometimes generate critical shear stresses as, for example, when a strong but heavily loaded shelf rests on small support pegs. The pegs could possibly be sheared through.

Torsion or twisting stresses, those that tend to generate rotation, are also not often critical in furniture but can arise in unusual situations. Base structures for tables or desks and shelf units have sometimes been developed with bracing that is vulnerable to twisting applied in a horizontal plane. Triangular bracing (discussed below), if introduced with braces in only one diagonal position across the spaces braced, may be vulnerable to torsion (see diagram).

The overall strength of a piece of furniture (or of any other object) can be analyzed into several components as follows:

Torsion (twisting force) applied to top may cause disturbing movement.

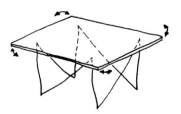

Diagonal braces, which will appear in elevation to be adequate stiffening, may still permit movement.

1. The strength of individual parts resulting from the inherent strength characteristic of the material chosen and the sizing and formation of the part.
2. The strength or integrity of joints between parts.
3. The overall geometry of the object as it affects the distribution of stresses to parts, relieves stresses on joints, and contributes to inherent structural efficiency in the total object.

Everyday familiarity with the common materials of furniture, woods, metals, and plastics gives a sense of the strengths of these materials. Everyone knows that steel is stronger than wood, or that plastic can be either surprisingly weak or surprisingly strong according to its particular formulation. More exact information about the strengths of materials—plywood compared with solid hard or soft wood, steel compared with aluminum, acrylic plastic compared with glass—must come from tables of data that can be found in engineering handbooks and in the literature provided by the manufacturers of various materials. Unfortunately, the ways in which different materials behave varies so greatly that it is not always possible to show strengths in strictly comparable terms. The limit of useful strength of a brittle material may be established by its tendency to break on impact (e.g., glass), while a more ductile material (e.g., plastic) may be immune to this problem but may sag under load and become set in a sagged curve that makes it unsatisfactory. Table 3 lists allowable working stresses of some common furniture materials as they are given in various references and provides some idea of how these materials compare, even where strictly comparable values cannot be established.

Most furniture parts have forms and sizes established for reasons other than strength, so it is only necessary to be sure that parts exceed the minimums that strength would require. Usually a tabletop, a bookshelf, or a chair frame are shaped and sized to satisfy functional and visual requirements as primary values. Having decided that a wood shelf is to span three feet and that it needs to be almost an inch thick for visual reasons, observation and experience will confirm that resulting strength will be adequate for the loads such a shelf will usually carry. Judgment would indicate, similarly, that ⅛ inch thick aluminum would not serve the same purpose without some special forming or other support to limit its flexibility. It is possible to use calculation to get exact answers to certain questions; for example, exactly how much will a shelf of a given material and span deflect under a particular load. Yet most furniture designers, realizing that the loads to which furniture parts are subjected are very unpredictable, prefer to check such questions through simple experiments. A rough model or mock-up test situation tends to be more informative than calculation. A shelf of a proposed material can be spanned between two bricks or boxes,

TABLE 3
WORKING STRESSES FOR TYPICAL MATERIALS

Note: Unfortunately, strengths of materials cannot be indicated by one simple figure. Materials respond differently to various types of stress, have directional characteristics (notably in the case of wood), and respond in differing ways short of failure. The form of parts also influences their strength in ways that make direct comparison of different materials confusing. To compare a wood two-by-four with a steel bar of the same dimensions is misleading, since the latter would not be a logical alternative to the former. The steel would surely be used in the form of a tube, a channel, or an I-section, forms not suited to wood.

The data given below will provide a sense of relative strengths and some hints as to suitability of different materials for specific uses.

Material	Allowable Extreme Fiber Stress (psi—pounds per square inch)			
	Bending	Tension	Compression	Shear
Wood, soft				
Southern yellow pine, select structural grade	1700			80
Parallel to grain		975	1050	
Right angles to grain			270	
Southern yellow pine, utility grade	225			70
Parallel to grain		125	400	
Right angles to grain			230	
Wood, hard				
Birch	1225			
Parallel to grain			900	
Right angles to grain			450	
Maple, hard	1200			
Parallel to grain			960	
Right angles to grain			500	
Oak	1120			
Parallel to grain			800	
Right angles to grain			500	
Walnut	1200			
Parallel to grain			975	
Right angles to grain			480	

Plywood and particle board
> These are not homogeneous materials and have strength characteristics that vary with thickness and the composition of layers of which they are made. Data must be obtained from the manufacturer as to characteristics of a particular board thickness and grade

Material	Bending	Tension	Compression	Shear
Metals				
Steel, mild	24,000	22,000	24,000	14,500
Aluminum		19,000	19,000	12,000
Stone				
Limestone and marble			800	
Granite			500	

TABLE 3
WORKING STRESSES FOR TYPICAL MATERIALS (CONTINUED)

Material	Allowable Extreme Fiber Stress (psi—pounds per square inch)			
	Bending	Tension	Compression	Shear

Plastics

Strengths of these materials vary greatly with chemical formulation, types of fillers, and nature of fabrication. Foaming, for example, can produce material of varied strength from one particular resin. Also, the varied characteristics of plastics make direct comparison with such materials as wood and metal difficult. Manufacturers' literature on a specific plastic used in a particular way is usually the best practical guide in determining strengths to be anticipated. The table below gives some idea of the ranges of relative strength that can be developed by different types of plastic

	Tensile strength (psi)
Acrylic	5,600–12,500
Fiberglass (polyester)	
With short glass fibers	4,000–20,000
With woven glass cloth	25,000–50,000
Melamine	5,000–11,000
Nylon	3,900–12,500
Phenolic	3,000–9,000
Polyethylene	900–5,400
Polystyrene	2,800–7,300
Polyurethane	4,500–8,400
Polyurethane (foams)	5–20
Vinyl, rigid	5,000–8,000
Vinyl, fiexible	1,000–4,000

loaded with a variety of objects that might be placed on it (books, records, dishes, canned goods), and its tendency to sag or bounce can be observed as the span is varied. A steel tube, proposed for use as a chair or table leg can be clamped in a vise with the appropriate leg length extending free, and shaken, and (if possible) bent by hand to get a clear idea of its adequacy for the purpose. Such primitive tests will usually indicate a need to increase cross sections of parts, to change configurations or parts, or to change the overall geometry of the design in doubtful cases.

Which of these three remedies to use, (or what combination of the three) can usually be established by considering the visual and economic impact of each. A wood shelf that shows a *slight* sag under a very heavy load might suggest the substitution of a thicker piece of wood; if the sag is significant, however, this route to a solution may be both costly and unsightly. A deep brace set back under the shelf (see diagram) would be a change in configuration that would give better results with less material and, possibly, with

Brace at center of shelf aids in resisting bending. (Right) Shelf of sheet metal stiffened against bending in two different ways.

preferable appearance. The ⅛ in. aluminum shelf with a 3-foot span *could* be made adequate by increasing its thickness, but the result would be a costly slab that would be very heavy even in that light metal. A more reasonable step would be a change in cross-sectional configuration to one of the shapes shown (see diagram). In both cases since the part is a shelf acting as a beam, a member subjected to bending stress, the problem is to make a shelf also act as an efficient beam.

The most efficient beams (e.g., the steel I-beams used in construction work) are "deep," that is, they are taller than they are wide, and have most material at top and bottom where maximum compressive and tensile stresses will develop (see diagram). A ruler laid flat between two supports (e.g., a shelf) will bend easily, but the same ruler turned up on edge becomes quite stiff, and would be stiffer still if given an I-shaped cross section. Unfortunately, the useful shape for a shelf makes a poor beam, while a good beam is not typically an ideal shelf. Shelves are usually the result of compromise between the need for width to provide utilitarian surface and the need for depth to provide efficient structure. Tabletops and desk tops are also beams, special cases of shelf construction. Because they may have a greater span than most shelves, it is often best to separate the solutions into the need for surface and the need for structure. When this is done, thin, light surface material is made stiff by deep edges or braces set back under the top or by some combination of these approaches (see diagram).

Other parts of furniture often act as beams—the term applies to any part that is subject to bending stress. The frame of a sofa or bed, for example, is usually supported at or near its ends and makes a kind of bridge between supports. Such frame members must be large enough and strong enough not to break and also

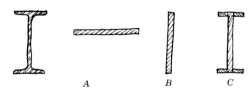

A   B   C

Structural steel I-beam at left. Flat beam A has limited resistance to bending. When turned on edge B the same beam becomes stiff. I form at C has even greater structural stiffness.

Shelf at left stiffened by edge brace; shelf at right has braces set back from edge.

not to sag or vibrate in a way that is disturbing. In all such parts structural efficiency is increased if the deep dimension of the part is turned in the direction of the forces that may tend to bend it; this usually means up and down, since the gravity forces that are frequently the source of bending stress are always vertical. There can also be bending forces in other directions. The back rail of a sofa might be subject to bending in a horizontal plane when users lean against it.

Vertical supporting parts of furniture, legs, and upright ends of cases and cabinets are not subject to bending stress in an important way in most cases but act as "posts" or columns subject to compressive stresses that tend to crush or squeeze the supporting part. The materials used for such parts are usually so strong that failure by actual crushing is very unusual. Long before crushing would occur, another problem usually would become evident—the problem of "buckling." When a support is made too thin for its height, a load much smaller than would cause crushing can make the support suddenly bend outward and actually bend or break. It is easy to visualize this kind of failure by picturing yourself leaning on a cane. Although it will readily support any weight you put on it, if we substitute a piece of thin wire (e.g., coat-hanger wire), which may be just as strong as the wood cane in simple compression, it would surely bend and fail through buckling. The same amount of metal made thin and rolled into a tube as thick as the wood cane would be of ample strength. The issue in this case is the ratio of the length (usually height) of the member in relation to its thickness, called the "slenderness ratio" of the member. In furniture, conveniently, the modest height of most objects means

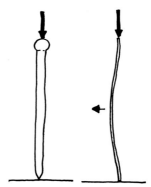

Thick compression member at left supports substantial load; thin member at right may buckle.

that the convenient sizes of materials usually provide an adequate slenderness ratio. It is not likely that any designer would propose supporting a grand piano on coat-hanger wire.

In addition to direct compressive stresses, vertical supporting parts are frequently subjected to sideway forces, often dynamic, which can produce bending in the vertical supports. Side stresses of this sort are not likely to cause collapse, but they often produce objectionable vibration, particularly when the material of the vertical parts is naturally springy (as in the case with metals and, to some extent, with wood and plastic when the parts are thin). Everyone has experiences of this kind of vibration in a desk or table and knows how irritating it can be.

Still another type of stress results when a part is loaded in a way that tends to pull and stretch it, the stress that is known technically as "tension." Tensile stresses do not appear often in most historic furniture, but in modern times the realization that many materials are very efficient when used in tension has led modern designers to seek forms that place parts in tension. Wire and cable, although thin and flexible, can withstand high stresses in tension. Objects that are suspended from above place the suspension members in tension, and braces that take advantage of triangulation (as will be discussed below) can act as tension members. Bracing members often turn out to be either compression members or tension members according to the direction of the forces working on them. In such cases, the brace must usually be designed as a compression member to ensure that it has an adequate slenderness ratio. It will then almost surely prove adequate when stressed in tension. When materials (e.g., wire or cable) that are only effective in tension are used, it is usually necessary to provide two or more braces so that one will become effective in tension when the other (or others) are slack and therefore ineffective (see diagram).

When all the individual parts of a piece of furniture are both shaped and sized to be adequate to sustain the stresses that anticipated load will generate in them, it is time to consider the connections or "joints" by which they are assembled. Everyone can think of examples of broken furniture where the failure has not occurred in any part but in a connection. Legs come off chairs, bottoms drop out of drawers, and shelves fall, probably most often

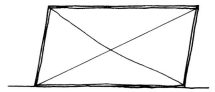

Diagonal braces resist tendency of rectangular unit to distort to parallelogram form.

because the connections intended to hold them in place fail. Connections vary tremendously in detail. The shaping of parts, adhesives, screws, and other hardware devices are all used singly and in combinations to put together similar or dissimilar materials. Details of joining methods for various materials and combinations of materials will be discussed in connection with specific materials below, but the general, structural issue is simply that every joint must be tested in concept, and possibly in that it can sustain the stresses that will be placed on it. In many cases the areas needed to permit an adequate joint will determine the size of a part rather than the stresses that will be developed in the part itself. Parts must often be shaped to grow large in cross section at the places where joints are to be made. Joints, like the parts joined, may be subject to compression, tension, shear, or torsion, in many cases in combinations or with different types of stress developing under varying conditions of use.

The joint between a leg and the tabletop it supports will normally be stressed in compression, but it is most likely to be broken when shear, torsion, or tension result as the table is dragged along the floor or upended for moving. The joints of chairs are broken again and again when users tip back to drag chair and occupant together along a thick carpet. A joint that appears secure when new can be gradually weakened with the continual flexing that may loosen screws, or as a result of dampness or excessive drying that can loosen many adhesives over a period of time. Frequently, designers establish configurations that include joints which are almost impossible to make sturdy. A thin table leg joined to a thin top at an outside corner establishes a condition in which many materials (wood, as a typical example) become almost impossible to join in a way that will withstand any rough use. Good judgment suggests that such situations should be avoided by substituting some different relationship of parts.

Actually, many of the more difficult problems of strength of parts and strength of connections can best be solved by the development of overall forms that avoid troublesome problems. The basic geometry of any structure determines how its parts will be stressed and what joining problems will be present. In structural geometry, one geometric form has peculiar properties that make it a solution, almost a "secret of success," in many situations. This is, of course, the triangle, the only figure having inherent rigidity because of the relationship between its angles and lengths of sides that makes it impossible for any angle to change while the sides remain constant in length. This becomes clear if we make a simple demonstration by putting together geometric figures with three, four, five, or more sides of cardboard strips joined at their angles by pins or thumbtacks (see illustration). The triangular figure will be rigid, while any other polygon will distort into a variety of shapes as the

Cardboard strips pinned together demonstrate rigidity of triangle as compared to square or pentagon.

pins at the angles act as pivots. The nontriangular figures can be made rigid by fixing the angle joints in some way (with glue or a second pin or tack), but that rigidity will depend on the strength of the joints. The triangle's rigidity is inherent in the geometry of the shape. This is the reason for the prominence of triangular shapes in such utilitarian structures as radios or electric high-tension towers, bridges, and the structural trusses used to roof large open spaces. It also explains the appearance of the diagonal wire braces on early airplanes.

Triangulation appears in the structures of many pieces of modern furniture in such forms as a simple tension brace (*A*), a pair or group of three braces placed so that one will be in tension with any one direction of side force (*B*), or in the form of the ubiquitous X-brace consisting of two overlapped triangles (*C*). In the last case one leg of the X works in tension while the other is slack and unstressed or, if it is made of a stiff material, becomes a compression strut. While these braces make triangulation very visible, the more usual route to structural rigidity through total configuration conceals the theoretical presence of triangulation. This happens when solid panels, sheets, or bars are used as a means of stiffening an otherwise nonrigid configuration. An ordinary open bookshelf such as (*A*), for example, will only be as stiff as the strength of its corner joints makes possible since its rectangular open shape can easily distort into a parallelogram (*B*), as can easily happen if it is loaded with heavy books stacked at an angle (*C*). If the back of this unit is covered by a panel reasonably well attached along its edges (*D*), the case becomes remarkably stiff. In fact, the panel contains an X-brace within itself, an infinite number of triangular braces all fused into one surface. Sheet material used in this way can also be thought of as the "stressed-skin" of aircraft structure. Any box having five or six surfaces is an excellent demonstration of the effectiveness of putting together sheets of material to generate mutual bracing. Since many articles of furniture are boxes or

Shelf unit **A** *with weak corner joints may distort as at* **B** *when loaded as shown at* **C***. Solid back panel* **D** *prevents "racking" distortion.*

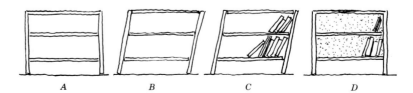

A   B   C   D

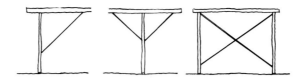

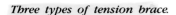

Three types of tension brace.

combinations of boxes, this is a particularly effective route to stiffness in furniture.

Ideally box constructions should not be used for tables and chairs (although it is not unusual, see illustration page 108), but the hidden triangulation within solid panels is often used in the less obvious forms of deep stretchers (*A*), or beamlike top braces (*B*) that both strengthen a top against bending and provide concealed triangulation or, in seating, in backs or back slats (*C*) that stiffen an otherwise questionable form. The type of brace of (*B*), if not considered as a beam, but only as bracing against side-sway (called "racking"), actually contains excess material. When this material is cut away, as at (*D*), the triangles that are its working principle become more visible. Many variations of these approaches are possible. Triangular braces may be introduced only at corners, for example, as at (*E*), or in solid plates at corners as at (*F*) called "gussets," a favorite detail of engineering structures.

The use of curvatures is also a possible route to improved strength through overall configuration. It is easy to demonstrate that a thin, flat sheet (e.g., a piece of paper or cardboard) is flexible until curved (see illustration page 109) when it becomes relatively stiff along one axis. Double curvature introduces stiffness along both axes of a surface, as in a shell or cup. Such forms have had little utility in furniture of the past because of the difficulties involved in manufacture, but modern materials, metals, and especially plastics encourage shell shapes, particularly in seating units where the curvatures favor comfort as well as strength. In order to apply the general structural principles discussed above to specific situations, it is best to consider the common materials of furniture individually and discuss the special characteristics of each. The ma-

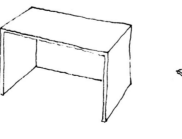
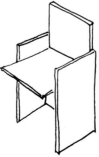

Boxlike table or chair will be highly rigid.

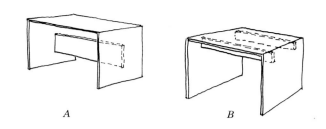

A   B

C

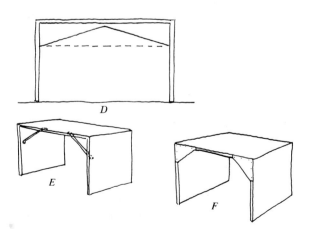

D

E   F

*(D) Removal of portion of brace
(dotted line) still preserves rigidity.*

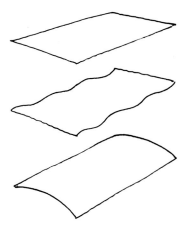

Flat sheet of paper (top) will ripple easily (center). When curved (bottom), same sheet becomes quite rigid in one direction.

terials used in furniture in any important structural way are, as of the present, limited to three main types. In the order in which they have been commonly used historically, these are wood, metals, and plastics. A large technical literature is concerned with each of these material families, but the important basics are summarized here.

Wood

The basic characteristics of wood as a material all arise from its origin as a natural material, the stem or trunk of a growing tree. The human processing that converts a live tree into the raw material we call timber or lumber does not alter its basic characteristics very deeply; instead, it is limited to reduction in size and shape for convenient transportation and working into completed products. If we omit the special cases of plywood and particle board, relatively recent inventions that alter the tree-trunk characteristics of wood extensively, we must confront wood in the forms of "solids" structured as they were by nature in the tree. The growth processes of plants depend on a stem structure consisting of compactly massed tiny tubes that rise from the roots up into the branches to permit the flow of sap that is involved in the plant's life process. Cut solid wood is still a mass of tiny tubes, clearly visible under strong magnification. Generally these tubes run in one direction— in the tree, upward from the roots; in cut lumber, in the "direction of the grain." This "grain" is the dominant characteristic of solid wood. The natural form of a wooden part is linear, long and narrow, a stick. All woodwork must consider grain structure, its usefulnesses, and the problems it presents.

Woods fall into two main types that correspond to the two main types of trees. The wood families are called hardwood and softwood in a roughly accurate identification of the qualities of the

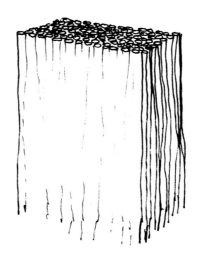

The tubular structure characteristic of wood.

materials, and the trees are often given the same group names. The softwood trees are the evergreens, or conifers whose leaves are spinelike and remain year-round. These trees have the familiar "Christmas tree" conelike shape. The common varieties are pine, spruce, fir, hemlock, cedar and redwood. The hardwoods are the deciduous trees that change color in the autumn and lose their leaves in the winter. These include fruit and nut trees. Typical examples are oak, maple, birch, and walnut. Many exotic woods from tropical climates are also hardwoods, although in most cases their rarity makes them less known as solid lumber for furniture production. These include rosewood, ebony, zebrawood, and even less familiar species. Mahogany and poplar are hardwoods, although they are actually somewhat "soft" in character. Teak is a unique hardwood because of its unusually oily makeup.

The softwoods are, in general, the materials of building construction, of carpentry, and of simply constructed woodwork intended for paint finishes. With a few unusual exceptions, only low-cost, utilitarian ("kitchen") furniture is made from softwoods. Furniture of good quality, the product of "cabinetmaking" as compared to "car-

Typical conifer (softwood) at left; deciduous tree (hardwood) form at right.

pentry" is made from hardwoods. The typical amateur craftsman uses softwoods because they are the only woods available in the typical lumber yard, because they are more modest in price, and primarily because they can be worked easily with hand tools and do not dull the cutting edges of power tools. It is often a shock to the home craftsman to hear that, despite the exceptional examples from colonial America and various other historic times and places, most furniture made of solid wood that has lasting qualities is hardwood. The hardwoods are difficult to cut, almost impossible to nail, and require special treatment when worked with power tools. Cutting blades will often become dull and burn rather than cut when working hardwoods, unless they are run at high speed and are of special material or design. The modern cabinet shop and furniture factory are prepared to deal with these problems when working solid hardwood, and traditional craftsmen dealt with them in making fine furniture in the past, but anyone experienced only in the softwoods of carpentry must make some major adjustments in working hardwoods.

The preference for hardwoods in quality work derives from their higher strengths, from the precision cuts, edges, and surfaces they can provide, and from their ability to develop surfaces of high quality, durability, and lasting qualities. Many hardwoods have much admired color and grain patterns, generally superior to those of softwoods that tend to be lighter in color and without prominent grain or interesting character. There are exceptions to these generalizations. A handsome pine panel, for example, can be beautiful and take a fine finish, but most softwood is best painted or finished with some other totally obscuring finish. The traditions of "cabinetwork," fine woodworking developed originally for hand craftsmanship, are primarily techniques for working hardwoods although often some of the softer types (such as mahogany) became preferred materials.

Cabinetwork using solid stock must consider grain structure and some of the incidental peculiarities that natural wood generates. Wood will shrink and swell with changes in humidity, and will change dimension more across the grain than along its length. In addition to shrinking and swelling, the dimensional change in cut lumber will include a re-creation of the changes in shape that the same piece would go through as a part of the log from which it

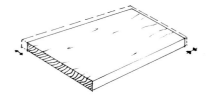

Wood shrinkage is greatest across the grain, least in lengthwise direction.

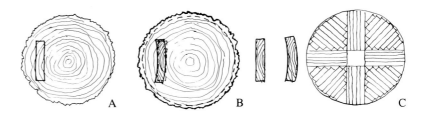

A   B   C

was cut. Thus, the board outlined in its position before cutting in a log (A) would, as the complete log swells with an increase in humidity, change its shape as shown at (B). The same board, cut from the log, can be expected to show a comparable change from flat to curved. This is the peculiar behavior called "warping," often considered to be a defect of wood but actually a wholly natural characteristic. Boards cut from a log in a radial position are least subject to this problem, and logs are often cut in special ways to produce a maximum yield of boards in radial, or near-radial positions. Quarter sawing (diagram [C]) is a favorite system for maximizing the production of boards with minimal tendency to warp. Any object made of solid wood must take into account the inevitability of shrinkage and swelling and some amount of warp. To make up wide panels by simply edge-gluing boards together, although often done in making drawing boards or cutting boards, almost ensures that cracks or splits will occur as well as some warping. Examination of any wide tabletops or boards made this way that have been in use for some time will usually show splits or "checks," partial splits beginning at an end.

Furniture craftspeople and furniture designers have developed several lines of defense against these problems. The choice of wood used will affect the seriousness of the problems to a considerable degree. Pieces chosen cut from radial positions in the log will be most stable—a matter of increasing importance as the board in question is to be wide in the finished product. Unfortunately, when wood is obtained already cut, it is not possible to ascertain what position it had in the complete log. The makers of historic furniture, who started with a complete log, had an advantage in this way over the modern worker whose wood comes from a mill precut. The second issue involves dryness of the wood. Freshly cut trees contain moist sap, and wood in this condition, called "green," is not ready for working. Ideally, drying should be as slow as possible. Wood staked to permit circulation of air and left to dry for many years (ideally for generations!) reaches a stable level of dryness which minimizes shrinkage and swelling. Modern lumber production does not, in most cases, provide time for air-drying and substitutes drying in a kiln, a kind of large steam-heated oven. Moisture is driven off rapidly in this way but, because of the rapidity of the process, is taken up from humid air again

Rail and panel construction.

very easily. Although not ideal, kiln-dried stock is now widely used. Its stability can be improved by arranging for some air-drying before use, several years if possible.*

Given wood reasonably dried, the furniture designer needs to consider conceptual planning that will minimize the need for wide, uninterrupted areas. Traditional furniture is full of demonstrations of how this can be done. The basic technique is usually to design in terms of a cagelike linear structure that can be built up of lengthwise, straight (or slightly curved) strips. A frame of this kind tends to be stable and serves well as structure for chairs, upholstery, and table support. Tabletops and cabinets require wider surfaces. The best means of developing these in solid woods involves building a frame around the four sides of the area needed, and inserting thin panels into the frame with the use of a tongue and groove (see illustration). The thin panel is restrained from warping by the thicker frame and, left unglued at its edges, is free to shrink or swell without splitting. This is the basis for the familiar "rail and panel" construction used for a wide variety of wood furniture. Drawers, when needed, can usually be kept small enough to avoid problems, and are inserted into the frame. Ends, backs, and doors are built with inserted panels. Tops present a problem since they must usually be smooth. They can be built up in a similar way with a surrounding frame, but with the central area made of thicker panel material flush with the rails on top, although some danger of checks always remains when this is done (see diagram). The popularity of leather tops for desks and marble tops for chests probably had its origins in this problem.

The sticklike members that make up a frame are sized with awareness of the unsupported length they will have, the loads they must bear, and the areas needed to join them successfully. Parts of chairs can be as small as $1/2 \times 3/4$ in., but usually will be $3/4 \times 1$ in. or more. The main elements of a chair may be as large as 2×2 in., but sizes greater than this tend to generate excessive weight. A large upholstered chair or sofa may have larger rails, but a cross section over $1\frac{1}{2} \times 3$ in. is unusual. Although members may be tapered or shaped, the section at connections must be large

Panel set flush with surrounding rails.

---

* Five or six years is considered a minimum aging time for wood to be used in violin making. Some piano makers age wood for a generation or more!

enough to permit a strong joint, as discussed below. Frames of cases usually have sections ranging from 1 × 1½ in. up to 2 × 4 in., although members at the top of this range tend to seem excessively massive and heavy. Panels can be anywhere from ¼ in. in thickness (unusually thin) up to ¾ in. Greater thickness negates the usefulness of panel construction. Solid drawer fronts are usually about ¾ in. thick, while sides and backs are ⅜ or ½ in. Bottoms of drawers are usually ¼ in. In modern practice, plywood is often substituted for solids in panels, drawer bottoms, drawer fronts, and doors even in furniture that is built up from solids elsewhere.

Plywood is now a widely used manufactured wood material that has its historic origins in the use of veneer. When a log or plank is sawed or sliced into very thin sheets, usually only 1/28 in. thick, a very large surface area is produced from a small quantity of wood. This almost paper-thin material becomes quite flexible if bent in only one direction (like paper or card, it will tear or crumple if double curvature into a cup or bowl shape is attempted). It is commonly thought that veneer was developed and is used to cover poor material with a surface of better material and many people are convinced that "solid wood" is always best. Actually veneer was developed to make maximum use of rare or valuable woods, but it quickly became clear that it was a new route to some solutions to the problems of using solid wood in case construction. A flush panel can consist of solid wood, glued together strips of indifferent appearance, and this "core" can then be covered with two layers of veneer on each side with grain direction running the opposite way in each successive layer (see illustration). The resulting core panel will be relatively immune to problems of splitting, expansion, and warping, and will have good appearance with limited use of good-quality veneer. In traditional furniture this technique was also exploited to generate decorative grain and inlay patterns in exposed surfaces.

In modern practice, most wood case furniture is made from such core panels. The core may be solid wood, usually poplar, layers of veneer (always an odd number to preserve balance) or, most recently, particle board or even plastic foam. In the latter

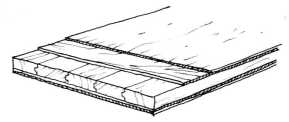

Typical panel construction with face veneer and cross-banding on top cut back to show layering.

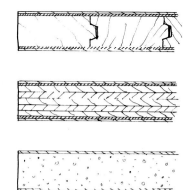

Panel construction: solid core (top), veneer core (center), and particle-board core (bottom).

cases, since the core material is grainless, the under layer of "crossbanding" veneer can be omitted (see diagrams). Such panels, made up in factories in standard sizes, can be bought in a variety of woods, good on one side or on both as desired, and is a favorite material of small shops and home craftspeople. Furniture factories usually make their own panels to required sizes (to avoid waste) and can then position solid strips of the desired kind of wood at edges and other locations where they will be machined. Modern plywoods, made with excellent modern adhesives are very durable and generally superior to solids for most parts of cabinet furniture. Desks and tables usually use some combination of solids and plywood panels while wood chairs and upholstery frames are most often mainly of solid stock.

A large number of wood species are used in furniture construction. Unfortunately, because of the careless and wasteful cutting of many trees of the slow-growing hardwood species, many woods are becoming increasingly rare and expensive. In plywoods, the species name describing the face appearance refers only to the outermost veneer layers that use relatively little material, but the cost is still strongly influenced by the rarity of the particular wood used for the faces. A summary of the characteristics of the most used woods is given in Table 4.

When a solid section of a log is sliced into veneer, the successive sheets or layers will be almost identical in appearance, since any color of grain patterns will be repeated through the stack (called a "flitch"), as with slices of bacon cut from a side. This fact can be used to generate patterns through "matching" of veneer in repeating or symmetrical ways (see illustration). Where such patterns are not wanted, instructions should be given to ensure that the maker does not produce them by accident or in an effort to achieve some extra decorative effect. Grain direction always needs to be shown in drawings or specified, since it is often optional when veneers and plywoods are being used and can be a strong factor in the appearance of wood furniture.

TABLE 4
CHARACTERISTICS OF MOST USED FURNITURE WOODS

Note: A large part of the wood visible in modern furniture is *plywood*, in which only the outermost thin layer of veneer is of the species named. In this case the only significant characteristics are the color and finish surface of the face veneer. Where *solid* wood is used, as in legs, rails, and stretchers, other characteristics are also signifcant. Woods that are rarely used as solids, but are common as decorative veneers, are not included in this list.

Species	Typical Color	Relative Cost	Current Availability	Typical Uses and Special Characteristics
Hardwoods				
Birch	Light beige-tan to near-white	Medium	Good	Hard, strong, compact grain, works and finishes well, generally useful in all furniture applications
Cherry	Reddish-brown	High	Limited	Works and finishes well, well suited to hand craftsmanship
Ebony	Brown with near-black grain	High	Limited	Dense and heavy wood with striking grain pattern. Often stained black
Mahogany	Reddish-brown to red	Medium	Good	Relatively soft, easy to work and finish. Typically red color often deepened with stain
Maple	Light beige-tan	Medium	Good	Similar to birch (see above), with which it is sometimes mixed in one product
Oak	Light grayish-brown	Medium to high	Good	Hard and strong with marked, coarse grain. Often stained to darker browns
Poplar	Light tan with pink and greenish streaks	Low	Good	Soft and easy to work. Color and grain not attractive. Much used for hidden parts and panel cores
Rosewood	Deep red with black graining	High	Very limited	Striking and highly decorative appearance. Most used as veneer, often in matched patterning
Teak	Warm, light brown	Medium to high	Fair	Close, uniform grain, easily workable. High oil content makes oil finishes desirable
Walnut	Grayish-brown	Medium to high	Fair to good	Strong, consistent grain and good appearance. Suitable to general furniture uses in solids and veneers. Medium-dark color often further darkened with stains
Softwoods				
Cedar	Orange to red	Low	Good	Occasionally used in furniture, most often as storage lining because of pleasant, aromatic odor
Pine, white	Clear, near-white	Medium	Limited	Soft, even grain and easy workability suited to hand craftsmanship. Limited strength
Pine, yellow	Tan, orange to yellow	Low	Excellent	Soft, grainy, and difficult to finish well. Primarily a material for carpentry. Limited use, low-cost, roughly worked applications
Redwood	Reddish-brown	Low	Excellent	Natural oil content makes usable outdoors without finish. Soft and easy to work, limited strength

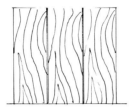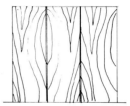

Veneers may be "matched" in various ways; to form a repeating pattern (slip match), left, or to form symmetrical patterns (book match), right. Where no pattern is desired, a "random match" is specified (not shown).

Frame members and panels (solid or plywood) that make up a piece of furniture must be assembled with suitable connections, usually made by shaping ends and edges of the parts to be joined in special ways. The art of "joinery," the selection and making of suitable joints, has been the heart of the traditional cabinetmaker's craft. This tradition is becoming obsolescent because some of its basic assumptions are no longer applicable, and the long and demanding apprentice training that was always required to make a good cabinetmaker is no longer appealing to newcomers to the field. The traditional cabinetmaker works in ways derived from several rules and assumptions, as follows:

1. Glue can never be relied on as a joining medium. Every joint must include some type of interlocking that would make it secure in normal use without glue. Glue is only added to eliminate rattles and to secure against forces in unusual directions. This conservative assumption has been largely invalidated by the development of modern synthetic glues that are often stronger than the materials which they join.

2. End grain (the grain exposed when wood is cut transversely, as opposed to lengthwise grain) may never be exposed. This tradition is based on a dislike for the nonmatching appearance of finished end grain, but became a mark of skill in its own right. While this practice is usually adhered to in modern times, it is no longer regarded as an absolute.

3. Edges may never expose cores or laminations of veneer or plywood. This rule is also still largely observed, but occasionally is deliberately violated when laminations are exposed and exploited for visual effect.

4. A technical means of joining must, in the finished work, be completely concealed. Even traditional work sometimes violates this rule and uses dowels, mortises, wedges, and so on for decorative and expressive effect. This has become increasingly common in the work of modern handcraftsmen.

5. Utilitarian hardware (screws, hinges, catches, etc.) must be completely concealed. The only exceptions are deliberately designed "decorative" hardware elements such as pulls, knobs or, occasionally, hinges.

Making sturdy furniture while observing these rules required the development of a large vocabulary of wood joints and other details. Modern woodworking still uses some of these details, in some cases in simplified form, and it is necessary to know some of the associated terminology. Many complex and interesting joints have become obsolete except as curiosities. Information about the most useful joining details is organized into the following series of charts.

Rail Joints
(Joints between solid-stick parts)

BUTT JOINTS
These do not conceal end grain if used at a corner, and are therefore most useful when one rail end meets the midpoint of another rail. They can also be used where the end grain would occur below eye level (as the bottom corner of a case frame) or where exposed end grain is tolerated or desired.

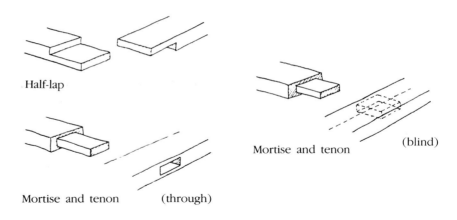

Half-lap

Mortise and tenon   (through)

Mortise and tenon   (blind)

Rabbet mortise and stub tenon

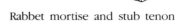

Dowel

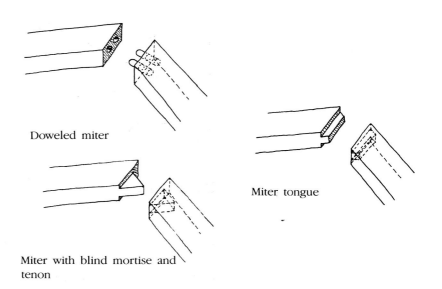

Doweled miter

Miter tongue

Miter with blind mortise and tenon

MITER JOINTS

These conceal end grain by bringing the two ends together on a diagonal of the joint. The diagonal is a 45° angle when two parts of the same width meet. When parts of unequal width meet, the 45° angle is usually maintained by combining a miter with a partial butt.

PANEL TO RAIL JOINTS

The first two types are relatively crude, while the latter two require assembling the frame of rails around the panel or, at least, adding the fourth rail last. The rails are joined using one of the joints illustrated above to make up a complete element of panel surrounded by assembled rails.

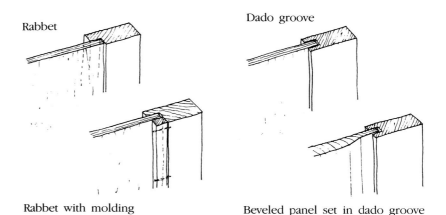

Rabbet

Dado groove

Rabbet with molding

Beveled panel set in dado groove

Case Joints

(Joints used to connect wider boards or panels and, in modern practice, to join plywood panels)

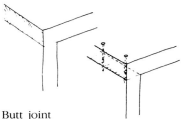

Butt joint

(often nailed to secure glue joint)

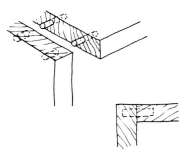

Dowel (or doweled butt)

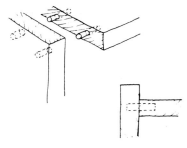

(more secure because of extra material beyond dowel)

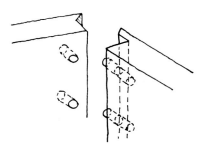

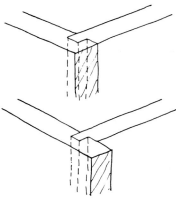

Tongued (or box) corner (also best when made more secure by extra material beyond joint)

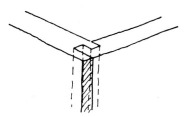

Milled corner

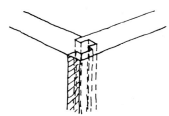

Lock butt

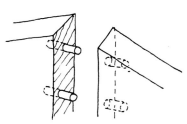

Doweled miter (two types above and left, the first more common)

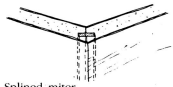

Splined miter

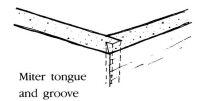

Miter tongue
and groove

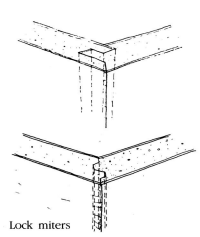

Lock miters

Offset miter

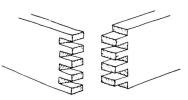

Box joint
(rarely exposed in good cabinetwork)

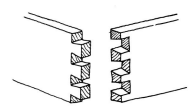

Dovetail joints: through dovetail

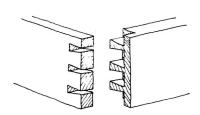

Multiple dovetail (handcut)

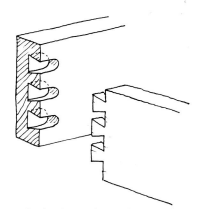

Multiple dovetail (machine cut)

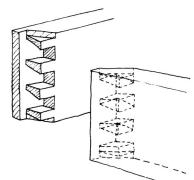

Blind, double-lap dovetail

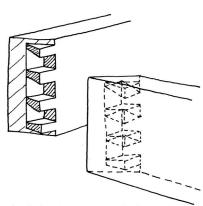

Blind (secret or miter) dovetail

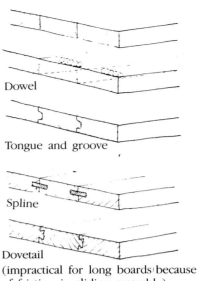

Dowel

Tongue and groove

Spline

Dovetail
(impractical for long boards because
of friction in sliding assembly)

Joints of Three or More
(Used to make up wide panels from many narrow boards, often to
make cores which are then veneered)

Edge Treatment
(Most often used with plywood in modern practice, but also applicable to solid wood, particularly along end grain)

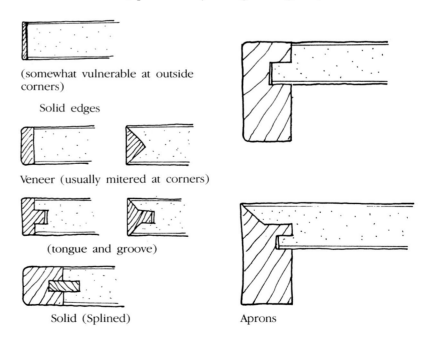

(somewhat vulnerable at outside
corners)

Solid edges

Veneer (usually mitered at corners)

(tongue and groove)

Solid (Splined)

Aprons

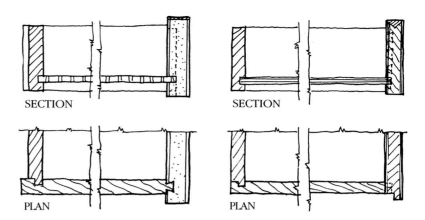

SECTION   SECTION

PLAN   PLAN

Drawer Construction Joints

(Joints illustrated above can be combined in various ways. The following combinations are typical)

In selecting wood joints the designer should remember that is easy to indicate on drawings joints or combinations of joints that are almost impossible to make. It is good practice to avoid or minimize "three-way joints," where three parts must meet at one point because there is often not enough material area to make secure joints possible when the parts are rails, and because the problems of fitting become difficult when panels are involved (see illustration): It is also necessary to consider assembly sequence. It is possible to design a box (e.g., a drawer) that cannot be put

Difficult: Easier:

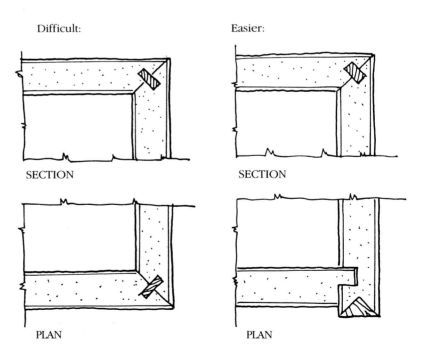

SECTION   SECTION

PLAN   PLAN

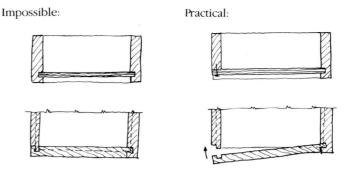

Impossible: Practical:

together—there must always be a way to put in the last part. When the craftsperson or factory that will make a design is known and trusted, it is often best to leave decisions about joinery to those who will be doing the work. Yet it is desirable for the designer to know at least one good way to deal with every joinery problem that his or her design will present.

Wood can be processed in special ways that produce particular qualities which almost generate a special name designation. Three of these processes are discussed here.

Particle Board

This material was referred to above as an alternative to solid or veneer cores in plywood panels. It is a manufactured sheet made by bonding together wood particles, chips, or sawdust, with adhesives under heat and pressure. It is made by automatic equipment in a continuously produced band in highly efficient factory production. The basic wood material used would ordinarily show up otherwise as waste in other woodworking processes, so that particle board is a highly economic material. Its strength and weather-resistance depend on the bonding agent used and the manufacturing process, but it is available in a number of grades suitable for many applications. Usually it is not as strong as solid wood, but when wood veneers are bonded to its surface the resulting panel is only slightly less strong than the solid core equivalent—more than strong enough for most furniture applications. Its ability to hold screws and to accept joinery details at edges is also slightly inferior to solid wood or plywood, but is usually adequate. Special fastening inserts are often advisable when making screw connections to particle board ¾ in. or less in thickness.

Since the material has no directional grain, it is immune to splitting or checking and tends to be stable against shrinking and warpage (although not fully immune). Its surface appearance is generally unsatisfactory for furniture uses, so it is usually veneered (with or without crossbanding) or otherwise surface-coated. Special

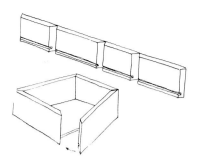

V-groove drawer construction.

grades are available with a factory-made surface for painting. Common trade names are Novoply and GPX.

A recent development in particle board uses a face surfacing of a plastic film (usually vinyl) of good strength and flexibility. A panel large enough to make up front and ends of a case is cut in one piece and then V-grooved at the points that will become corners. Adhesive is spread in the grooves and the sheet is folded to form the intended case parts (see illustration). This technique makes for excellent production economy but has not yet been exploited in furniture of any particular design excellence.

Hardboard

This is a generic term for sheet materials similar to particle board but made up of more finely shredded fibers similar to those used in making paper or cardboard. Masonite is the trade name of a well-known example. Hardboards are made in a range of thicknesses, usually ⅛ to 5/16 in., and in various grades of density and hardness. Perforated and prefinished panels are available. Hardboard is most often used in utility parts of furniture, drawer bottoms, and case backs, but manufacturers demonstrate ways in which complete furniture units can be constructed from hardboard through the use of suitable edging and joining details.

PAPER and cardboard have possibilities as furniture materials that may come to be more fully explored as wood products become increasingly scarce and expensive. Some experimental paper furniture has been developed that seems to have good possibilities, particularly in lowcost applications where portability or disposability may be considered.

Hollow cores for panels are made from paper strips glued together at points in staggered lines and then expanded into honeycomb form. Paper honeycomb impregnated with a plastic resin is adhered to a surface sheet material and forms a panel of great strength and very light weight. Edges must be specially treated, and joining presents problems. Doors are the most common application of this material at present.

Bentwood

It has long been known that solid wood can be made flexible by the application of heat, a fact used by violin makers for many centuries in making the curved parts of instruments. In 1841 Michael Thonet, the Austrian furniture inventor-manufacturer, obtained patents on his method of making complete pieces of furniture from bentwood parts. The wood used must have a straight, uniform tight grain. European beech is ideal. Long parts are shaped to desired cross sections while still straight sticks. These are placed in steam chambers and heated under pressure until they become flexible. The parts are then placed on forming molds, bent to their shape, and held clamped in place until they dry and cool. When removed from these formers, the parts retain their bent shape except for some slight spring-back. Parts are then assembled with screws and glue into frames that can receive caned, padded, or plywood seats and backs or tops of any material. Thonet's firm developed excellent lightweight low-cost designs that are still widely used. Bentwood requires the availability of ideal material and the use of special equipment and skills. It has not been developed as a significant manufacturing technique in the United States, although there are a few small firms that specialize in making bentwood parts for other manufacturers.

Thonet chair No. 18, a classic example of bentwood construction. (From an early Thonet catalog.)

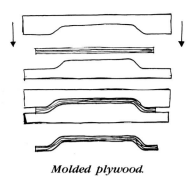

Molded plywood.

Molded Plywood
(also called bent plywood)

There is some confusion of terms in relation to this process. "Bent" plywood implies that flat plywood is bent in some way similar to solid bentwood. This is not possible except for very limited cold bending of very thin plywood, rarely attempted. What is often called "bent plywood" is actually molded, that is, made in a mold so that the "bend" or molding is a characteristic of the piece of plywood from the time it is made. This process takes advantage of the fact that wood veneer is, because of its thinness, quite flexible. If glue (or adhesive in dry sheets) is placed between a number of layers of veneer, the prepared stack can be placed in a press between forming molds. When the press is closed, the veneer flexes to conform to the molds. Heat and pressure cause the adhesive to set and the part, when removed from the mold, retains the curvature given it. Curves in one direction can be quite sharp as long as the radius of curvature has a reasonable relationship to the thickness of the part; about one thickness is a minimum inside radius. The design of the part and the design of the molds must be worked out to make it possible for the press to exert adequate pressure to push the veneer layers together, and to permit the part to be removed from the mold easily (see diagrams). Shapes that include undercuts or approach complete loops present special difficulties. Molds of more than two parts, including center cores may be needed. In some cases an inflatable air bag is interposed between the surface of the mold and the part as an aid to obtaining even pressure over the surface. Dry adhesive layers require a radio-frequency current field to produce internal heating to meld and set the adhesive.

Long parts of molded plywood with the bend running the long way of the part can be made and are often used as seats for benches or church pews. It is also possible to make such long parts to be sliced after molding to produce many small parts. Straight slicing is often used to make legs or chair side frames. Slicing in a

Contours must permit easy release from the mold.

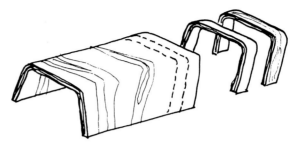

A plywood molding to be sliced at an angle.

Solid material converted to molded plywood for a part of its upper end.

complex pattern can produce frames with complex curvatures that seem at first glance to be impossible.

Multiple curvatures to produce dish or bowl shapes are possible to a very limited degree because the veneers tend to split or buckle when forced into such forms.

Occasionally parts are made partly solid and partly molded. To do this, the end of a solid is saw cut into a comb, and layers of veneer are slipped into the resultant slots. Molding of the layered area proceeds as described above.

Finishes

Wood requires a finish coating to protect it from dirt and gradual wear. Many types of finish that have been used in the past remain available, but a small number of finishing systems that are practical in modern industrial production have become dominant in recent years. Such finishing materials as wax, shellac, natural base lacquer, varnish, or "French polish"* used to finish historic furniture now survive only as materials for handcraft production and for refinishing or reproducing historic examples. The following are widely used modern finishes:

Oil Finish. Boiled linseed oil (or, in some cases other oils or oil mixtures) is brushed or wiped on to the wood surface, allowed to soak in, and any excess on the surface is wiped off. Two or more coats are usually required. With small objects or parts, the entire unit may be dipped in oil to avoid wiping or brushing.

An oil finish has a particularly "natural" appearance since the wood grain is left open and unchanged. The oil only causes a darkening and color shift comparable to wetting the material with water.

Oil finishes may show water or other liquid spotting and do not offer much surface protection, but spots and damage can be easily repaired with reoiling. Even scratches or dents can often be sanded or steel-wooled and oiled over with good success. Minor damage, oiled over, can become with the passage of time a kind of "patina" of wear similar to the worn finishes of antiques that are often greatly admired.

Natural Lacquer Finish. The word "natural" as used here refers, confusingly, to the natural wood color, not to the lacquer material. Modern lacquers are usually synthetic chemical formulations applied with a spray gun. Three or more coats are usually given with a heat-drying period between. Objects to be finished can move on a conveyer through a spray booth and through a drying oven for several cycles before being given a final hand rubbing. A high gloss can be developed, or a mat or satin finish can be maintained. The lacquer forms a surface skin that is tough and resistant to stains and spots. Once damaged by scratching, denting, spotting, or staining by a material that is a solvent for the lacquer, this finish is difficult to repair satisfactorily.

When lacquer is applied to wood without previous preparation, an open "close to the wood" finish results similar in appearance to an oil finish with the grain of the wood open and visible. If a filler is applied first (a paste spread on the surface and wiped off so that it will remain in the open grain pores), the surface can be made totally smooth. The color of the filler can match or contrast with the color of the wood and so alter the appearance of the finished surface considerably. Filler color and stains can

---

* "French polish" is shellac, alcohol and oil hand applied with pads and hand rubbed according to many different "secret" routines.

be used together to obtain a wide variety of appearances from a particular wood. Finishes of this type seem to be most popular to obtain variety in commercial furniture of indifferent quality. Most quality furniture is finished in a way that retains the natural appearance of the wood.

Stains. Before finishing with either oil or lacquer, stains may be used to change wood color. Mahogany, for example, which has a natural light orange color, is often stained to deep red or red-brown before finishing.

Light staining may be used to help match parts made from wood of slightly different color. In some cases wood of one species is stained to match another wood. Birch, for example, can be stained walnut with fair success, although the grain will remain somewhat different.

A black stain, often called ebonizing, can be used to produce a solid black color before finishing. The traditional black finish of many pianos is of this type.

Paints. In most cases, only inexpensive wood furniture of lesser quality is brush painted with ordinary house paint. Where colored surfaces are desired on better quality wood furniture, spray painting can be used with the same routines as are used for lacquer finishes. In fact, the material is usually of the same synthetic used for natural or clear lacquer finish with the addition of opaque color pigment. The terms "paint" and "lacquer" are used interchangeably for such finishes.

Epoxy plastic resin as a base for paint or lacquer develops a very tough and durable surface skin that can approach the durability of plastic laminates. It is wise to make tests of any such finishes before accepting uncritically any claims to total invulnerability, particularly when white or other light colors are to be used.

An alternative to finish coating on wood furniture is surfacing with plastic laminate. This possibility is discussed below in the section on plastics.

Metals

Modern industrial production of various metals has made these materials available as possible alternatives to the traditional wood. Metal parts were first introduced into furniture cautiously as decorative accessories or as strengthening elements, but furniture made entirely of metal became common in the 19th century. Its use is currently accelerating as the cost of wood rises with increasing scarcity.

Steel is the metal most used in furniture, and aluminum also has extensive applications. Other metals such as brass, bronze, or magnesium are used occasionally for special reasons, and the alloy called "die-casting metal" shows up in parts made with that technique. Metal furniture can be stronger and more durable than wood (although it is not necessarily so), has the advantage of being virtually fireproof, and can be worked with great efficiency in industrial production based on techniques developed for the production of automobiles and appliances.

The woodworker can, if he or she wishes, start with a log, but the metalworker must accept his material in forms established by the basic producers of the metal in question. There is no such thing as a small, backyard steel mill. The large steel members that are rolled for use in heavy construction such as building frames, bridge members, and railroad rails rarely have furniture applications because their weights and strengths are excessive for furniture uses. A steel beam 30 inches deep might make a good table base, but weighs 240 lb. per foot of length! Metal used in furniture is usually in the form of sheets, bars, and tubes or small "structural sections" similar in form to the heavy steel sections, but miniature in scale. Since steel and aluminum both come in these forms, it is convenient to discuss them together, noting that aluminum weighs only about one third as much as a steel part of comparable size but is also far less strong by a factor that varies with different alloys and temperings.

Frames for many furniture types are made from metal tubes, bars, or other sections by cutting pieces to length, in some cases bending the cut lengths and assembling these parts with one another and with parts of other materials. Tube bending can be done by hand with simple devices or a powered tube bender can be used. The tubing is held in place and bent at the right point to the desired angle by swinging a movable arm while a wheel-like form guides the bend. In general, tube is difficult to bend to a radius less than twice the diameter of the tube (inside radius). Thin-walled tube will often show some flattening even at this radius. Spring-like inserts may be put in the tube to reduce crushing, or the tube may be packed with sand for the same purpose. A costly and elaborate means of getting perfect bends, even with

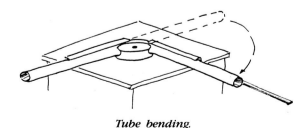

Tube bending.

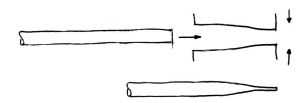

small radii, is to pour molten lead into the tube. After bending while cool, the tube is reheated to recover the lead. Very sharp bends are sometimes made by making a V-cut on the inside of the bend and welding and polishing over the cut area after the bend has been made.

An unusual way of working tube is called "swaging" and produces tapers at any desired point in a tube. Tube of the maximum diameter desired is used and the portion to be tapered is pushed into a swaging machine, where dies shaped to the needed taper pound the tube down to the desired lesser diameter (see illustration).

Metal to metal joints can be welded or mechanical. Gas welding or brazing use a line or "fillet" of weld-metal fused to the parts by high heat to hold the parts together with a kind of metallic "glue." Neat welding to make strong joints requires skill and can be costly. Polishing and finishing after welding is needed, to ensure neat appearance if the location of the weld will be visible. Resistance welding uses electric current passed through the metal to be welded to fuse the parts at a line or point of contact. Spot-welding machines make a small, round weld at a particular point and are very convenient for joining sheet metal through a number of such small spot-welds.

Mechanical joints of metal parts can use rivets, screws with or without nuts, and various specialized fastenings that have been developed for particular purposes.

Wood, plastic, and upholstered parts are usually attached mechanically, often with special purpose fastenings. Frames for chairs and other seating, for beds, tables, desks, and storage functions are commonly made in this way. Where furniture is constructed entirely of metal, similar frames can support parts of sheet metal, formed as needed and connected to frames by welding or mechanically. Stock sections and sizes commonly used for frames are listed in Table 5. Sheet metals are available in a range of thicknesses usually designated by gauge numbers, as listed in Table 6.

Sheet metal, like all thin sheet materials, tends to be flexible but can be made stiff by curving or folding like paper or cardboard. Although paper will not permit curvature in two dimensions to form a dish or bowl, metal, because of the quality called ductility, can be shaped into complex forms (as automobile body parts clearly demonstrate). Complex curvatures in metal require expen-

TABLE 5
AVAILABLE SIZES OF METAL SECTIONS

Note: Other sections (e.g., Is, Hs, and Zs), sections of larger sizes, and sections in other metals (e.g., bronze) and special alloys are also available as standard, but are omitted from the listing above because of their limited use in furniture.

Metals can be obtained in almost any practical cross-section if sufficient quantities are involved to justify setting up production. A large number of sections are "stock," although any one distributor will usually carry only a limited range. The listing below shows sizes that are generally available on a stock basis.

In aluminum, extrusion of any desired section is possible with a relatively low tool cost, as compared to the very high cost of tool for rolling special steel sections.

Steel
Rod, bar, and flat (rectangular) sections:

	1/8	3/16	1/4	5/16	3/8	7/16	1/2	9/16	5/8	3/4	7/8	1	1 1/8	1 1/4	1 1/2	1 3/4	2	2 1/2	3
Round	O	O	O	O	O		O		O	O	O	O	O	O	O	O	O	O	O
Square			O	O	O		O		O	O		O		O	O		O		
Hexagonal							O			O		O							
Rectangular 1/8									O	O	O			O	O	O	O		
3/16													O		O	O	O		
1/4												O		O	O	O	O		
5/16														O	O		O		
3/8														O	O		O		
7/16														O	O	O			

Angles, channels and Ts:

		0.062 1/16	0.078 5/64	0.093 3/32	0.109 7/64	0.125 (1/8)	0.187 3/16	1/8 Top 1/4 Leg
Angles	1/2 × 1/2					O		
	5/8 × 5/8					O		
	3/4 × 3/4	O				O		
	1 × 1					O	O	
	1 1/4 × 1 1/4					O	O	
	1 1/2 × 1 1/2					O	O	
	2 × 2					O	O	
	1 × 5/8					O		
	1 1/4 × 3/4					O		
	2 × 1					O		
Channels	1/2 × 1/2			O				
	3/4 × 3/4			O				
	1 × 1					O		

TABLE 5
AVAILABLE SIZES OF METAL SECTIONS (CONTINUED)

Steel
Rod, bar, and flat (rectangular) sections:

		1/8	3/16	1/4	5/16	3/8	7/16	1/2	9/16	5/8	3/4	7/8	1	1⅛	1¼	1½	1¾	2	2½	3
	1¼ × 1¼												O							
	1½ × 1½												O							
	2 × 2														O					
	5/16 × 5/8							O												
	3/8 × 3/4												O							
	1⅛ × 1¾												O							
	1 × 2														O					
Ts	7/8 × 9/16																		O	
	25/32 × 1														O					

Tubing:

		1/32	3/64	1/16	5/64	3/32	1/8	9/64	5/32	3/16	1/4
Round	3/8		O								
and	1/2	O	O	O							
square	5/8	O	O	O							
tubing	3/4			O	O		O				
	1	O	O	O	O		O				
	1⅛			O							
	1¼	O	O	O	O	O	O	O		O	
	1½	O	O	O	O		O	O		O	
	1¾			O	O		O	O		O	
	2			O	O		O	O		O	O
Rectangular	3/8 × 3/4			O							
tubing	3/8 × 1			O							
	1/2 × 1			O							
	1/2 × 1¼			O							
	5/8 × 2				O						
	3/4 × 1			O							
	3/4 × 1½			O	O						
	1 × 1¼			O	O						
	1 × 1½			O	O		O				
	1 × 2			O	O		O		O		
	1 × 2½			O							
	1¼ × 1¾			O							
	1¼ × 2			O							
	1¼ × 2½			O							
	1¼ × 3			O							
	1½ × 2			O			O				

Steel

Rod, bar, and flat (rectangular) sections:

	1/32	3/64	1/16	5/64	3/32	1/8	9/64	5/32	3/16	1/4
1 1/2 × 2 1/2				○		○	○		○	
1 1/2 × 3				○		○			○	
2 × 3				○		○			○	○

Stainless Steel

Rod, bar, and flat (rectangular) sections:

	1/8	3/16	1/4	5/16	3/8	7/16	1/2	9/16	5/8	3/4	7/8	1	1 1/8	1 1/4	1 1/2	1 3/4	2	2 1/2	3
Round							○	○	○	○		○		○					
Square							○		○	○		○		○					
Rectangular 3/16							○		○	○		○		○	○		○		○
1/4										○		○		○	○		○	○	○
7/16										○									

Angles and channels:

		0.062 1/16	0.078 5/64	0.125 1/8
Angles	1/2 × 1/2	○		
	5/8 × 5/8	○		
	3/4 × 3/4	○		○
	1 × 1	○		○
	1 1/4 × 1 1/4	○		○
	1 1/2 × 1 1/2	○		○
Channels	1/2 × 1/2	○		
	3/4 × 3/4	○		
	1 × 1	○		
	5/8 × 5/16		○	
	3/4 × 3/8	○		
	1 × 1/2	○		
	1 1/4 × 1/2	○		
	1 1/2 × 1/2	○		
	2 × 1/2	○		

Tubing:

	Wall Thickness →	0.049	0.065
Round and	3/4	○	
square	1	○	○
tubing	1 1/4		○
	1 1/2		○
	1 3/4		○
	2		○
Oval tubing	1/2 × 2		○
Rectangular	3/4 × 1		○
tubing	3/4 × 1 1/2		○
	1 × 1 1/2		○
	1 × 2		○
	1 1/4 × 2 1/2		○
	1 3/4 × 3		○

TABLE 5
AVAILABLE SIZES OF METAL SECTIONS (CONTINUED)

Aluminum
Rod, bar, and flat (rectangular) sections

	1/8	3/16	1/4	5/16	3/8	1/2	5/8	3/4	7/8	1	1 1/8	1 1/4	1 1/2	1 3/4	2	2 1/2	3
Round	O	O	O	O	O	O	O	O	O	O	O	O	O	O		O	O
Square			O			O	O	O	O	O							
Flat 1/8						O	O	O		O	O	O	O	O	O	O	O
Flat 3/16						O		O		O		O	O	O	O	O	O
Flat 1/4						O	O	O		O		O	O	O	O	O	O
Flat 5/16										O		O	O				

Angles, channels, and Ts:

Angles	1/16	3/32	1/8	3/16	1/4	5/16	3/8	7/16	1/2
1/2 × 1/2	O		O						
5/8 × 5/8		O	O						
3/4 × 3/4	O	O	O	O					
1 × 1	O	O	O	O	O				
1 1/8 × 1 1/8			O						
1 1/4 × 1 1/4		O	O	O	O	O			
1 1/2 × 1 1/2		O	O	O	O	O	O		
1 3/4 × 1 3/4		O	O	O	O	O	O		
2 × 2			O	O	O	O	O	O	
2 1/2 × 2 1/2			O	O	O	O	O	O	O
3/4 × 3/8		O							
1 × 5/8			O		O				
1 × 3/4			O						
1 1/4 × 3/4		O							
1 1/4 × 1			O						
1 1/2 × 3/4			O	O					
1 1/2 × 7/8				O					

	0.109 7/64	3/32	1/8	3/16	1/4	5/16	3/8
1 1/2 × 1				O	O		
1 1/2 × 1 1/4			O	O	O		
1 5/8 × 1 1/4			O				
1 3/4 × 1 1/8				O			
1 3/4 × 1 1/4			O	O	O		
2 × 1 1/4			O	O	O		
2 × 1 3/8					O		
2 × 1 1/2		O	O	O	O	O	
2 × 1 3/4					O		
2 1/4 × 1 1/2					O		

Channels	0.109		
	7/64	3/32	1/8
3/8 × 3/8	○		
1/2 × 1/2		○	
5/8 × 5/8			○
3/4 × 3/4			○
1 × 1			○
1¼ × 1¼			○
1½ × 1½			○
2 × 2			○
3/8 × 1/2 W			○
3/4 × 1/2 W			○
1 × 5/8 W			○
3/8 × 3/4 W			○
1/2 × 3/4 W			○

	0.109						
	7/64	3/32	1/8	3/16	1/4	5/16	3/8
1/2 × 1 W			○				
3/4 × 1 W			○				
1/2 × 1¼ W			○				
5/8 × 1¼ W			○				
3/4 × 1¼ W			○				
1/2 × 1½ W			○				
5/8 × 1½ W			○				
3/4 × 1½ W			○				
1 × 1½ W			○				
1/2 × 1¾ W			○				
3/4 × 1¾ W			○				
1/2 × 2 W			○				
1 × 2 W			○				
7/8 × 2¼ W			○				
3/4 × 2¼ W			○				
1½ × 2½ W			○				
Ts 1 × 1			○				
1½ × 1½				○	○		
2 × 2					○	○	
2¼ × 2¼					○	○	
2½ × 2½						○	○
1½ × 1¼			○	○			
1½ × 2				○			
2½ × 1¼				○			

TABLE 5
AVAILABLE SIZES OF METAL SECTIONS (CONTINUED)

Aluminum Tubing:

		0.028	0.035	0.049	0.058	0.063	0.065	0.078	0.083	0.094	0.095	0.125
Round	1/4		○									
tubing	3/8		○	○	○		○					
	1/2	○	○	○	○		○					
	5/8	○	○	○	○		○					
	3/4		○	○	○		○		○			
	7/8		○	○	○		○					
	1		○	○	○		○		○		○	
	1 1/4				○	○		○		○		○
	1 1/2					○	○	○		○		○
	1 3/4					○		○		○		○
	2					○		○		○		○
	2 1/2					○		○		○		○

	Nominal Size	Outside Diameter	Wall Thickness
Extruded	3/4	1.050	.113
Pipe	1	1.315	.133
	1 1/4	1.660	.140
	1 1/2	1.900	.145
	2	2.375	.154

		0.063 1/16	0.078 5/64	0.125 1/8
Square	1/2	○		
tubing	5/8	○		
	3/4	○		○
	1	○		○
	1 1/4		○	○
	1 1/2		○	○
	1 3/4		○	○
	2			○
	2 1/2			○
Rectangular	1/2 × 1			○
tubing	3/4 × 1 1/2		○	○
	1 × 1 1/2		○	○
	1 × 2			○
	1 × 3			○
	1 1/4 × 2 1/2			○
	1 1/4 × 3			○
	1 1/2 × 2			○
	1 1/2 × 2 1/2			○
	1 3/4 × 2 1/2			○

TABLE 6
SHEET METAL GAUGE NUMBERS

Note: Sheet metal gauges are *not* the same as wire gauges. Several differing wire gauge systems are (or have been) in use but are not ordinarily significant in furniture design.

Gauge Number[a]	Thickness (Decimals of Inch)	Thickness in (Fractions of Inch)
3	0.250	1/4
11	0.125	1/8
14	0.078125	5/64
15	0.0703125	
16	0.0625	1/16
18	0.050	1/20
19	0.04375	
20	0.0375	
21	0.034375	
22	0.03125	1/32
23	0.028125	
24	0.025	1/40
25	0.021875	
26	0.01875	
27	0.0171875	
28	0.015625	1/64
30	0.0125	1/80

[a]United States Steel, in general use for sheet steel.

sive stamping tools and are therefore only used in furniture where high production is expected (e.g., the seats of metal folding chairs). Simple bends in one direction can be made with simpler equipment, and a whole vocabulary of office and kitchen furniture made in this way has become familiar. The thin sheet steel of which this furniture is constructed takes on strength as it is bent at corners and edges into pan or box forms. Parts are then welded together to increase strength and generate the forms needed for shelves, doors, drawers, cabinets, and so on. Enclosed parts made in this way may be supported by legs or frames made from linear metal materials.

Lengthwise stock metal sections (bars, tubes, and small structural sections) may be rolled, but in the case of aluminum are often made by the process of extrusion, in which the metal in a semimetaled form is forced through a steel die, a plate with a shaped opening that acts somewhat like a nozzle. The metal is squeezed out in a continuous ribbon having the shape of the die opening. Extrusion dies are relatively inexpensive to make so it is possible to extrude special and unusual shapes, even very complex ones, as long as they are of reasonable size (usually to fit within a circle

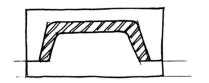

Tapers to permit easy release in die-casting.

no more than 4 or 5 inches in diameter). Extruded sections are used extensively in such products as aluminum window frames and can solve some furniture problems more easily than furniture designers seem to realize.

Small parts, legs of small sizes, knobs, handles, and even parts as large as bases for swivel chairs can be made in a foundry by casting. For limited production where great precision is not required, the process of sand casting may be used. A wood pattern is pressed into packed fine sand to form a mold in which aluminum and certain other alloys can be cast. Permanent mold casting substitutes a more lasting mold for the sand, while die casting uses metal molds in a machine that automatically produces casting at high speeds. Die castings can be made with very high precision and are widely used in making mechanical parts. Die castings used in furniture are usually pulls, knobs, shelf supports, or other components of limited size. The metals used for die casting are alloys developed specially for this purpose. Parts to be cast should be designed with some thought for the location of the "parting line," the line along which the mold will open, difficult to obliterate completely; with rounded corners and angles to make the flow of metal into the mold easy, and with "tapers," slight angles in the deep dimension of the part to aid release from the mold (see illustration).

With the exception of stainless steel, a very hard and strong steel alloy that is expensive and difficult to work because of its hardness, all metals require finishing. Steel rusts rapidly even from the effect of humidity in the air, while aluminum (although not subject to rust) will develop a surface oxide that makes it dull, grey, and unattractive. The types of finish available for metals include the following:

Paint is usually sprayed on over carefully chosen primers. Cleaning and priming determine how well paint will adhere, but even at best a paint finish is inclined to chip and peel unless it is baked on. A wide variety of enamels and synthetic coatings are intended for baking at high temperatures to achieve the hardness of porcelain enamels, and at lower temperatures to arrive at the reasonably good surfaces developed in the paints used on automobiles and appliances. In the latter cases, baking heat is provided by infrared bulbs in a so-called "oven," a chamber through which the freshly painted parts pass on a conveyer. Baked finishes have reasonable durability, but are always subject to scratching or chipping and are hard to repair once damage has occurred.

Plastic Coating through dipping results in a softer, thick coat that is less likely to chip but may have an undesirable texture. Kitchen accessories such as dishdriers are usually finished with a plastic dip. Fluid-bed coating is a variation of plastic coating that has become useful on furniture parts. In this process, the part is heated and then dipped into a box in which the suitable plastic in the form of a dust or powder is fanned up into the air. The heated part causes the plastic to melt and fuse onto the metal surface. Fluid-bed coatings are tough and lasting and may have a slight leatherlike texture that is often suitable for furniture applications.

Plating is the finish that seems paricularly characteristic of metals. Through electrolytic action, a thin deposit of a hard, nonrusting metal is deposited on the less attractive metal underneath. The silverplate of tableware is a typical example. Chromium is a metal with a bright glitter and a very hard surface. It can be plated onto steel or die cast parts (after preliminary plating with copper) and, when the plating job is well done, becomes a permanent and durable finish. The appearance of the surface can be modified by differing final finishing steps that can produce a bright, mirrorlike surface or softer finishes called "brushed" or "satin." Other metals, such as brass, can be plated onto steel or cast parts.

Anodizing is a special finishing technique possible only on aluminum. It coats the metal with a kind of plating that can be clear (virtually invisible) or have color. Transparent anodized finishes preserve the metallic look of the aluminum but can introduce various colors, including those that suggest brass or gold (usually rather garishly) or bronze (with better success). Dark, opaque colors such as blues or black can be very successful.

Various other metals show up in occasional furniture uses. Cast iron, the favorite of the Victorian age, remains available for parts where mass and weight are desirable. Lead appears occasionally as a concealed element adding weight but, because of its cost, iron is usually preferable for this utilitarian role. Brass is often admired for its color, but because of its cost, brass plating or even aluminum with a brass anodized finish is usually substituted except in small accessory parts.

Plastics

The third family of materials available for use in making furniture is relatively new, subject to continuing change and development, and more complex and confusing than the traditional materials. Plastics are synthetic materials and can be formulated in an infinite variety of chemical compositions and processed in many ways. As a result, generalizations about plastics are difficult, and one must usually discuss a particular plastic formulation processed by a particular manufacturing technique. To add to the problem of clear discussions, the naming of plastics is not well standardized. Each plastic has a generic, chemical name, often long and hard to remember or pronounce. In addition, it will have one or more trade names adopted by manufacturers to aid marketing. Thus the same plastic may have several different names, while a particular name may apply to forms of the same material so different as to be hardly recognizable. Plexiglas and Lucite are different manufacturers' trade names for the same material, transparent acrylic; the trade name Nylon describes both the knitted fine filament of stockings and the solid mass of an antifriction roller or glide. In an effort to make some order of the common uses of plastics in furniture, a brief index of plastic materials is provided below followed by a listing of the more common processes for working plastics. It is usually necessary to name both material and process to give a clear idea of plastic material—for example, foamed urethane, cast acrylic, extruded vinyl, or injection molded polystyrene.

The essential characteristic that justifies calling a material plastic is the passing through a soft or semiliquid stage during manufacture which permits shaping or otherwise processing the material. Once formed, the plastic becomes more or less stiff and retains its form in a finished product. The transition from the soft form to final stiffness can be accomplished in two different ways, depending on the material used. All plastics are classified into two "families" according to their way of hardening.

Thermoplastics, as the term suggests, become soft when heated and harden when cooled, behavior familiar with such preplastic material as wax. Thermoplastics can be remelted and hardened by cooling any number of times. Thermosetting (or thermoset) plastics are hardened by a chemical action that takes place in the presence of heat. Once set, heat does not cause softening so that the set form is permanent. The chemical action occurs when two elements are combined: the resin, which is the basic material of the plastic, and a catalyst which interacts with it to cause hardening. The heat required may be no more than normal room temperature, or may be much higher. Setting is more rapid in the presence of high heat. This kind of plastic is now familiar in the form of the modern adhesives sold in two tubes. The tubes contain resin and catalyst which must be combined to start the glue setting.

Room temperature is all the heat required with such adhesives. Thermoplastics are unsuitable for uses that include exposure to high heat. In general, the thermosetting plastics offer more strength although great strength is not an inherent characteristic of most plastics. Strength must come from forming to make best use of the material, or from the addition of strengthening elements of other materials.

Thermoplastics

ABS (acrylonitrile-butadiene-styrene). A tough and strong material processed by injection molding, extrusion or vacuum forming. Used for small parts and complete chair shell units.

Acrylic. Strong and tough material of glasslike transparency. Available clear and in colors, in sheets of various thickness, rods, and tubes. May be cast, but most often used in fabrication by cutting, heat bending and, where required, assembling parts with cement or mechanical connections. A favorite material for complete furniture products because of its striking appearance and the ease of working without expensive tooling. Plexiglas and Lucite are well-known trade names.

Cellulosics. Early celluloid and cellophane were of this family. Used for thin sheets and coatings, often transparent or in light colors. Packaging materials and photographic film are common applications. Nitrate forms are inflammable to the point of being explosive (guncotton is cellulose nitrate) but acetates are less hazardous.

Nylon. Best known in thin filament used to knit or weave textiles. Molded or cast solid nylon is also useful in small parts because of its low-friction characteristics.

Polyethylene. A material with good strength and flexibility. It has a waxlike surface texture and is normally a translucent white, but may also be colored. Kitchen containers, ice trays, bottles, and toys are common products.

Polypropylene. A material with good surface hardness, used for pipe fittings and kitchen equipment parts. Also often laminated to other materials and used as a film.

PVC (polyvinyl chloride). A particular type of vinyl used for plastic piping (made by extrusion) and for electrical device parts.

Polystyrenes usually called:

Styrene. A material of medium strength, widely used for a great variety of commonplace objects and parts such as refrigerator door liners, kitchen containers, and similar small objects. Foamed versions include styrofoam, used for packaging and decorative craft applications.

Vinyls. Tough and rubbery materials, familiar in floor tiles (solid or in combination with asbestos fibers), wall coverings, and upholstery materials.

Thermoset Plastics

Alkyds. Widely used in liquid form as a paint base. Also used in solid form in electrical parts and other small devices.

Aminos. Of two different types, melamines and ureas (q.v.).

Epoxy. A plastic of exceptionally high toughness and strength. Used as a high-strength adhesive and as a paint base for extra-durable finishes. High cost limits its use in solid form to special applications where strength is important.

Fiber Glass. A term brought into use by the trade name Fiberglas for plastic reinforced by spun glass fibers imbedded in the material—most often polyester. This produces a high-strength compound material, the only plastic material able to compete with earlier materials in strength terms at reasonable cost. Chair shells of glass-reinforced plastic are the most widely known application of plastics in furniture.

Laminates. A term referring to the process of lamination (q.v.), which has come to denote sheet materials made by laminating papers with melamine plastic. These materials provide a very resistant surfacing for furniture, counter tops, and similar flat surfaces. Laminates are usually sold as sheets in a wide variety of colors and textures, often imitative of other materials. Laminates are also sometimes offered in sheets with curves suitable for formation of counter edges or splash-backs. Many trade names are used (e.g., Formica, Micarta, Textolite, and Parkwood).

Melamines. A very hard and tough plastic, resistant to scratching and abrasion. The only plastic that can stand up (to a degree) under knife cutting, often used in solid form for plastic dishes. Its hardness makes it suitable for use in laminates, as described above.

Neoprene. A synthetic rubber sharing most of the characteristics of natural rubber, but less subject to deterioration. Used for door gaskets, shock mounts, and as elastic webbing in upholstery.

Phenolics. One of the first types of plastic to come into wide use under the trade name Bakelite. A tough, hard material, brittle in thin sections. Of naturally dark-brown color, it can only be made in browns and black. A good insulator, relatively inexpensive, widely used in utilitarian ways in electrical devices.

Polyesters. Strong and rigid with good surface hardness, widely used with imbedded glass fibers to form fiber glass (see above). Reinforced plastic of this type is used for boat hulls, automobile body parts, and in furniture applications.

Polyurethane or **Urethane.** The most used type of urea plastic. Tough and shock-resistant. Used in molded or extruded form, but most widely used in furniture in the form of foam that may be soft (replacing foam rubber) or rigid as a structural material. Urea adhesives are also used in making plywood and applying various kinds of surface coatings.

Production Techniques:

Blow Molding. A bubble of thermoplastic material is formed on an air pipe end and inserted into a closed hollow mold. Air pressure blows the material up to fill the mold shape with a hollow shell. The mold opens to release the part. Most used to make bottles, this technique has been suggested for making bottlelike units with bellows bodies for use as upholstery or bedsprings, but the idea has never been implemented.

Calendering. The process used for making plastic material into thin film or sheet by passing it between sets of rollers.

Casting. Plastic material is poured into an open or closed mold, allowed to harden, and removed from the mold. The term mold-

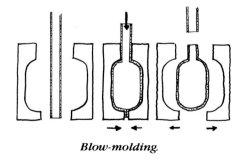

Blow-molding.

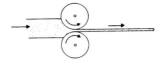

Calendering.

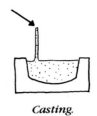

Casting.

Compression molding.

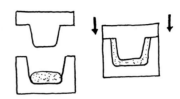

Extrusion.

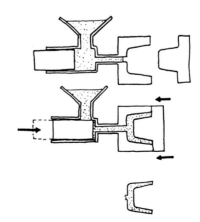

Injection molding.

ing is used when material is forced into a closed mold under pressure, casting when no pressure is used.

Compression Molding. Thermosetting material is forced to take the shape of a closed mold under heat and pressure.

Extrusion. This process is similar to metal extrusion previously described. Plastic material is heated and forced through an opening in a die, which shapes it to a desired cross section in a continuous ribbon. Used for making tubes, rods, and special shapes for gaskets, table edge trim, and so on.

Fabrication. A general term for simple working of plastic materials by cutting into parts and assembling. Typical fabrication operations may include cutting, drilling, polishing, lathe-turning, tapping, and threading, dry or cemented assembly, thermo-forming (q.v.) heat sealing (q.v.), and sewing.

Foaming and Foam Molding. A number of plastics including styrene, polypropylene, and urethane can be processed to cause air bubbles to form, transforming the material into a "foam" in which a small amount of plastic material generates a large mass. The foam can have a wide range of rigidity according to the chemistry and process used. Foam produced in sheets or slabs can be cut and shaped for a variety of uses. In foam molding, the foaming action is produced in plastic material inside a mold which determines the shape of the finished part. Molded foam can be produced with a closed or stiff skin which will take a textured surface from the mold. Foams of various densities can be glued together or, in some processes, several densities of foam are formed in the mold to make a part of multiple density (e.g., stiff for support structure and soft for cushioning in upholstery). Reinforcements or parts of other materials can be placed in the mold to become embedded parts of the finished unit.

Heat Sealing. Plastic sheet or film can be sealed, or "welded" together by application of heat along a thin line. This process is widely used for package sealing. It has been used in the manufacture of "inflated furniture," hollow plastic baglike units which, when air-inflated, take on useful furniture forms.

Injection Molding. The most common way of making parts from thermoplastic. Plastic material is heated until soft, then forced into a closed mold where it cools in the shape of the mold. The mold opens and the part is forced out by ejection pins. Small parts can be made in this way at high speed on automatic molding machines. Molds can be very costly, but the efficiency of production makes this process highly usable when large quantities of an object are required.

Laminating (high pressure). The method by which a tough plastic, usually melamine, is used to adhere together and surface other sheet material, normally paper, to make a hard surface sheet. The materials to be laminated are stacked in layers and then cured in a press under heat and pressure.

Pressure Forming. A variation on vacuum forming (q.v.), in which compressed air is used to force material down into a mold at the same time that vacuum is used below the material.

Reinforcement. The process of combining another material, usually spun glass fiber, with plastic to increase strength (as discussed under fiber glass, above). Fiber glass parts may be made on a single mold by the process of hand lay-up in which glass cloth is dipped in the resin-catalyst mix and positioned on the mold in layers by hand, or by spraying a mixture of chopped glass, fiber, and plastic onto the mold from a special spray gun. These processes use inexpensive molds, but are slow and only suited to low production. For quantity production, costly matched steel molds are required. A "preform," roughly shaped mass of glass fiber is placed in the mold, and molding follows as in other compression molding of thermosetting materials.

Rotational Molding. A process used to make hollow units. A small amount of plastic is placed in a large mold, which is kept heated while it is rotated about two or more axes. The material builds a skin of desired thickness on the inside of the mold. When the mold is opened a hollow, completed unit is removed. The hollow shell can be filled afterward with a foam. This process is often called "rotomolding."

Thermoforming. Thermoplastic sheet material is heated where forming is desired, and gravity, air pressure, or mechanical pressure is used to shape the softened material. Simple bends in flat

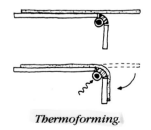

Thermoforming.

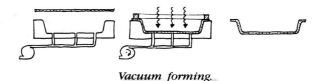

Vacuum forming.

sheet can be made easily over a suitable heat unit of tubular form. This process has been used extensively in making furniture of sheet acrylic. Pressure forming and vacuum forming (q.v.) are special cases of thermoforming.

Transfer Molding. This process is similar to both compression and injection molding. It is used for molding thermosetting material, but the material is heated to an appropriate degree of softness before being forced into the mold (rather than being softened within the closed mold). Hardening takes place in the mold, and the finished part is forced out by ejection pins as in the other two processes.

Vacuum Forming. Thin-sheet thermoplastic material is placed over a mold with an airtight seal around the edges. The material is heated and air is evacuated from the mold by a vacuum pump. Air pressure forces the material into the mold, where it cools before removal. This process is suited to forming parts of thin sheet such as trays, door liners, and so on. Tools can be relatively inexpensive, but deep draws and sharp corners are difficult or impossible because of the difficulty of obtaining a flow of plastic sufficiently good to maintain a satisfactory thickness.

In designing objects that are to be made from plastic, it is essential to have a clear idea of the type of plastic and the process that will be most appropriate so that the design can take best advantage of the material's characteristics and avoid unexpected problems. Since most plastics are not materials of inherently high strength, it is unsafe to suppose (as is often possible with wood or metal) that the size and shape of parts desirable for other reasons will provide adequate or excess strength. Objects of plastic, particularly those as large as most pieces of furniture, must be carefully planned to deal with stresses through forms that place material where needed and distribute stresses to minimize high stress concentrations. It is also unsafe to assume that any shape can be made easily; processes using forms or molds require that the designer consider not only the form of the final part but also the relationship of that form to the molding tools. There must be a way to remove the part from the mold easily, and parting lines, marks of sprues, and ejection pins are realities that affect appearance and need to be taken into account when the part is being planned. Sharp corners, sudden changes of thickness, and very deep, narrow cavity draws can present difficult molding problems that are easier to avoid than to solve.

It is easy to forget that plastics are not cheap materials. The early, and still commonplace, use of plastic as an inexpensive (and often inferior) substitute for other material has led to an expectation of economy that is often unrealistic. In small objects, where the cost of material is small while the cost of workmanship is, in traditional materials, relatively high, plastic will often offer great economies. Complex detail molded in an automatic machine costs virtually nothing, while the same detail made by hand or with many separate mechanical operations may be far more expensive. As the size of an object increases, the cost of material becomes an increasing factor. Each type of plastic has a price per pound that can easily be discovered at a given time. An estimate of the volume of material can be converted to an estimate of weight and to material cost. When this figure approaches the cost of the comparable object made from conventional materials, the probability of major economies will vanish. Thus it becomes important to consider forming to maximum strength with a minimum of material, or the use of foamed materials where air bubbles distribute a minimum of material to generate needed form and mass.

Choice of material and process must relate to anticipated volume of production. Tools for plastic production, particularly matched molds, can be very costly and increase more than proportionally as the object to be molded grows larger. The cost of a tool must be paid out, amortized, by adding something to the sale price of the object. A large tool cost can easily be amortized with a tiny increment in the price of objects to be made in vast quantity—a small bottle for a mass-distribution product, for example. Most pieces of furniture of any one design are sold in limited quantities, and each item must then carry a heavy toll to ensure rapid tool cost recovery. When objects will be needed in only small numbers, it becomes necessary to use processes that do not require tools or that can use low-cost tools. This may limit what can be produced or may lead to large costs for hand labor per piece produced.

During the years when plastics were developed rapidly, prices of the basic plastic materials tended to decrease steadily giving rise to great optimism that plastics were destined to become universal materials. As metal and wood became more expensive with increasing scarcity and threats of depletion, plastics appeared to be a solution to all problems of shortage—as synthetic materials, they seemed to many observers to be synthesized from nothing and so to be endlessly and infinitely available. When petroleum depletion, shortages, and international price increases suddenly became a factor in modern life, it was shocking to realize that the basic chemistry of plastics depended on petroleum derivatives. The long era of declining plastics prices was suddenly reversed as actual shortages of materials began to appear. In long-range terms, it seems probable that plastics cannot possibly remain a source of accelerating quantities of increasingly cheap material. The assumption that plastic is usually a cheaper substitute for something else is fast disappearing, and it is necessary to be certain that plastic is the best material for a particular function or other practical or visual reasons before it becomes a material of first preference.

Finally, it should be noted that various unanticipated hazards have surfaced in connection with the manufacture and use of plastics. The chemicals involved are often toxic or can generate toxic fumes. Production situations can be hazardous to workers and can create environmental problems—usually solvable but only at a certain cost. Related chemical problems make some plastics flammable to a dangerous degree or create a hazard of dangerous fume production when exposed to fire. Many inflammable plastics can be modified to make them incombustible, but the problem of fumes may remain or be made worse. Increasing use of plastics in interior materials, floor coverings, wall coverings, paints, and furniture has led to new and difficult fire control problems. A number of bad fires in office buildings, hotels, and motels has led to increasing restriction on fire safety characteristics. Perhaps such problems could be dealt with better through provision of suitable extinguishing systems in buildings (such as universal provision of sprinklers where inflammable materials are present), but until this becomes a general practice, inflammability and fume hazards should be considered in furniture material selection.

Another problem associated with the increasing use of plastics, the ecological impact of materials that are difficult to destroy as wastes, seems to have a minor impact on furniture. Unlike packages and bottles, furniture has a long life and a high degree of usefulness in relation to the material quantity involved. Rivers and lakes can be expected to be filled with empty bottles long before they fill up with discarded chairs, tables, and beds.

Other Materials

Furniture makes surprisingly little use of materials outside of the three main families already discussed, except in the nonstructural elements of upholstery discussed below. Otherwise, it is only necessary to note the uses of glass and certain stones.

The transparency of glass made it a unique material until transparent plastics were developed. Although more fragile than plastic substitutes, the hardness of glass surfaces makes them desirable for certain applications such as tabletops or shelves. Glass is a stronger material than is commonly thought, but it is necessary to be sure that the thickness specified is adequate when its use generates beam action with significant loads. An unsupported glass shelf loaded with books or records by a thoughtless user can fail in bending or in shear. There is a limit to reasonable increase in thickness (usually 1 in. would be considered a maximum, and ½ in. thick is enough for most uses), and the designer must consider support by framing with wood or metal where span and load suggests that unsupported glass may be inadequate. In addition to the problems of static loads, impact can cause shattering and broken glass is particularly hazardous because of its sharp edges. Although tempered glass is hard to break and breaks into a harmless crumble, it is rarely used in furniture because it cannot be cut to size— it must be cast in the desired size before tempering at the factory. Exposed edges of glass need to be polished and should be rounded to avoid dangerous edges and corners. Glass can be cut and drilled, with difficulty, and some shapes, such as inside corners, are almost impossible to cut. Mirror is simply a special type of glass, usually used only for its special reflecting characteristics.

Both glass and stone present some problems in the development of connections to other materials. The easiest approach is to use the weight of these materials by allowing gravity to hold them within some kind of edging, clips, or other retaining devices. Large and thick pieces of glass and stone are often heavy enough to stay in place without retention if the points on which they bear are given a high-friction surface, such as a rubber button. In the case of stone, if there is adequate thickness, a blind hole can be drilled from below and plugged with a lead or plastic insert to accept a screw driven from below.

The most widely used stone in furniture is marble, which makes an attractive (and luxurious) top material because of its wide range of attractive color and veining pattern combined with a glasslike hardness and smooth, durable surface. Marble is less subject to shattering than glass, but shares many of its other characteristics. The most spectacularly veined marbles tend to break up along the vein lines and must be cemented to a backing (such as plywood) to hold them together. Travertine is a marblelike stone that is very porous. In furniture uses "filled travertine" is usually specified to obtain a smooth surface that results when the holes of the natural stone are filled with cement before surface polishing. Slate and granite are other stone materials that are used occasionally. They are treated as described above, are generally stronger than either glass or marble, and are less subject to impact damage. When specifying glass or stone parts, it is important to note resulting weight which can be great enough to involve problems of support and difficulties in shipping or moving. A granite top 36 × 72 × 2 in. thick will weigh about 1000 lbs.!

Hardware and Fastenings

Over the years a vast variety of hardware and fastening devices have been developed that are used in furniture. In most cases where the appropriate device (a screw, a hinge, or a drawer slide) is obvious, its choice can be left to the craftsman or to factory personnel who will install it. When difficult or special problems arise, or when appearance will be affected, the designer needs to select

TABLE 7
FASTENINGS AND HARDWARE

Generally available and useful common fastenings are shown with the range of sizes that are useful in furniture applications. Unusual fastenings and other types of hardware are made in such great variety that a complete listing would not be practical. Typical examples of types in wide use, and a few examples of less common types, are shown to give some idea of the range of available products.

Nails. These are the primary fasteners of carpentry, but have only a minor role in furniture. They are hard to drive and may cause splitting in harder woods unless a pilot hole is predrilled, and their holding power is inferior to that of screws. They are used to some extent in concealed locations (e.g., to retain backs or hold internal drawer guides) and to reinforce glued joints while the glue is setting. Upholstery nails and tacks have considerable use in upholstered furniture, although staples are replacing them because of the ease with which they can be driven with a power tool.

COMMON NAILS: with large, flat heads

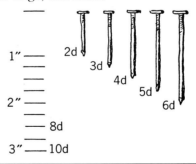

FINISHING NAILS: with small head that can be driven below the surface of the wood with a nail-set so that the hole can be filled and concealed (shown half size)

TABLE 7
FASTENINGS AND HARDWARE (CONTINUED)

BRADS: very small nails, usually with small heads
(shown half size)

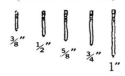

TACKS: short nails with large heads

UPHOLSTERY NAILS (OR TACKS): often with heads intended to be exposed)

STAPLES: available in a wide range of sizes and types

Screws These are available in a wide variety of types, including the familiar wood screw (tapered shape) and "machine" screw for use in tapped holes in metal or with nuts. A "bolt" is a large screw or may refer to any screw used with a nut. Screw heads are of many types and shapes; not all screw sizes and types are available with all types of heads. Screws are used in wood furniture to reinforce glue joints and provide clamping action while glue dries, and to make dry joints that can be disassembled repeatedly. They are useful in making metal to wood connections (attaching hardware, legs, etc.), in connecting metal parts without welding, and in many aspects of mechanical assembly, especially where repeated disassembly is anticipated.

In wood furniture of cabinetmaking quality, screw heads are not expected to show. They must either be driven from a concealed location or covered with a plug or other trim. Visible screw heads are more readily accepted in metal parts, although a desire for neatness often leads to efforts to conceal them. Where screw heads are exposed, Phillips or Allen heads are often preferred because they avoid the arbitrary angles of the slots of regular, slotted heads.

Selecting or specifying a screw requires decision about some or all of the following:

Type
Size (diameter)
Length
Thread
Head type
Head shape
Material
Finish

Head sizes: (shown half size)

◯ ◯ ◯ ◯ ◯ ◯ ◯ ◯ ◯ ◯ o o
No. 16 14 12 11 10 9 8 7 6 5 4 3 2

Head shapes:
  Flat
  Oval
  Round
  Pan
  Truss
  Filister
  Hexagon
  Washer

Head types (driver required):
  Regular (slotted)
  Phillips (cross)
  Allen (socket, or hex socket)
  One-way (prevents easy removal)

For use in wood:
  Wood screw
  Dowel screw
  Lag bolt

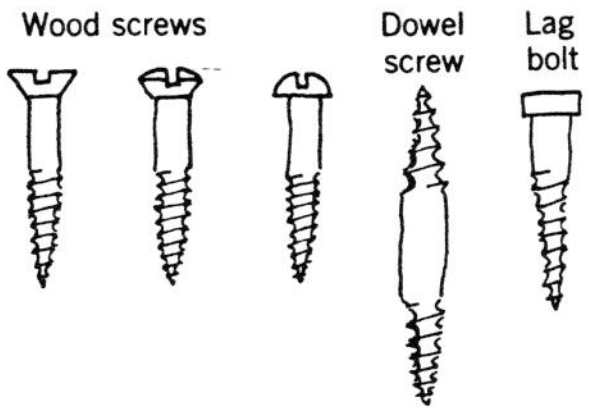

Wood screws   Dowel   Lag
                     screw   bolt

For use in metal:
  Machine screw
  Sheet metal screw
  Thread cutter (self-tapping) screw

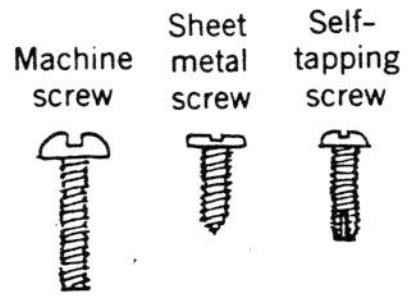

                Sheet   Self-
        Machine metal   tapping
        screw   screw   screw

Bolts:
  Machine bolt
  Carriage bolt
  Stove bolt

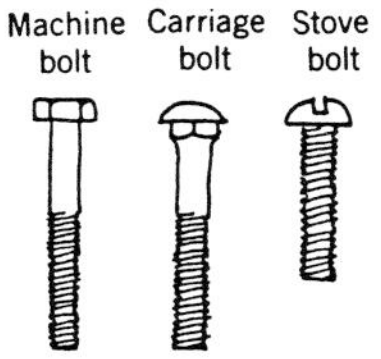

Machine Carriage Stove
bolt   bolt   bolt

Nuts and Washers are used with screws and bolts to avoid threading the materials to be joined. Size and thread must match the screw or bolt.

  Hex nut
  Square nut
  Wing nut
  Plain (flat) washer
  Lock washer
  Toothed washer

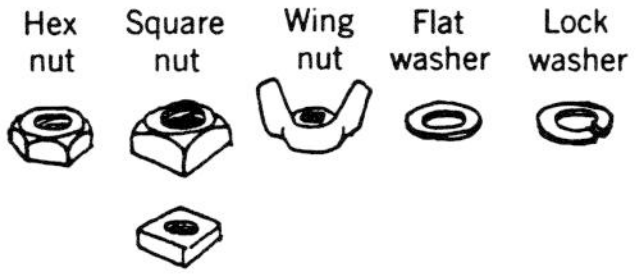

Hex   Square Wing Flat   Lock
nut   nut   nut   washer washer

TABLE 7
FASTENINGS AND HARDWARE (CONTINUED)

Tee-nut

Threaded insert (Southco)
  expands as screw is driven.

Corner (or chair) brace

Leg plate

Table corner plate

Keyhole plate

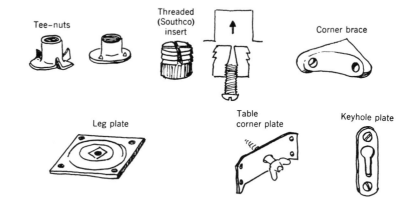

Other Furniture Hardware. Typical examples of widely used standard types appear below. Special hardware is often designed and produced for exclusive use in a particular design.

Hinges:
  Butt
  Knuckle
  Semiconcealed
  Concealed (Soss)
  Pivot
  Piano (continuous)

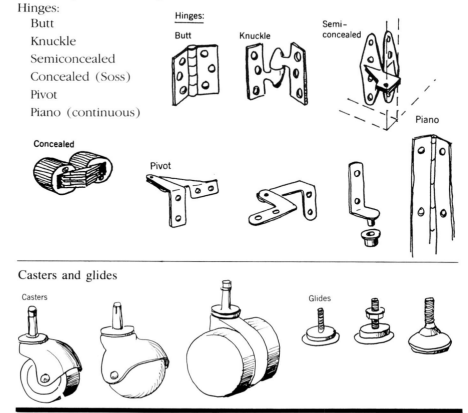

Casters and glides

Catches:
    Friction (clip)
    Roller (single and double)
    Magnetic
    Touch-latch (hidden, releases on pressure from front)

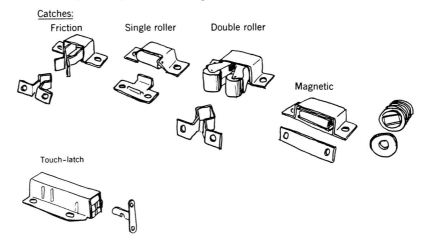

Catches:

Friction   Single roller   Double roller

Magnetic

Touch-latch

Drawer rollers and guides

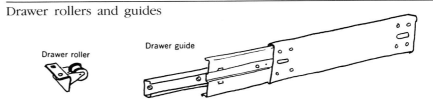

Drawer roller   Drawer guide

Lid support

Sliding door hardware

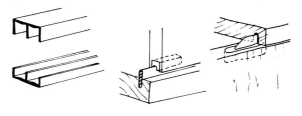

Shelf supports (adjustable)

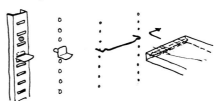

TABLE 7
FASTENINGS AND HARDWARE (CONTINUED)

Extension table hardware

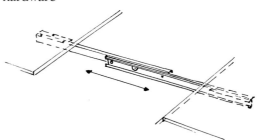

Chair swivels and "controls"

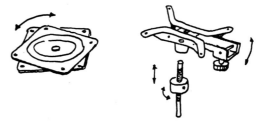

Chair bases

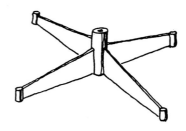

Cabinet locks

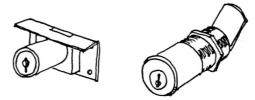

Upholstery Hardware Materials
Coil spring
Sinuous (No-Sag) spring
Flat coil spring

Coil
spring

Sinuous
spring

Flat coil
spring

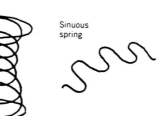

Rubber (Pirelli) webbing

Complete units of metal framing with springs are available as stock or semi-stock items for chair and sofa seats and backs, and for upholstery incorporating mechanical movements such as sofa-bed convertibles and reclining chairs.

the precise device to be used or, in some cases, even to design a special part. A complete listing and discussion of available hardware could fill a large book. Table 7 illustrates and lists a number of typical fastenings and widely used types of furniture hardware and provides some notes to aid in their selection. A furniture designer will want to build a substantial library of manufacturers' catalogs to aid detailed specifications.

Upholstery

Traditional upholstery construction makes use of complex handicrafts and a great variety of materials to build up soft surfaces in seating. Upholstery has remained difficult to industrialize fully and continues to involve a major element of handwork even in such products as automobile seating. The use of foam rubber and plastic foams has reduced the need for hand upholstery work and the development of all plastic foam seating may come close to eliminating it, but the craft of upholstery remains important in most nonplastic soft seating. Because of the complexity and specialized nature of the craft, it is not unusual for furniture designers to develop external forms for upholstered furniture while leaving the details of internal construction entirely to the shop that will manufacture the product. Some knowledge of upholstery construction is useful to ensure that difficult or impossible situations do not develop, and also to establish a basis for specification of intended quality of construction and degree of comfort.

All upholstery construction is based on the concept of providing a support structure that relates to a certain body posture, but separating this structure from the user's body by a space filled with soft, springy material capable of adjusting to individual body size and shape and of conforming to changes in body position. This tends to distribute pressure over larger areas of body surface and to encourage more change in body position. As a result, discomfort and fatigue are reduced and the sensation we call "comfort" is increased. The basic shape of any piece of upholstered furniture is established by its frame, a rigid construction that follows the bottom, rear, and general outer form of the unit. Traditionally this frame is built of wood members, hardwood in good quality work (oak is ideal), straight or bandsawn to curves as the intended shape requires, and doweled and glued together with reinforcing corner blocks at joints subject to heavy stress. Extra members are introduced as needed to provide anchorage for the upholstery construction—the "pull-through" strip at the bottom of unit backs is particularly important to allow independent movement of seat and back cushioning. Plywood can be substituted for solid members in some cases, and entire frames can be made of metal angle or tubing in place of wood (as in automobile and other transport seating). Wood makes tacking and nailing easy, while metal frames require other ways of attaching the upholstery elements. The upholsterer begins work with a completed frame as a foundation. On this frame he or she builds a soft structure by one of several methods or combinations of techniques.

The best traditional upholstery uses steel coil springs as its basic system of soft structure. A base of canvas webbing is used as a bottom plane and individual springs are tied and sewed to it, four or five in each direction to form each seating position. These springs are partly compressed and tied down so they can compress further, but not rise above the established plane of their tops—a travel of two to four inches is usual. The springs are tied so that lateral movement is prevented, enabling them to compress independently without touching. The top plane is padded over and surfaced with a "deck" of canvas. A cushion goes on top of this, either anchored in place ("tight-seat" construction) or as a removable loose unit. This seat cushion may be stuffed with hair, felt, down, foam, or a combination of these materials. It may even contain additional coil springs in a unit made up of separate springs sewn

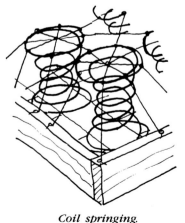

Coil springing.

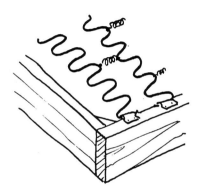

Sinuous (No-Sag) springs.

into muslin bags, then sewn together and surrounded by soft padding. The back of the unit can be of the same construction, or may omit the springs or substitute a different system of springing. In less expensive construction (currently more usual), the coil springs are replaced by flat springs that require no depth but run across the seat area from front to back. The most common spring type is called "sinuous" (No-Sag is a well known trade name). Rubber webbing can also be used in place of springs to form the main seat deck. Cushioning is placed on top, as described above, and similar back construction can be used. Since back pressure is generally limited, a hard base may be used for the back cushion, canvas webbing or even plywood or fiber board with the cushioning directly on it. Occasionally a hard plywood base for seats is used, but it limits comfort and can be unpleasant if a user drops into a seat from a standing position. Arms, when present, are padded over their framing with some cushioning on the top surfaces.

Typical conventional upholstery construction using coil springs for the seat, sinuous springs for the back. The back might, alternatively, use webbing in place of springs. Cushions may be foam, down or hair, and felt, or combinations of these materials; they may be "loose" (removable) or "tight" (stitched in place.)

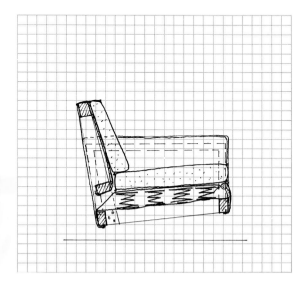

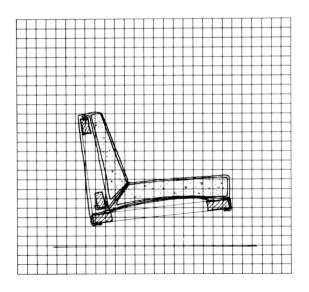

Typical "light" upholstery construction using sinuous springs for the seat, webbing for back support.

The cover fabric (or other cover material, possibly of plastic or leather) is sewn together into units rather like articles of clothing. Seaming is done from the back or inside so that the units can be turned inside out and slipped over the upholstered frame. The "pull-through" strip makes it possible to pull the seat cover and back cover through to the rear for tacking without their being attached to one another. This permits the seat to compress without being restrained by the back material. The exterior back material and all the outside edges are pulled down to the bottom of the frame and tacked in place. Hand sewing of exterior edges is often needed to close seams that cannot be dealth with otherwise. A wide variety of special details such as tufting, buttons, welts, sprung and padded edges, and so on can be used to vary comfort and appearance.

Many variations on traditional upholstery techniques have been

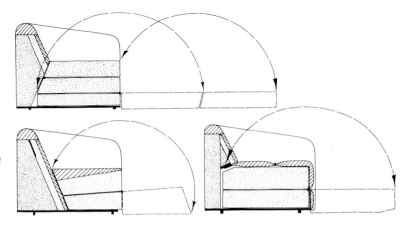

A manufacturer's proposals for three different types of all-foam upholstery. In each case the unit opens to form a bed or lounge. Different foam densities are indicated by dots or hatching. (Illustration courtesy of Dow Chemical Co.)

developed in recent years to reduce hand labor, produce less massive, more comfortable units, and yield more durable construction systems than those that depend on the traditional materials subject to wear and decay. Whether any of these systems can equal the comfort of traditional upholstery remains a matter for debate, but the increasing cost of handcrafted techniques makes use of the new techniques increasingly common.

Bedsprings and mattresses have become highly specialized products not normally provided by furniture manufacturers. Most beds only provide a support frame that can carry any desired combination of spring and mattress units.

Factory Processes and Equipment

In the small, craft-oriented cabinet or upholstery shop, the product under construction stands in one place while the craftsperson makes parts and brings them to the unit for attachment or installation. Modern factory efficiency had its origins in the well-known assembly line concept, in which identical units in production move along a line past workers who perform a repeated operation on each item as it passes. This ideal "mass-production" factory has only had limited applicability to furniture production because the relatively small size of even the largest furniture plants, and the great variety of products in both type and design that they must produce, often makes the number of identical operations to be performed too small to justify a specialized work station for each production step. Nevertheless, the furniture factory is usually planned to take advantage of some production machinery, and is planned around a logical flow of work from starting point to finished product. Some large factories take advantage of conveyers to move work from step to step and use automatic equipment to feed machines and assemble parts. Unfortunately, the demand for well-designed modern furniture of any one unit type is usually insufficient to justify an automated setup of this sort. As a result, ironically, the most efficient and modern factory processes are generally used to produce furniture of poor quality and archaic design. Factories that make well-designed furniture must usually settle for less efficient production methods.

No two factories are alike. In many cases a factory producing the final product is primarily an assembly and finishing plant using parts, frames, metal and plastic elements, and other sub-assemblies made elsewhere. Even plants that do a major portion of the manufacturing often obtain materials (plywood, lumber, tubing, plastic moldings) made outside.

Part of a modern furniture factory. (Photo courtesy of Herman Miller, Inc., Zeeland, Michigan.)

Production Machinery

Even "hand work" requires tools, and most tools have been developed into powered devices using air or electric power to replace human muscle, with a resulting increase in speed and often in precision. Even home craft shops are now usually supplied with a variety of power tools for sawing, planing, drilling, shaping, routing, sanding, and other operations. The reader is referred to craft manuals for information on hand and power tools and their uses in furniture making. The term "machine" is usually reserved for a more complex device that goes beyond the power tool in combining operations, providing automatic feed and/or positioning of work and makes possible repeated operations at high speed, with good precision and a minimum of human work, supervision, and control. Many machines can be automatically controlled and work can be fed from one to another by automatic conveyers leading, in its extreme form, to the "automated factory" in which human work is almost eliminated. Usually furniture factories use some machines and become more efficient as the proportion of machine work increases. Some common factory machines are prescribed below:

Saws. Most factory production saws use the familiar rotating circular saw blade, but include automatic feed of material. The basic ripsaw is a production version of the craft table saw. Cutoff saws are similar to the home radial saw and are used to cut stock to length.

A gang saw has a number of blades spaced to produce a number of thin boards from one pass of a thick piece of material. Panel saws are set up to cut thin panels to size in both dimensions.

The band saw is not based on the rotary blade, but on a continuous thin saw blade. It makes curved cuts possible, but automatic feed is difficult (although guides are used to aid the operator).

Jointer. A machine using knife blades set in a rotating head to cut a straight and true edge along the edge of a board.

Planer. Similar to the jointer, but with a wide cutter to smooth-plane the face of wide boards to take out warp, establish precise thickness, and make smooth surfaces. Some planers are now made using abrasives in place of cutter knives for the same purpose.

Molder. A machine used to convert lengthwise strips of wood into

Rip saw (Photograph courtesy of Royal Industries, Evans Division.)

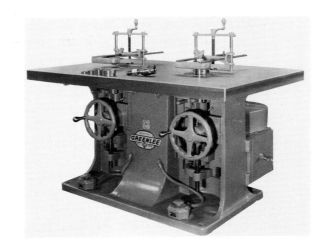

Double spindle shaper. Knives on the spinning cutting heads cut edges of material to desired profile. The two spindles rotate in opposite directions so that the operator can select the direction appropriate to the direction of the grain of wood being fed. (Photograph courtesy of Greelee Bros. and Co.)

moldings of any needed shape or complexity by feeding the strip past a number of rotating-knife cutting heads.

Shaper. A machine in which a rotating-knife cutting head projects upward from a flat table. Wood passing the cutting head is shaped in the profile of the knife. Curved parts can be fed past the head to cut a shape along the curving edge. The double-spindle shaper has two heads rotating in opposite directions to permit the operator to choose the direction of cut appropriate to the direction of the wood grain, which may change along the length of a curved part.

Router. Similar to a shaper, but with the cutting head lowered from above and moved along stationary wood. Used for cutting

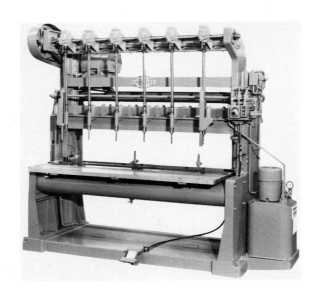

Multiple boring machine. As many holes as there are spindles are bored at once, positions are adjustable as desired. (Photograph courtesy of Greelee Bros. and Co.)

grooves and "routs." Portable routers, power hand tools familiar in home shopwork are also used for some factory applications.

Boring Machine. Used to drill holes positioned precisely and to controlled depth, typically in preparation for doweling. Multiple head, or simply "multiple boring" machines, bore a number of holes at once in precise dimensional relationship.

Dovetail Machine. (multiple spindle). With many cutters to cut the typical dovetail shape in each of the parts to be dovetailed together. The use of the same cutters on both parts produces the equal dovetails characteristic of the machine-cut (as distinguished from hand-cut) dovetail. (See page 121.)

Mortising Machine. Used to cut small and short mortises. A hollow-chisel mortising head cuts square or rectangular mortises. Often combined with a boring function to produce bored holes and mortises simultaneously in the same piece wood.

Lathe (automatic). The well-known wood turning machines used for making round parts from square stock. Stock is automatically fed, chucked, turned to pattern, and removed.

Double End Machine. (also called double end tenoner). The most important of factory woodworking machines. Wood parts are fed automatically past "heads" at either side, which hold a number of revolving spindles that can carry various cutting heads. Cutters can be set in various positions, at different angles to cut any needed complex shape. The heads can be moved to adjust to different size parts. Modern double end machines often include automatic controls operated by push button and punched tape to make setting easy to change and repeat. By passing panels through along one dimension and then rotating 90° for a second pass, all of the edge machining needed on a panel can be accomplished in two passes. Cuts for grooved edges, miters, and splined or lock miters are commonly made on this machine at high speed and with excellent efficiency.

Edge Banding Machine. Used to glue a thin band of veneer to the

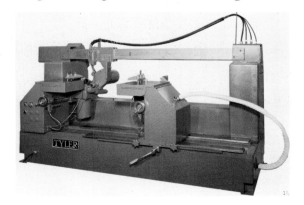

Dovetailer. Dovetail cuts are made on both sides of a drawer front while a third head makes a groove for the drawer bottom at the same time. (Photograph courtesy of Tyler Machinery Co., Inc.)

Automatic lathe. Wood-turning operations are performed without handwork. (Photograph courtesy of Mattison Machine Works.)

Double end tenoner (double end machine). The most universal production woodworking equipment. Work is automatically fed past a number of cutting heads on each side. (Photograph courtesy of Greelee Bros. and Co.)

Edge bander. Applies wood, veneer, or plastic edges to panels in a continuous automatic flow. (Photograph courtesy of Richard T. Byrnes Co., Inc.)

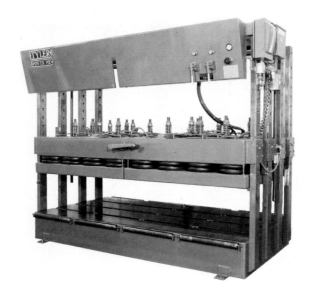

Press for laminating and similar operations. This example uses air pressure; hydraulic presses are similar. (Photograph courtesy of Tyler Machinery Co., Inc.)

Final finishing sander with automatic feed-through. (Photograph courtesy of Precision Concepts Corp.)

edges of panels in a continuous process somewhat like rolling gummed tape off a fixed roll onto material passing by the roll.

Presses. Many types are used for face veneering, laminating, making plywood, and similar steps in the production of flat panels. Special presses are used in making bent or molded plywood.

Sanders. A variety of large production sanders are simply enlarged versions of common home shop power tools. Edge sanders, drum sanders, and belt sanders are fairly self-explanatory. Large belt sanders use a long, continuous belt pressed against the panel to be sanded by an operator using a moving pressure roller.

Air Clamps. Clamps are necessary for most glued assembly operations. Hand screw clamps are replaced in most factory operations by air-powered clamps that operate more rapidly. Clamp arrangements often include conveyers that position the unit for easy clamping and hold the work during drying.

Machinery for metalworking and plastic production is not characteristic of the typical factory producing quality modern furniture. Welding equipment is not uncommon for metalwork, and plants that produce all metal furniture sometimes use powered shears, presses, and forming breaks with work fed by conveyer. More specialized metalwork (e.g., die casting) and plastic molding are usually done in specialized plants or in special departments of the furniture factory. Upholstery work remains largely unmechanized except insofar as complete units of metal frame construction or foam have come to replace conventional construction.

Well-designed modern furniture of good design is too expensive is a common complaint. Certainly, other kinds of products often seem to better value at a given price. A radio or television set, a typewriter, or an automobile seem to offer, at their respective prices, far more performance than good furniture at comparable cost. It is even more disturbing that furniture of poor design is often a better value in terms of performance in relation to cost than comparable products of good design, simply because the poorly designed products are made in sufficient quantity to justify production in more highly automated assembly-line plants. Until good modern furniture is made in the same way, its purchasers will usually confront a premium price that results solely from inefficient, low quantity production. This situation has its roots in the belief, widely held by manufacturers and (even more important) by retailers, that the mass buying public will not accept good design. Most designers are convinced this is a myth that will perpetuate itself as long as only bad furniture is offered to the buying public at a reasonable price.

Construction Details

The great variety of furniture types and materials, as well as the infinitely varied approaches to design that are possible, makes it very difficult to generate a set of "standard details" for furniture construction. The details provided here describe a few typical circumstances that include the most frequently recurring situations and several details that relate to unusual or specialized problems and solutions. Additional details are included in the examples of working drawings provided in the following chapter.

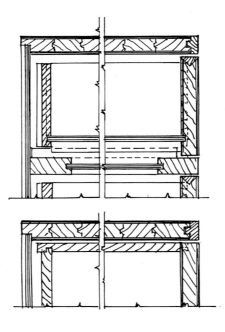

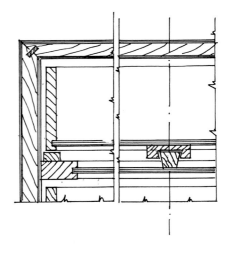

Typical details for conventional wood case construction. Drawers are dovetailed and run on center guides. A frame occurs between each drawer and the next, and makes possible the "dust panel" shown; the frame may be visible (as shown here) or concealed if it is set back and covered by the drawer fronts.

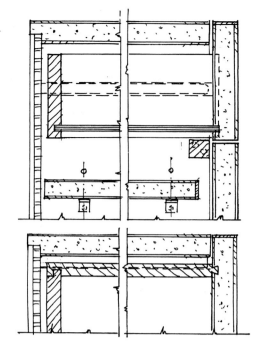

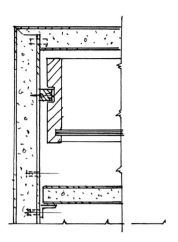

Simplified case construction. Drawer runs on side guides and uses "French" or continuous dovetails. Door compartment with adjustable shelf is shown below. Drawer fronts and doors cover edges in this example, although construction with visible edges is also possible.

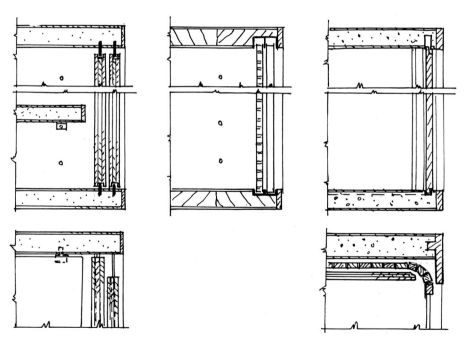

Two types of sliding doors: (left) running on plastic guides, and (right) using metal channel tracks. Far right shows details of wood tambour. Strips are glued to a canvas back to permit running on curved groove track. Metal and plastic tambours are also available.

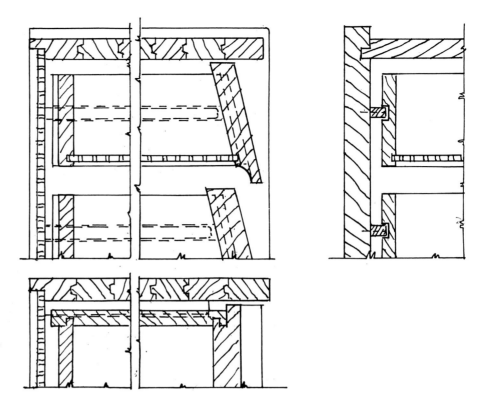

Case construction in solid wood. End grain will be visible along the top edges of the sides. The slanted drawer fronts make a finger-grip pull possible. Vertical drawer fronts are also possible with conventional pulls.

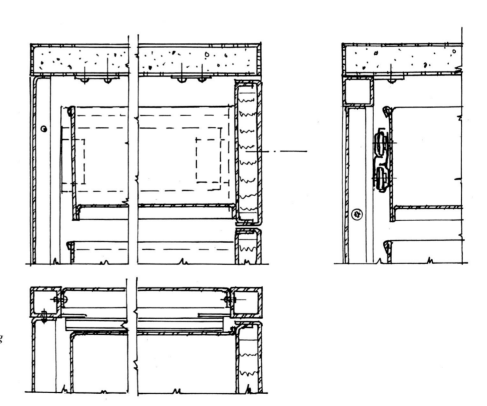

Metal desk or case construction using a square tubular frame and a particle-board top with plastic surfaces. Drawers are carried on metal roller side guides.

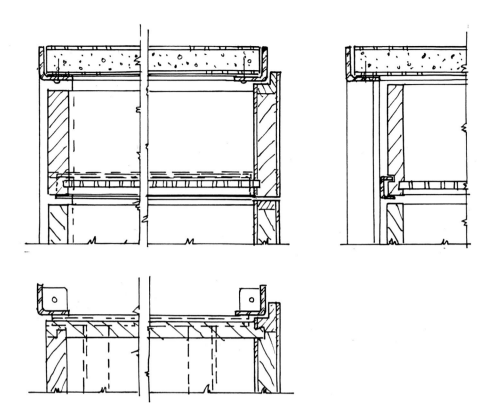

Simple case construction using a metal angle frame. Drawer sides and backs are visible externally and must be finished.

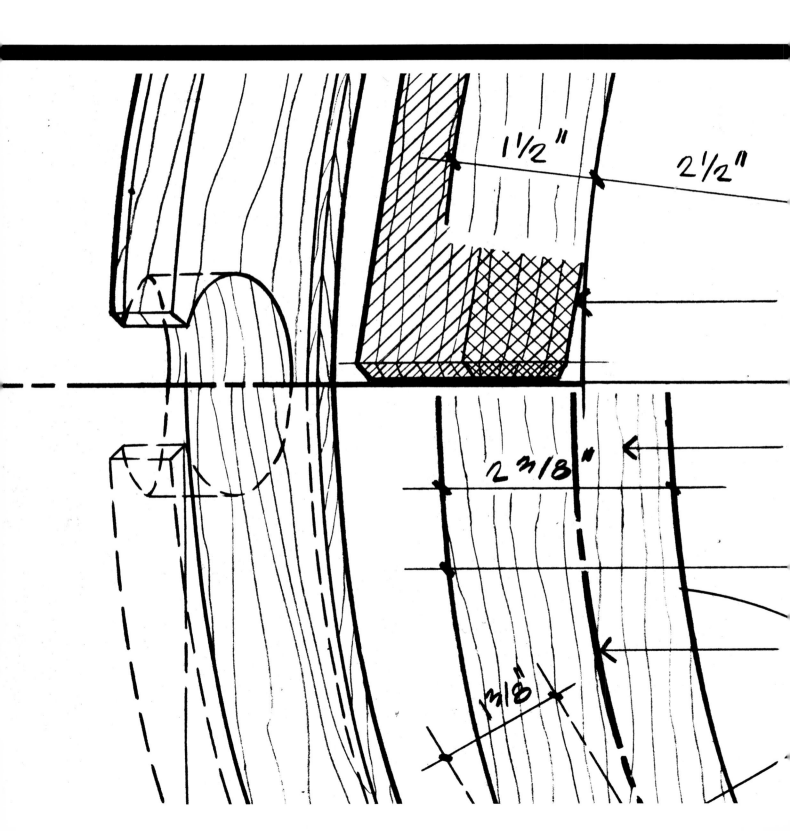

1½"

2½"

2 3/8"

3/8"

5

DESIGN PROCESSES AND METHODS

Since the objects we call furniture are relatively small and simple (as compared to large buildings, ships, or aircraft), and because their uses are so familiar to everyone, it seems a simple matter to "think of" a new design for a table, a chair, or a cabinet. Almost anyone who tries can produce such a thought, but this simplicity is deceptive. With the thought in mind, a design process must begin that will continue through a number of steps before a first concept can become a reality. In practice, the first thought usually has some of the illusory quality of a dream—when an effort is made to reduce it to reality, it turns out to be hazy and imprecise, full of unresolved problems and unanswered questions. Thus any serious attempt to design furniture must include a series of steps with some logical order that move from first thought to finished product with a minimum of detour and waste motion.

Furniture design projects can start in several different ways and the nature of this beginning will almost surely exert some control over the end result. In many areas of design projects begin in fairly consistent and well-established ways. A client may approach an architect with a specific need for a house, a factory, an institutional building, or a similar project knowing, in some rough way, what is needed and why it is needed. Manufacturers of industrial products, with competitive advantage over their opposite numbers in mind, ask their designers to produce "new models," changed

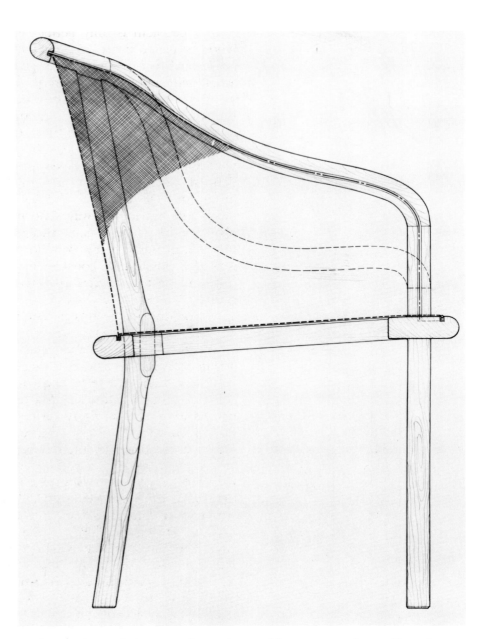

Full-size working drawing side view of a wood-framed chair designed by Ward Bennett for Brickel Associates. Drawing by Norman Diekman. (Courtesy of Ward Bennett and Brickel Associates.)

and, it is hoped, improved versions of known products. Occasionally they may ask the designer to seek out a human need that a new product could fill. An engineer designing a bridge, a highway or a radio tower is initially aware of what is needed and may then proceed to develop ways to fill that need economically and efficiently.

In these cases it is customary to start a project with a first stage called "programming." In this stage the needs that have brought the project into being are explored in detail and are expressed, usually in writing, in the most specific possible terms. It is a truism that once a problem is fully defined the solution will begin to emerge. When a furniture project originates in similar ways, it is useful to go through a programming stage, even a brief one, to arrive at an *exact* statement of what is required. What is its intended function? Are there restrictions on materials, production method, or cost? For example, usually it is much easier to design a typewriter table to hold a standard office machine to be built of steel, in large quantity, and to sell for 10% less than any similar product now on the market than to design "a new piece of furniture" not otherwise defined. Nevertheless, because of the simple and familiar nature of furniture, it is perfectly possible for a project to begin in a far less organized and logical way. One may notice a fault in some familiar object and be led to think about ways to avoid that fault. One may notice a personal, fairly common need that justifies a new design. It is also possible to consider a particular material, perhaps a new one, and be led to furniture products that could use it advantageously. The specific character of an existing building or interior space, or one in the design development stage, may suggest the need for a new furniture design that will be more satisfactory than anything currently available. This last possibility has made many architects turn to furniture design at various times.

Although any of these kinds of project beginnings are acceptable, some are much better adapted to precise "programming" than others. As long as a furniture concept fills some need it has a degree of legitimacy, and many furniture designs have found uses that were unanticipated by their designers. It is unikely that anyone would begin to plan a building or design a machine without a clear idea of its use, developed in considerable detail, but a chair or a table can be designed with no more exact program than the name of the object implies. Contrary to expectations, a "tight," or precise program is likely to simplify the design process while a "loose," or undefined program may make the process more difficult and the result less useful. The reasons for this will become clear as the process of design is considered. The basic pattern of the design process, insofar as it has been defined with any clarity, includes the following steps:

1. A problem is recognized and defined. The definition may be detailed and precise, or (as is often the case with furniture design) it may be slightly vague and general.
2. The designer proposes a tentative solution to the problem, arrived at through the kind of thought that is usually called "creative." Exactly how the tentative proposal is synthesized in the designer's mind remains a matter for discussion, but it seems to involve a search of the memory for any and every trace of information that might have some bearing on the issue. The experience of being "struck by an idea" or of "hitting on some-

thing" is probably a matter of recognizing the way in which some group of memory traces can combine to form a suggestion, a proposal, for a problem solution.

3. The tentative proposal is visualized as a form having a potential physical reality, and this reality is described in some definite way that makes it a "matter of record." Words are a possible medium for such a description but, because of their abstract quality, they are often unsatisfactory for defining a proposed physical reality. It is, of course, possible to proceed at once to create the physical reality. One can think of a new sort of chair and proceed to the shop and construct that chair. Craftspeople often work this way to some extent, but experience has shown that it may be more efficient to insert some steps between concept and production. Designers have become accustomed to two particular techniques for making a proposal specific in ways less costly in time and materials than constructing a complete realization of a concept. These are the sketching or drafting of drawings and constructing models. Each is a system for producing, quickly and easily, a concrete and specific physical record of a concept in a form that can be viewed by the designer and by others, that can be shipped, stored for long or short periods and (particularly in the case of drawings) that can be easily duplicated. Pencil lead and paper are inexpensive materials but, when used properly, they can record a concept in ways so specific as to leave very little room for doubt. Models can add the three-dimensional aspect of the proposed reality and may often be (in furniture) full size. Models are usually slower and more difficult to construct than drawings are to sketch or draft, and tend to be more difficult to revise and change than drawings. Thus, even when a model is planned, it is often advantageous to make sketches or drawings first. In any case, a first sketch or rough model makes it possible to proceed to the next step.

4. The visible statement of the proposed object, whether it is a sketch, a model, or an actual constructed realization, is now ready for a critical evaluation that can lead to improvement. Sketches—which may take only minutes to make—have the advantage that, with so little time invested, revision seems easy if desirable. Models and prototypes are more specific and realistic, but sometimes discourage revision by their very realistic completeness and the magnitude of the chore of revision. In any case, the purpose of the drawing or model is to make it possible for the designer to evaluate his or her own proposal and to devise improvements. This leads to many cycles of revision and evaluation. The evaluation can be the designer's own, or it can come from others—possible users, other designers, or experts in a particular field (e.g., constructional techniques, physiology, specifics of utility)—but its purpose is to improve the quality of

Designer Norman Diekman who develops products for several furniture manufacturers works with scale models and with drawings, often using color tones
applied to prints of perspectives and orthographic drawings. Application of
color tones can convert a construction drawing print into a highly realistic
presentation drawing. A number of examples of these techniques are shown
here.

The "Norman" chair designed by Norman Diekman for the David Edward firm.
Color tones are applied to a black and white print showing side and front
view and a partial top view above. (Illustration courtesy of Norman
Diekman.)

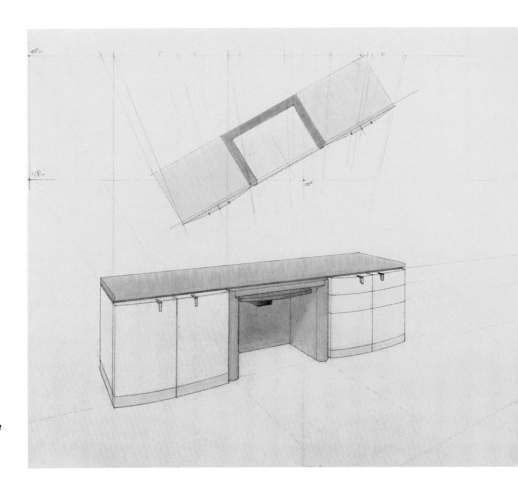

A credenza, part of the "Canto" group designed by Norman Diekman for Stow/Davis shown in a color drawing. (Illustration courtesy of Norman Diekman.)

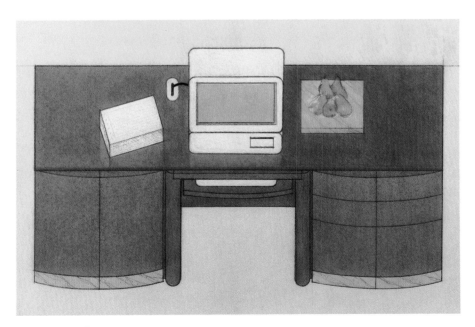

The credenza illustrated above shown in a combined top view-front elevation color drawing. (Illustration courtesy of Norman Diekman.)

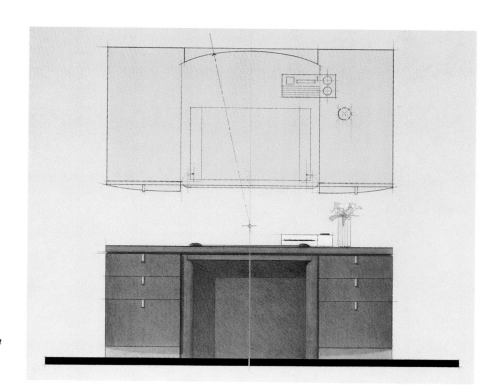

Stow/Davis "Canto" desk in elevation and plan by Norman Diekman. (Illustration courtesy of Norman Diekman.)

"Canto" desk and credenza in combined plan and elevation by Norman Diekman. (Illustration courtesy of Norman Diekman.)

A large elliptical table designed by Norman Diekman for a new furniture company "360 Designs." The drawing shows a top view above and a front elevation below partly overlapping the top view. The black edge and base inlays are ebony inlaid into ash burl. The large black squares in the top are granite inlays. A square box appears in top view and elevation. The vase of flowers in elevation overlaps the vase as drawn in top view. (Illustration courtesy of Norman Diekman.)

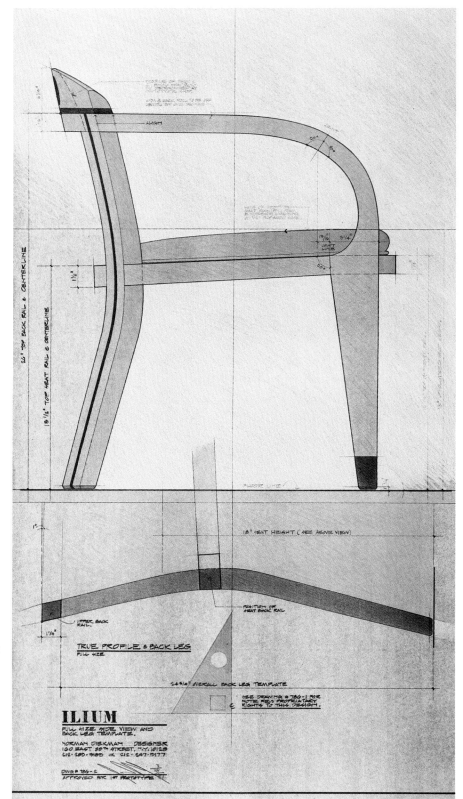

An arm chair designed by Norman Diekman for Vecta: Beylerian Collection. The drawing is a full size construction drawing shown here in a print made into a rendering with Prismacolor pencil color tones. In the drawing at left, a side view is shown with a true elevation of the back leg (laid out horizontally) below. The drawing at right shows a half front-half rear elevation with a plan (top view) partly superimposed below. The left half shows the frame only; the right half adds the seat cushion. (Illustration courtesy of Norman Diekman.)

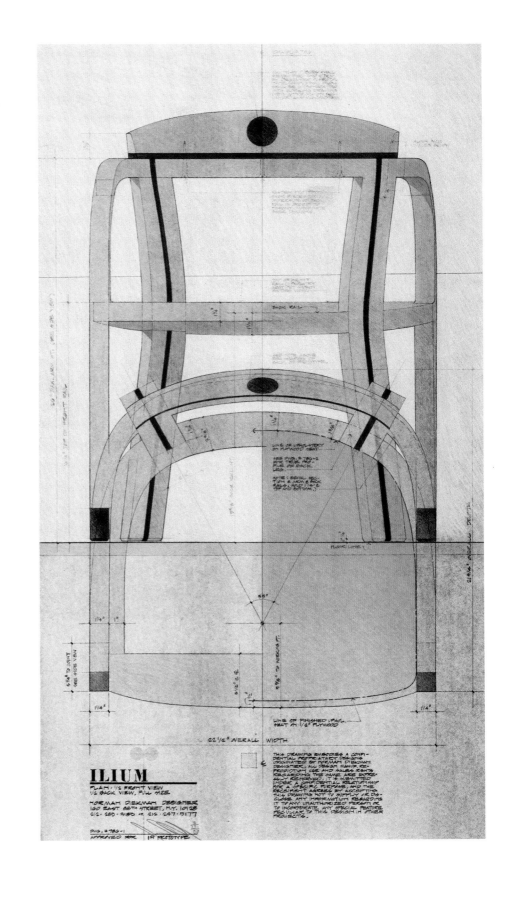

ILIUM

PLAN · 1/2 FRONT VIEW
1/2 BACK VIEW, FULL SIZE

NORMAN DIEKMAN DESIGNER
150 EAST 98TH STREET, N.Y. 10128
212 · 289 · 9180 OR 212 · 247 · 5177

DWG. # 786-1
APPROVED FOR 1ST PROTOTYPE

22 1/2" OVERALL WIDTH

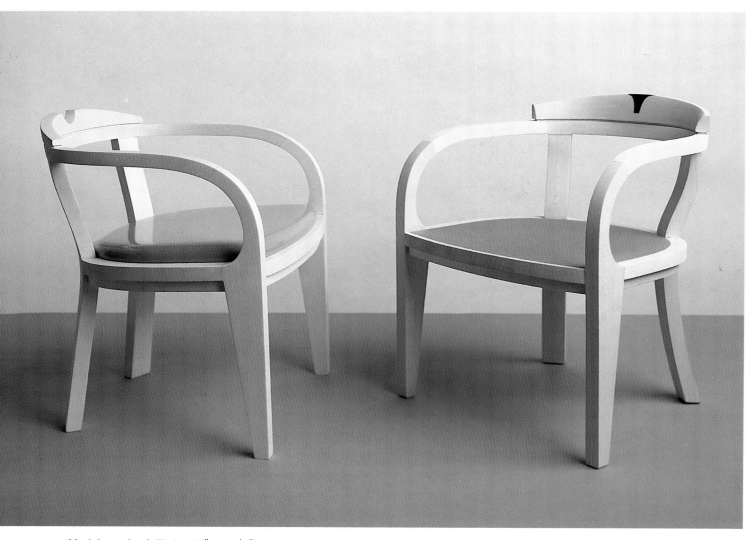

Models at ¹/₄ full-size (3" = 1'0") of the chair illustrated in drawings on the preceding two pages. Designs of Norman Diekman for Vecta: Beylerian Collection. (Photograph courtesy of Norman Diekman.)

the concept proposal as it becomes more specific at each cycle of reevaluation.

5. It is the designer's obligation to decide when a design has progressed to the point where further criticism, evaluation, and revision no longer produce significant improvement. The first few cycles of revision usually produce large gains, but these gains are then diminished, and sometimes revisions that lead to improvement in one way may lead to a step backward elsewhere. It is possible to continue working at a design that has reached a certain level of excellence in ways that gradually diminish its quality. The skilled designer knows, in some intuitive way, when it is time to stop and convert the developing design into a form ready for realization. This form may be a drawing (or set of drawings) that spells out every detail of the design in its final form, or it may be a full size "model" identical to the intended final object. Such a model is usually called a "prototype"—a single realization, often costly and difficult to make, that demonstrates what the produced version of the design is to be.

6. A full size prototype, or a first "sample" made from drawings calls for one more cycle of criticism and evaluation. It can sometimes return the project to its beginning, with the discovery that only sweeping revision or a totally new start can lead to a satisfactory end result. If things proceed well, however, it will usually require only small revisions in the nature of a final "fine-tuning."

7. The design is now ready for production. This may involve making tools, starting up special production lines or other complex steps, or it may merely mean making "shop drawings" or patterns that will be needed as the final products are manufactured. In either case, the designer needs to maintain contact with the process, to offer "supervision" and to make sure that adjustments made to ease production do not distort the design in some unfortunate way.

The entire process involves making a specific proposal, subjecting it to criticism, then making revisions and improvements, thus generating a new and better proposal until a level of quality is reached that seems to justify final production. The "proposal" is described above as taking a number of forms. Each of these forms requires detailed discussion.

Sketches

Designers of every kind (and artists as well) are accustomed to using a sketch as the quickest and simplest way of converting a mental image into a tangible reality that can be viewed, retained,

Rough sketch on a lined legal pad. (Author's drawing.)

A preliminary sketch using watercolor to suggest form. (Author's drawing.)

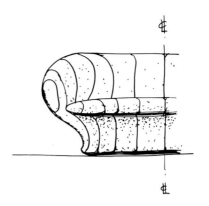

Ink line sketch on graph paper (Author's drawing.)

and shown to others. Beginning work on a furniture design project usually means many sketches—often even hundreds—in which the designer notes possible ideas on paper. The very process of noting tends to generate alternative ideas and certain directions emerge as most promising. Pencil is the favorite medium because of the ease of erasure, but pen and ink (or the recently popular felt-tip pen) are also commonly used even for initial design stages. Any kind of paper may be used; the legendary sketch on the back of an envelope or menu is often quite literally the first version of a furniture proposal. Sketchbooks and drawing paper are useful, but many designers seem more at ease with less formal materials; loose sheets of paper or (a particular favorite) sheets from a lined, yellow legal pad. The color and the ruled lines of these pads offer a background that is less intimidating than a clean, blank white page. Graph paper has the same quality and offers the possibility of

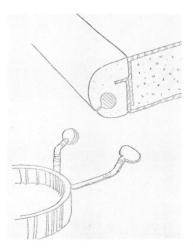

Detail sketch presenting a proposed idea to a client. (Author's drawing.)

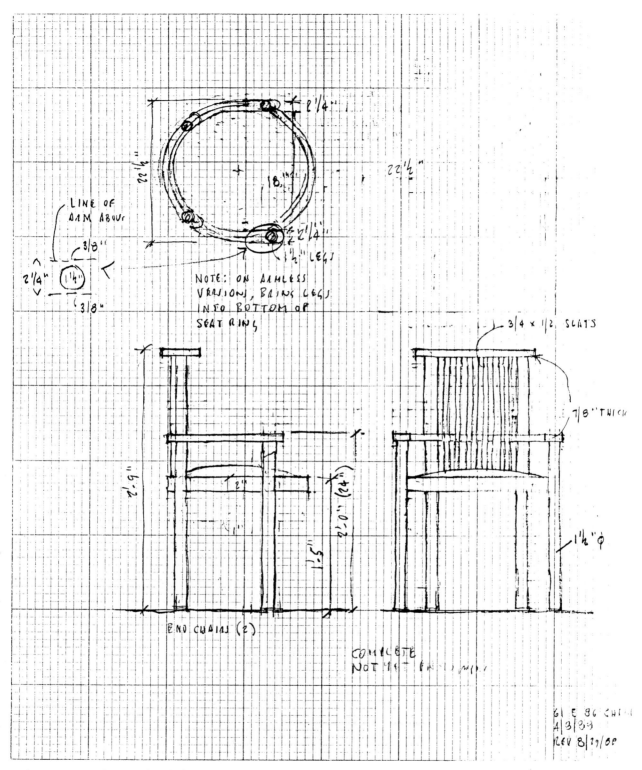

Design sketch for a wood arm chair by Alfredo DeVido. (Illustration courtesy of Alfredo DeVido, architect.)

Perspective sketches for an armchair under design development by Norman Diekman. (Illustration courtesy of Norman Diekman.)

maintaining 90° angles or establishing scale relationships, if desired. Tracing paper, particularly the inexpensive, thin yellow sketching variety, is also favored because of the ease with which layered revisions can be made by drawing over a previous sketch. A well-known designer is devoted to standard size index cards as a sketch medium because they are easily portable and encourage organized storage for future reference.

Whatever the media used, sketches may be vague and conceptual or more specific, with the former often leading to the latter. The proposed design may appear in perspective or in orthographic elevations. Details are often sketched early in the process of development, initially sometimes even when a total concept is generated by an improved detail. Sketches need not be to scale, but it is frequently useful to introduce scale at an early stage to avoid the discovery that drastic changes in form are needed when the design is considered in terms of real dimensions. Until metric dimensioning becomes standard practice in the United States, most designers will continue to use the scales that commonly appear on the familiar triangular architects' scale: 1 in. = 1 ft 0 in. (too small for any except general representations of large units), 1½ in. = 1 ft 0 in. (⅛ full-size), 3 in. = 1 ft 0 in. (¼ full-size), half full size, and actual full size. The last two scales are most often useful for developing details. Most sketches are made freehand, but a T square and a triangle may be useful where geometric relationships are important.

Sketch Models

Since so much furniture involves crucial three-dimensional relationships, it is often important to sketch in three-dimensional form at an early stage of design development, sometimes even at the very beginning. The terms "sketch model" or "rough model" refer to prototypes made quickly of simple materials, without great care for a realistic appearance and finish, that serve to aid visualization in three dimensions and to check aspects of certain designs (e.g., movable parts, fitting or stacking relationships) that are hard to work with in flat representation on paper. Sketch models are often done at very small scales and can be made from paper, cardboard, wire, soft woods, or any other convenient miscellaneous materials. Paper clips and coat-hanger wire, pins, toothpicks, tongue depressors, bamboo skewers, and similar odds and ends are often used although the materials offered in model-making shops may provide more accurate parts. Acetate sheets (for glass or transparent plastic), thin brass and aluminum, wood veneers, and various papers that simulate marble or plastic surfaces are also useful. It is convenient to collect scraps of all such materials in one place where they will be readily available for sketch models and more formal models as well. Model-making cements, quick-setting wood glues and, for dif-

Card and paper model for an office furniture group. (Design and model by the author.)

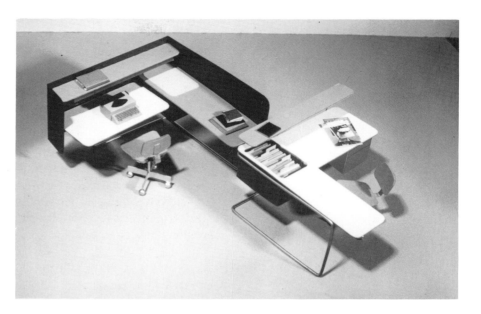

Office secretarial work stations modeled at a scale of 1" = 1'0". (Design and models by the author.)

1/4 full size (3" x 1'-0") models of two chairs designed by Norman Diekman. (Photograph courtesy of Norman Diekman.)

ficult to join materials, epoxy and other high-strength plastic adhesives are useful. Scissors, mat knife and razor blade, a metal straight edge, a small wire cutter, pliers, and some emery-board nail files are usually the only tools needed although a trimming board paper cutter can be convenient and time saving.

Often it is helpful to move alternatively from paper sketch to sketch model and back again as a design develops. Each sketching method helps to expose particular kinds of problems and encourages their solution. Choice of scale for sketch models is similar to that for sketches; it is possible to work without scale, but modeling in a scale leads to better precision in converting ideas into realistic forms. Models at 1 in. or 1½ in. = 1 ft 0 in. are ideal for most early design stages although full size models of details, intersections of parts, or items of hardware can be useful. Occasionally complete, full size sketch models are made and may be very helpful in visualizing the relation of an object to human scale. Sketch models tend to be fragile and must usually be considered expendable, but they can yield photographs that are convincingly realistic and easy to preserve.

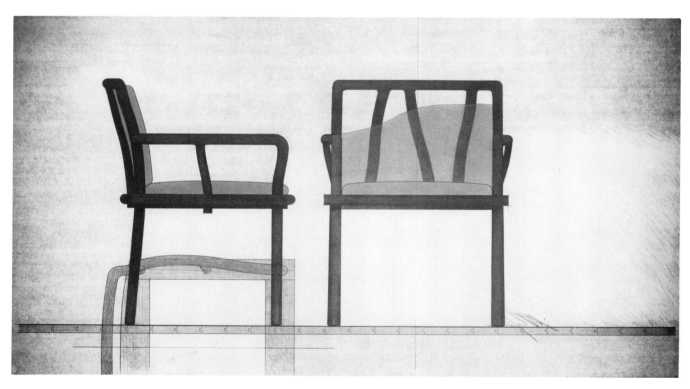

Orthographic drawings for a chair by Norman Diekman. Note the plan (top view) superimposed on the elevation, lower left. (Illustration courtesy of Norman Diekman).

Drawings

The term "drawing," not sketch or working (or construction) drawing obviously refers to a more formal, finished representation of a design on paper. Like sketches, drawings may be perspectives or they may be orthographic. In the latter case they are invariably done to scale and may include sections or plan sections to show details that would not otherwise be visible. The term "presentation drawing" refers to a formal drawing made to show a design to a client, competition jury, or similar audience. The use of drawings of this kind is resisted by most furniture designers as an unnecessary step that can often be misleading. The designers of mass-produced commercial furniture frequently produce presentation drawings in media such as pastel or air-brush (long popular in the more commercial phases of industrial design practice) for use in "selling." These are highly unrealistic and concentrate on surface appearance to the exclusion of any interest in serious effort at de-

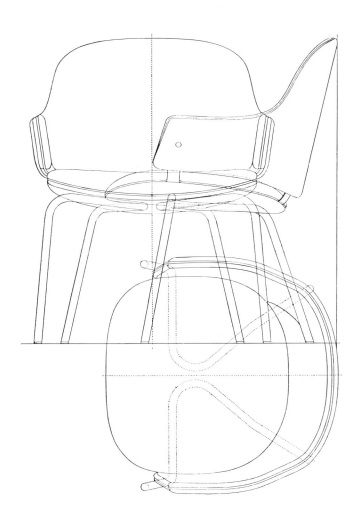

Complete design drawing for a chair. Drawings are superimposed to save space. Dimensions are omitted since the actual drawing is full size.

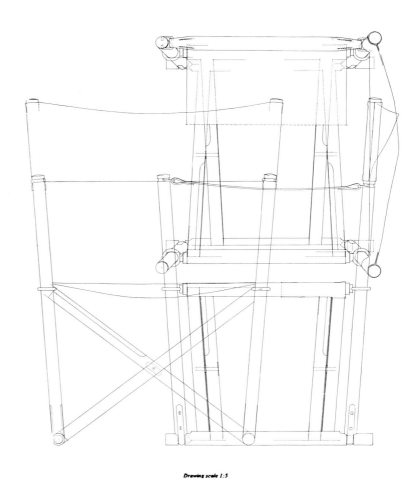

Drawing scale 1:5

Folding chair designed by Mogens Koch shown in typical European ink line working drawing. (Courtesy Interna, Copenhagen.)

sign creativity. Perhaps such drawings have led designers to mistrust all formal drawings. Thus, most designers seem to prefer to proceed from sketches and sketch models to working drawings or to prototypes.

Yet it is still possible to make careful, accurate drawings as a step in design development or as a means of showing a design. European designers seem to have retained more interest in this step than their colleagues in the United States. In Denmark, careful and precise drawings are often "rendered" in watercolor with colors that represent materials realistically, and may even include shading and shadows that suggest three-dimensional forms. Precise ink line drawings are also popular in Europe and (especially when drawn full size) often serve as both visual representations and construction drawings. These approaches are always available to any furniture designer who may find them useful.

Working Drawings

Construction drawings, or working drawings (the term normal to architectural practice) include all information necessary for actual production. These drawings can be delivered to a manufacturer or furniture maker's shop and, without additional verbal instructions, will serve to permit a realization of the designer's exact intent. Ideally, it should then be possible to accept production bids from various sources with an assurance that any product which complies with the drawings will be identical with any other, even one made at a different time and place. Ultimately, however, this is an ideal drawings can only approach. Differences in quality of workmanship and selection of materials are very difficult to control through drawings or verbal instructions. The qualities of furniture are also

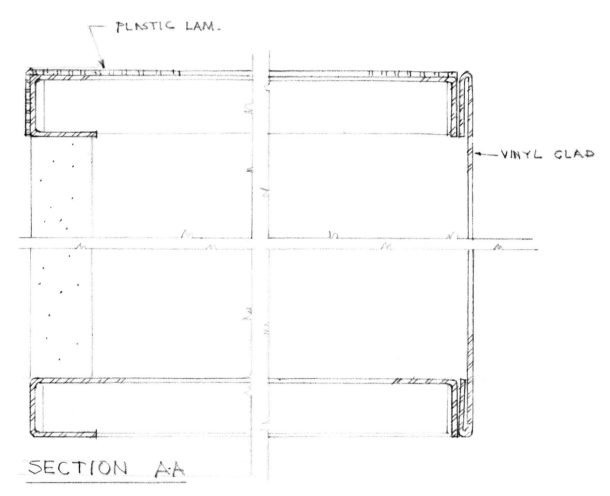

A detail of a drawing with "breaks," making it possible to condense full size details to reasonable size by omitting all but the significant portions.

very subtle, so that two examples that match drawings may still show noticeable differences in small ways.

Nevertheless, the only ways that furniture design can be recorded to form a basis for production are by drawings or prototypes (discussed below). Drawings are more compact, simpler to transport and file, and easier to reproduce. Although a prototype may be more specific, its very completeness may hide interior details that can be more readily displayed in drawings. Traditionally, furniture working drawings were always made full size. In modern practice this is still done when complex forms, irregular curves, and obscure details are present. When forms are simple and geometric, smaller scales are satisfactory and avoid the inconvenience of large drawing boards and large tracings and prints that are clumsy to handle and store. Full size drawings are frequently required for chairs, where complex shapes are common. Surprisingly, chairs are not normally large enough to lead to an inconveniently large sheet. It is customary to draw any symmetrical views (usually front, back, top, or bottom views) to show only one symmetrical half of the view. Drawings can often be superimposed (a plan onto an elevation, for example) without confusion so that a full size drawing of a chair will often fit on a sheet no larger than 33 × 42½ in.* Sofas may be extended versions of chairs and require only a scale drawing to show overall size and any modifications that development from the corresponding chair may require. Tables, desks, other storage furniture, and beds can often be shown at smaller scale with any critical details at full size. A complete cross section of a desk or cabinet at full size can usually be made conveniently small by "breaking," that is omitting, portions of the object that involve no constructional detail. A drawer chest, for example, can be shown in full size at front and back, while the depth is "condensed" by simply leaving out the full depth dimension and indicating this omission with "break" lines. The height can be similarly condensed by not including repeated drawers or otherwise empty space.

It is often best to show general views of a complete design at a moderate scale (e.g., 1½ in. = 1 ft 0 in.) and then to add a number of small, partial details at full size that show crucial intersections, special situations that may present problems or irregular shapes that might be distorted in the process of enlargement to full size. Curved forms present a particular difficulty. Curves that are parts of circles can be defined accurately by showing center and radius, but irregular curves must be set out at full size so they can be transferred directly to shop tools or parts. It is important to

---

* The odd figures reflect a widely adopted practice of making drawings in dimensions that are multiples of standard letter size paper (8½ × 11 in.). This makes filing convenient and avoids a confusion of random sizes.

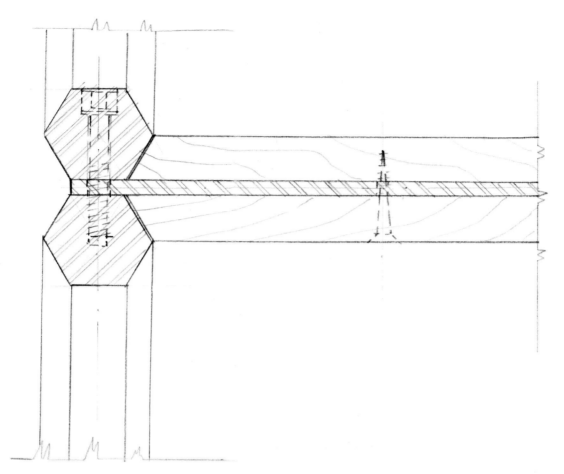

Portion of a full size working drawing reproduced at full size. (Author's drawing.)

guard against the mistaken belief that any curve can be expressed with parts of circles. Joining a number of circular arcs only produces a crude and faulty approximation of a free curve of the sort that occurs in organic forms.

Multiple curvatures that occur along two curvature axes simultaneously are the most troublesome forms to represent in drawings. Some designers give up the effort and resort to full size models or prototypes exclusively, but the problems of shipment and storage of a record of the form still encourage the use of drawings even if only as a supplement to a three-dimensional model. The practice of naval architects (who have had to deal with this problem for centuries in connection with forms far too large for prototypes) is the guide in dealing with these problems. A "set of lines" for a ship's hull shows a series of profiles that result from sectioning the desired shape at regular intervals. Three sets of lines taken in the three planes of orthographic projection record a curved form with great precision and make it possible to recreate the

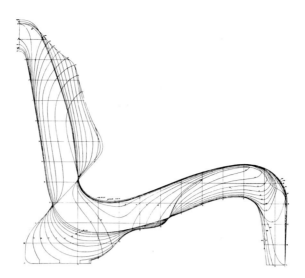

Side elevation of a very low chair with "lines" superimposed to show contour at successive planes. (Jørn Utzon design for Bramin, Denmark.)

form by cutting templates to control the form of a model, by building up laminations that conform to the successive profiles, or by some combination of these methods. When a three-dimensional model or prototype exists, making such a set of lines is simply an exercise in careful draftsmanship. If they are drawn on paper first to define a desired three-dimensional form, the lines of any two views generate the third view through a process detailed in any descriptive geometry text. Three sets of lines that include contradictions may be drawn, making it impossible to construct a form that agrees with all three views. The multiple curved forms of molded chair bodies are an example of the kind of furniture part that must be dealt with in this way. Curves of more conventional furniture, including curved upholstered seating, are usually only shown in one (or a very few) section and the maker's judgment (or the natural characteristics of the materials used) fills in the exact forms of the curves.

Working drawings for furniture of traditional materials, wood and upholstery, are generally "assembly drawings," that is, drawings that show all parts fitted together as they will be in the final product.

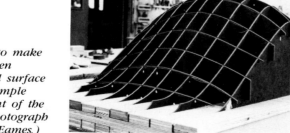

A set of "lines" can be used to make full size templates which, when interlocked, generate a curved surface in three dimensions. This example was a step in the development of the Eames plastic chair shell. (Photograph courtesy of Ray and Charles Eames.)

Where there are metal or plastic parts that involve more highly mechanized technologies, it is usually desirable to make "parts drawings," showing each part separately in accordance with good engineering drawing practice, as described in standard texts on that subject. This facilitates dealing with various sources that may be possible producers of separate parts of various types, suppliers who may be in widely dispersed locations and active in widely different fields of production. A diagrammatic or schematic assembly drawing can then be used to show the intended assembly of parts. Sometimes it may be logical for the designer to make a drawing of the complete, assembled unit and leave the making of the parts drawings to a production engineering department, but this always invites the intrusion of errors and changes as the information is translated from one drawing to many individual parts drawings. In such cases the designer should check all engineering drawings before they are issued to minimize errors.

In general, working drawings for furniture are made with less system and formality than is customary in architecture and engineering. Contact between designer and factory or shop is usually close and competitive bidding is not usually contemplated, so that the drawings become merely a device for conveying necessary information. Consequently, formality of drawing format, dimensioning, notes and references, and such details as borders and title blocks are usually improvised to suit the convenience of the particular situation. It might be best if more care, order, and system became accepted practice in the furniture field, and designers would be well advised to try to introduce some systematic routines into their drawing methods. Some architectural and engineering drawing routines that apply to furniture drawings include the following:

1. Use of standard size drawing sheets with border and binding space.
2. Use of a standard title block at lower right with project and drawing number, date, scale, and names and addresses of designer and client or manufacturer involved.
3. A space for recording revisions with number and date and a systematic way of locating the revision where it appears on the drawing.
4. A systematic way of indicating dimensions. In full size drawings, dimensions are only needed to indicate overalls (exterior totals) and to show critical dimensions that must be precise. On scale drawings every significant dimension should be shown, but shown only once. Where a series of dimensions occurs, it is best not to close the sequential series of dimensions, but to let an overall govern the total of the series. If all dimensions of a "run" and the total are both shown, there is always the chance of a discrepancy.

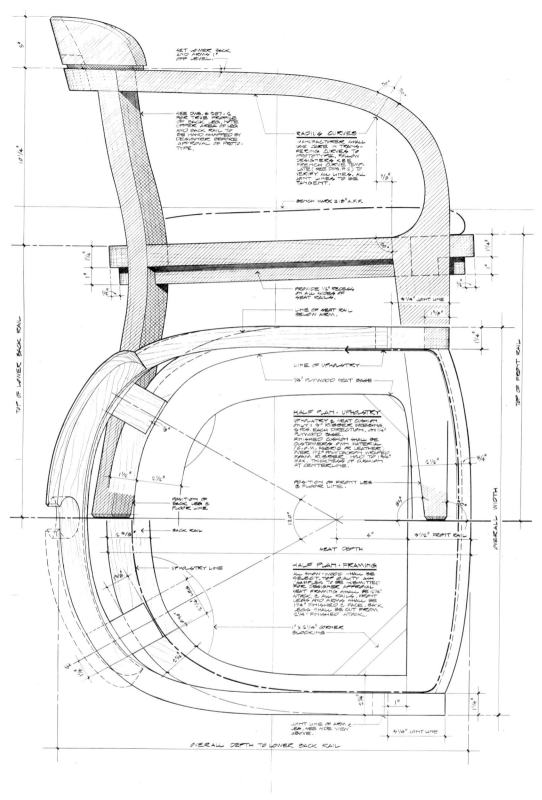

Full-size construction drawings for a chair designed by Norman Diekman
Side (profile) view at left with superimposed plan (top) view
Note the back leg shown in true profile at bottom with french
curve shown in place to establish curvature. Half front-half rear view at right.
(Illustrations courtesy of Norman Diekman).

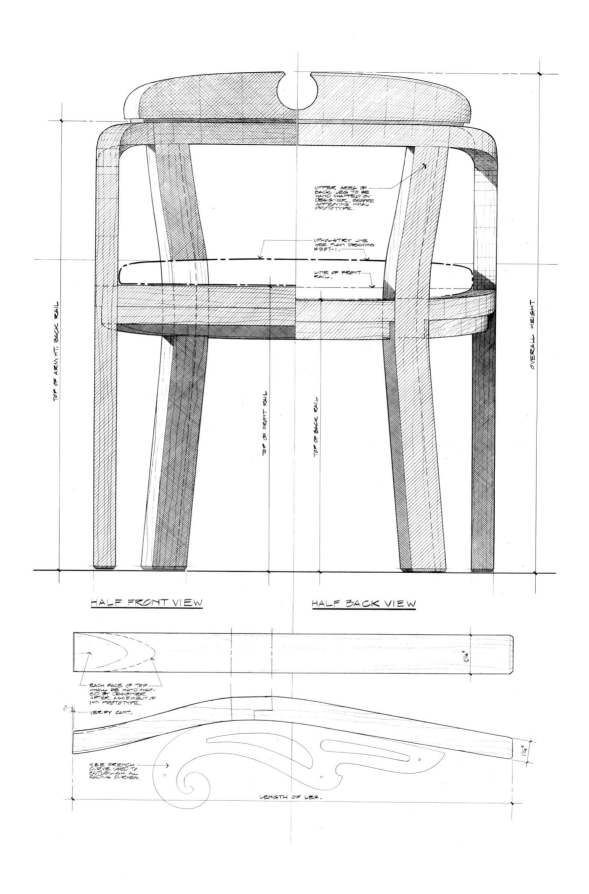

UPPER AREA OF
BACK LEG TO BE
HAND SHAPED BY
DESIGNER, BEFORE
APPROVING FINAL
PROTOTYPE.

UPHOLSTERY LINE
SEE PLAN DRAWING
#987-1.

LINE OF FRONT
RAIL.

TOP OF ARM HT. BACK RAIL

TOP OF FRONT RAIL

TOP OF BACK RAIL

OVERALL HEIGHT

HALF FRONT VIEW   HALF BACK VIEW

EACH FACE OF TOP
RAIL TO BE HAND SHAP-
ED BY DESIGNER
AFTER ASSEMBLY OF
1ST. PROTOTYPE.

VERIFY CANT.

K&E FRENCH
CURVE USED TO
ESTABLISH ALL
RADIUS CURVES.

LENGTH OF LEG.

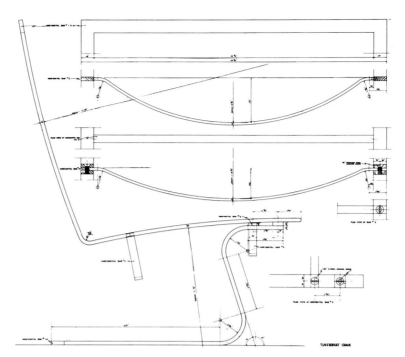

Metal parts drawings for the flat bar structure version of the Mies van der Rohe Tugendhat chair. (Courtesy of Knoll International, Inc., New York.)

The Mies van der Rohe Tugendhat chair as produced from the metal parts drawing illustrated above. (Photograph courtesy of Knoll International, New York.)

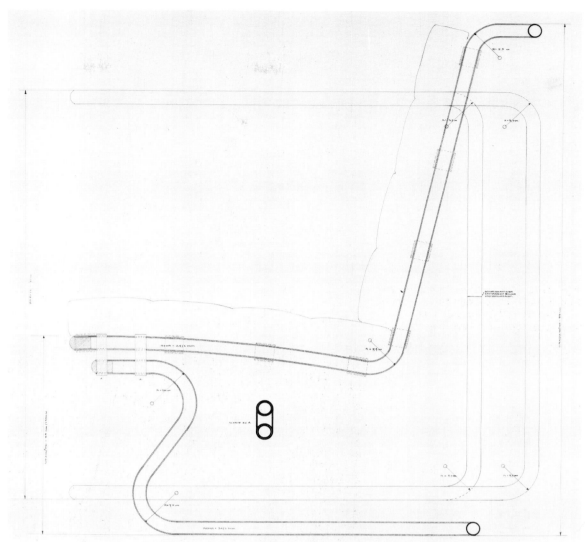

Full-size drawing of the Tugendaht chair from the Atelier of Mies van der Rohe, 1931. Main dimensions and radii of bend are shown even on the full size drawing. (Courtesy Mies van der Rohe Archive, the Museum of Modern Art, New York.)

Dimensions are usually given in feet, inches, and fractions. If dimensions over one foot are to be given in inches, that practice should be followed throughout a drawing (all dimensions in inches). Decimals are usually used in place of fractions of an inch for metal or plastic parts, where engineering practice rather than architectural or cabinet making practice governs. Tolerances may also be shown in such cases. A standard practice should be established and adhered to for the weight and location of dimension lines, type of dimension arrowheads or other identification, lines for reference notes, symbols for locating

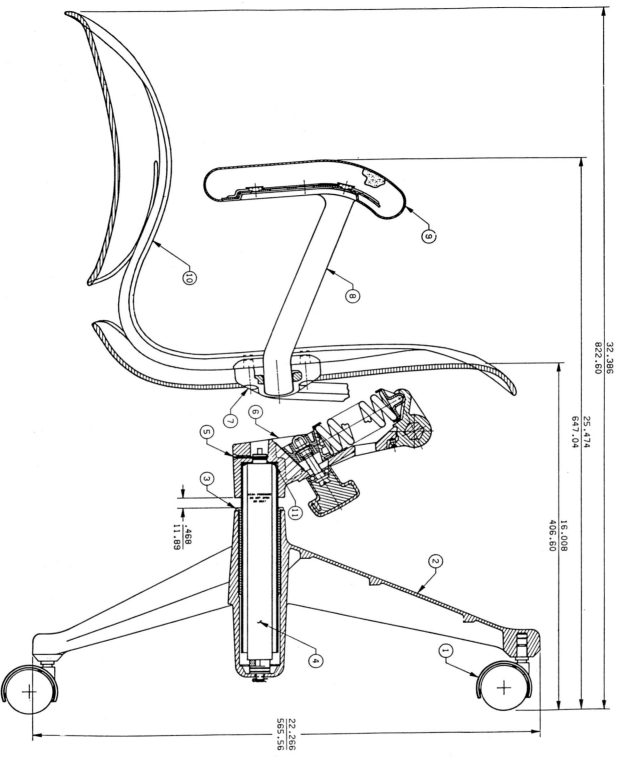

Engineering drawing showing highly detailed cross section of the "Equa" chair designed by Don Chadwick and William Stumpf. Note dimensions given in both inches and metric units. (Illustration courtesy of Herman Miller, Inc.)

sections and identifying the section drawings, and similar details. Indication of materials shown in section should follow standard practice.

5. Notes and specification information should be grouped on the right and made as clear and concise as possible. It is often convenient to include a small perspective of the complete object above the title block on general or assembly drawings to aid in visual identification of a tracing or filed print.

Any and all of these rules are frequently broken in furniture design practice, but it is best to adhere to them unless there is some logical reason for working in other ways.

The level of detail shown in furniture drawings should always relate to the designer's awareness of the needs of the production personnel who will use them. There is no need to include detail that is a well known standard on the part of the drawings' user. For example, a shop that routinely makes drawers, in a standardized and satisfactory way does not need drawings that show drawer construction in detailed sections. Generally, upholsterers and upholstery frame-makers have far more knowledge of the details of upholstery construction than most designers. There is no need to provide details beyond those necessary to ensure the forms and the quality of construction desired. Over-detailing of working drawings is a waste of time and often merely exposes the limits of the designer's knowledge and confuses the user of the drawing. A knowledge of exactly how much detail to draw under each set of circumstances is characteristic of the skilled and experienced designer.

CAD

Computer-aided drafting (CAD) or computer-aided design and drafting (CADD) have come into wide use in many architectural and interior design offices. Furniture design makes such modest demands of designer and/or draftsman that these modern aids are still not extensively used in furniture development. A typical chair, table, or storage unit can usually be drawn by hand in a few hours. It is nevertheless quite possible to work with computer techniques and, where the equipment is available and the designer has learned the (quite simple) necessary skills, CAD can be helpful and even, in its way fun. With keyed commands, a "slate," mouse or light-pen, drawings can be generated on the CRT screen of a computer terminal ready to be stored, printed out (by suitable printer or plotter) or even transmitted to remote recipients by telephone line. Changes are fast and easy and perspective views can be produced, rotated, varied, and modified with the results translated back into orthographic projection views as needed.

The ease with which all of these things can be done and the almost miraculous seeming abilities of the computer make its use a source of satisfaction to many users even when the benefits are not of major significance.

Finished Models

A finished model, as distinguished from a sketch model, attempts to simulate the final product in every visible way. It is an ideal way to show the appearance of a design and, when photographed, can stand in for an actual sample. Skilled model makers can simulate a final product very successfully at scales down to 1 in. = 1 ft 0 in. or less, but fine models at small scale can often be as difficult and costly to make as full size prototypes. Consequently finished models do not play an important part in professional furniture design. They are probably most useful when a large group of designs or a complex system is under development, where making many full size prototypes would be inconvenient. Frequently used close relatives of the finished model are the two model types called "mock-ups" and "prototypes." These two terms overlap to some extent but can be described as follows:

Mockups

A mock-up is a full size model that reproduces certain aspects of a design in full and realistic detail, but omits other aspects of realism in the interest of easy construction and revision with resultant economy in time and cost. A mock-up chair, for example, might present seat and back surfaces at full size and at intended angles, with finally planned seating construction, but be made of rough materials with no effort to simulate final appearance. This would permit study of seating comfort without the effort of making all the finished parts that a complete prototype (see below) would involve. A mock-up storage unit might be roughly built, but would serve to check convenience of storage spaces provided. Mock-ups are usually made of materials and with assembly details that encourage easy revision.

Prototypes

A prototype, like a mock-up, is a full size model, but is made as accurately and perfectly as possible, with all materials and finishes as they will be in the final product. A prototype is often called a "sample" and is a "one off" single example of production. Where furniture is to be made by hand (as in craft production) or with simple production machinery, the prototype may simply be the first unit made. It is then suitable for careful evaluation with an eye to revision that may improve subsequent production. Where more complex and industrially advanced production techniques are involved, as in the making of metal and plastic parts that involve costly tooling, a prototype may require difficult and expensive hand work to simulate the production parts that will be produced mechanically later, but it is still a useful device for checking success before a large investment is made in tools that may be difficult to alter once they are made. An ideal prototype is indistinguishable from the production units it simulates and is often considered to be the best possible record of a designer's intention. Thus it is frequently proposed as a preferable alternative to drawings. This view is held by a number of designers who prefer to move directly from sketch concept to production of a prototype. If several stages of redesign are then gone through, the cost of successive prototypes in terms of time, money, or both can be very high and the prototype always suffers in relation to drawings because it is difficult to transport and reproduce. Yet it remains a key step in the development of most furniture designs, particularly those involving forms or manufacturing techniques that depart from familiar norms.

Where a prototype is made by the designer or under his direct supervision, it can precede or substitute for the making of working drawings. If it is to be made by a model maker, or shop (or shops) not under the designer's direct control, it may be necessary to make complete working drawings as a guide to the prototype maker with the resultant possibility that revision of the prototype may require remaking of the working drawings. On the other hand, for the designer to have available all the skills, materials, tools, and facilities for working materials that any conceivable prototype might require makes demands that most designers find extend outside the reasonable limits of design activity. Prototype making can be part of design activity under certain circumstances, but it can also absorb time and resources to the extent of halting design development. Every designer must make decisions about his or her way of working and the kind of product under development that will lead to reasonable decisions about whether to attempt prototype making or to farm out this work to specialists in the skills and trades involved.

Designers with a background in architecture or interior design tend to rely on the production of drawings and sketch models as their primary way of working, and to turn to outside sources for the production of prototypes. This follows naturally from training and experience in these fields, where it is rarely possible to design directly through the building of an actual structure. Since major buildings are built from drawings, the architect must feel confident that what the drawings show will prove satisfactory with no more check than scale models and an occasional detail mock-up can offer. In contrast, industrial designers and craftspeople who usually work in full-sized samples of smaller products are more inclined to prefer this method over the production of drawings. Exceptions may be observed in each group of professions, but the tendency is to follow these habits. Tracing the history of successful designs does not offer clear evidence that one way of working is to be preferred over another. Either can be successful if used with intelligent awareness of its limitations and with some care to compensate for those limitations. Tracing the history of some furniture design projects may be helpful.

Projects

Development of an office chair group "Paragon" by Bruce Hannah for Shaw-Walker, Inc.

A full size rough mock-up using metal pipe support for seat and back units while seating comfort was under developmental study. (Photograph courtesy of Bruce Hannah.)

Two mock-ups with seat and back elements with arms mounted on caster bases to permit use testing. (Photograph courtesy of Bruce Hannah.)

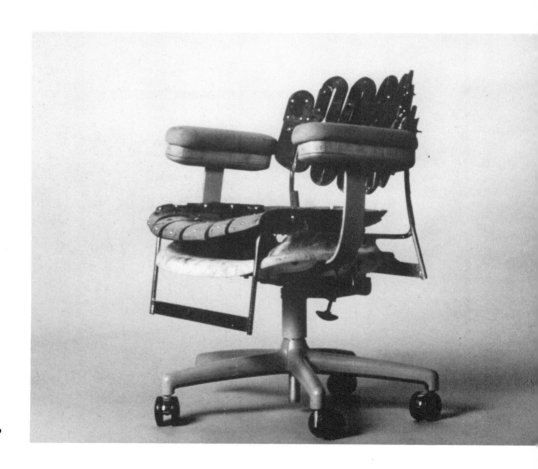

Mock-up on caster base. (Photograph courtesy of Bruce Hannah).

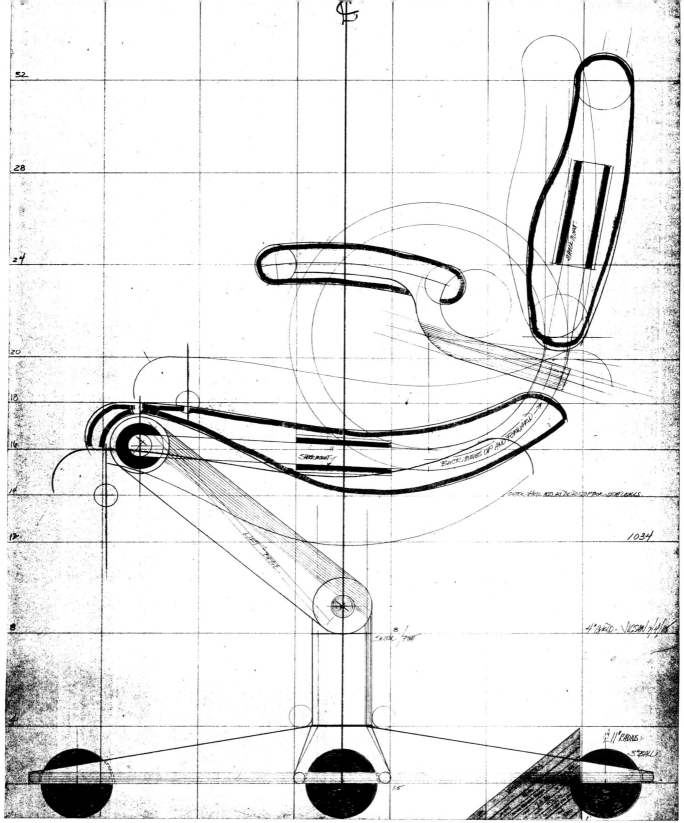

Full size drawing (profile) side view showing a stage in design development.
(Illustration courtesy of Bruce Hannah.)

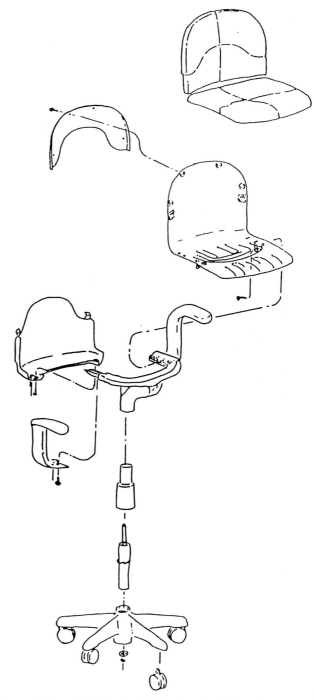

Explored view of Hannah desk chair showing individual parts in their correct relationship. (Illustration courtesy of Bruce Hannah.)

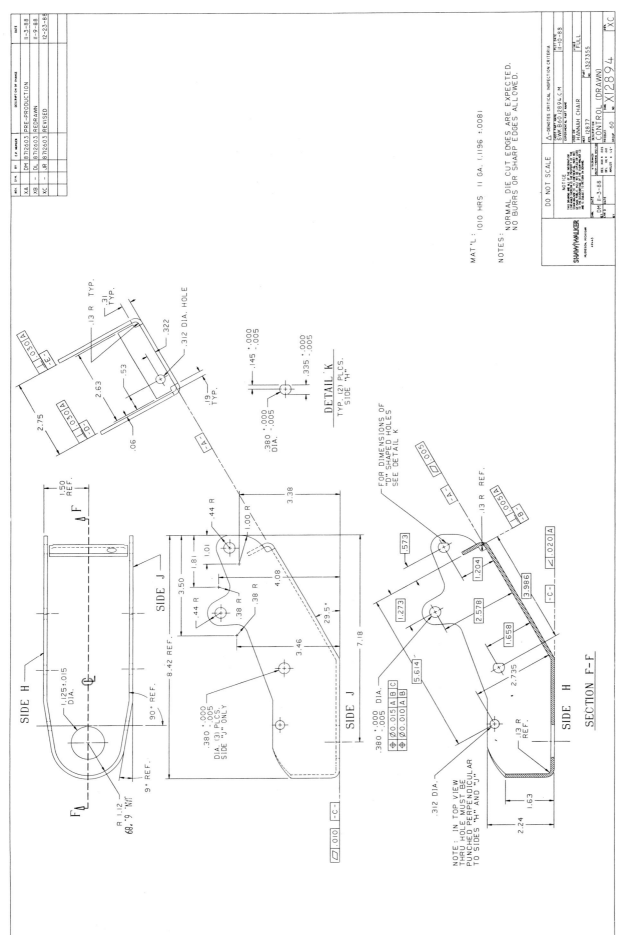

Engineering drawing at full size showing a steel bracket, one part of the complete Hannah swivel chair as detailed for factory production. (Illustration courtesy of Bruce Hannah.)

The complete Bruce Hannah designed "Paragon" chair as produced by Shaw-Walker shown in open arm (above) and closed arm (below) versions. (Photographs courtesy of Bruce Hannah.)

A group of molded plywood chairs designed by Robert Venturi for Knoll International. (see also pp. 76–78.)

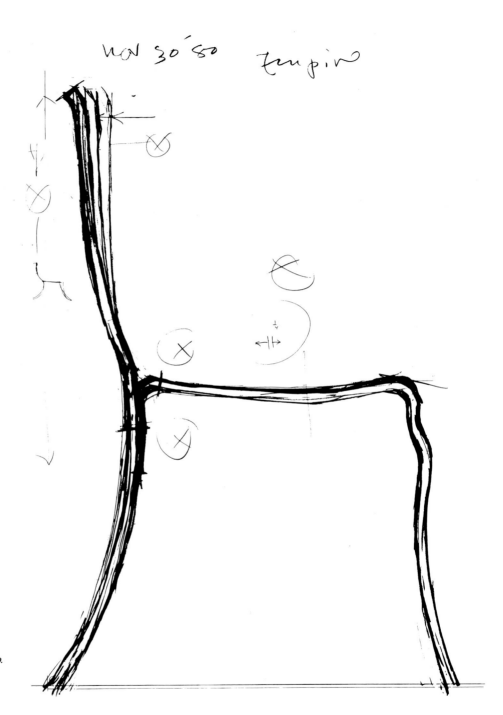

A sketch showing a side view (profile) of the two molded plywood parts assembled to make up a chair. This form applies to the entire group. (Illustration courtesy of Robert Venturi.)

A sketch elevation showing the cut-out pattern that became the "Chippendale" version of the Venturi chair. (Illustration courtesy of Robert Venturi.)

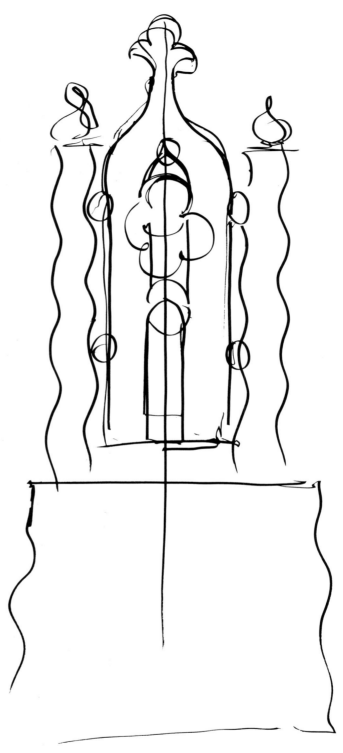

Sketch elevation for a "Gothic" version of the Venturi chair—not put into production. (Illustration courtesy of Robert Venturi.)

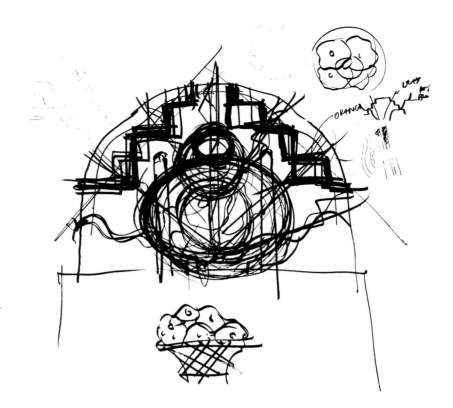

Sketch elevation drawing showing the back cut-out design for the "Art Deco" Venturi chair. The production version of this design was acquired for the collection of the Metropolitan Museum of Art in New York. (Illustration courtesy of Robert Venturi.)

Sketch elevation for the back of the "Sheraton" version of the Venturi side chair. (Illustration courtesy of Robert Venturi.)

Sketch front elevation of the "Sheraton" Venturi chair. (Illustration courtesy of Robert Venturi.)

The "Art Deco" (left) and "Sheraton" Venturi side chairs as produced by Knoll. (Photograph courtesy of Knoll International, New York.)

Furniture designed by architect Robert A.M. Stern of the furniture company H.B.F. with strong reference to traditional design generating a "post-modernist" character.

A design sketch for the "Signature" chair for H.B.F. The spiral volute arm recalls English Regency period design and related designs of the American Federal period. (Illustration courtesy of H.B.F.)

The H.B.F. "Signature" chair as produced in front and side views. (Photograph courtesy of Ken Litton, Omega Studios, Inc. and H.B.F.)

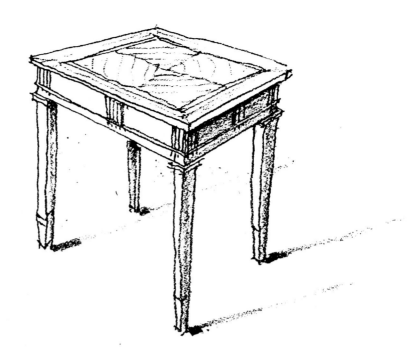

Sketch for the Stern table for H.B.F. named "Tryglyph". The name refers to the carved architectural ornament at the center of the apron on each side, a decorative element borrowed from the vocabulary of the classical "orders" of architecture. (Illustration courtesy of H.B.F.)

The "Tryglyph" table as produced. (Photograph courtesy of Ken Litton, Omega Studios, Inc. and H.B.F.)

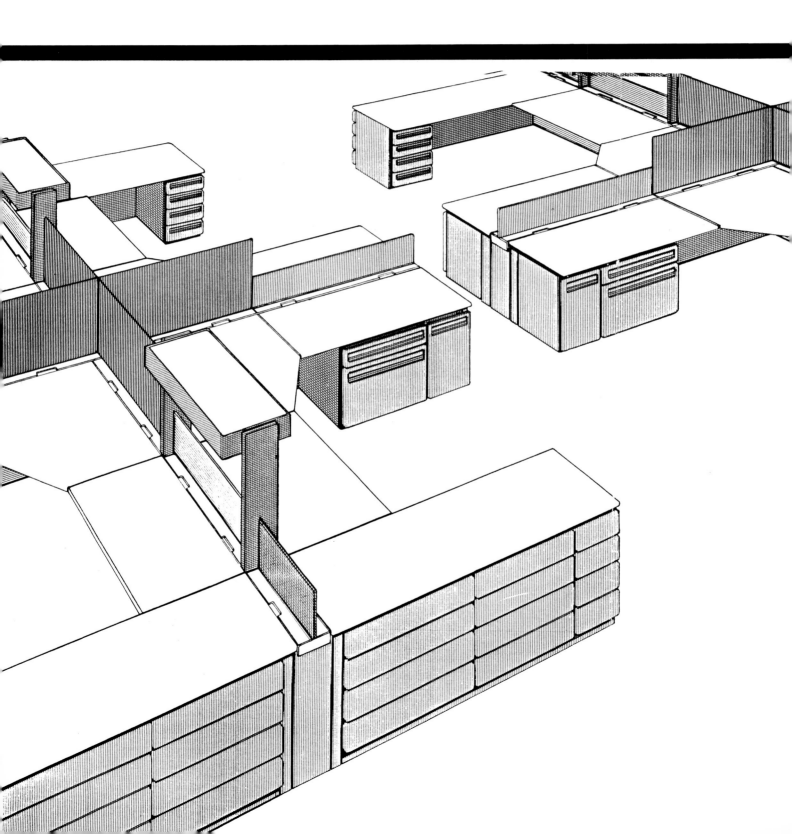

6

CONTEMPORARY FURNITURE: A PORTFOLIO OF ILLUSTRATIONS

Traditional Materials and Construction

Nothing requires the designer of modern furniture to seek out new materials or new techniques. By accepting the methods of furniture making that have developed over centuries, it is possible to avoid a whole family of problems related to the uncertainties involved in new technology. The primary material of historic furniture has been wood, which obviously remains a dominant material in modern furniture. It might be argued that plywood is a new material, but its use as an alternative to solid panels does not involve any major conceptual changes and so it is considered here as an alternative form of a traditional material. The second family of materials with a long history of furniture use are metals. Minor parts, pins or bronze bindings, steel springs, and similar elements have a long history and even all metal furniture is by no means new. Napoleon carried folding metal furniture on his campaigns and the brass bed seems the essence of Victorianism. Thus we can also list metals as traditional materials when they are used in traditional ways.

Viewed in this way, a large number of well-known modern designs (and their less famous counterparts as well) become "traditional" in constructional terms. The Barcelona chair has a steel X-frame supporting conventional cushions on leather straps. Its steel bar base could have been made in the 19th century, or even long before, if we assume that the steel of the armorer could have been used. The bent tubing of Breuer's Bauhaus furniture is no different from the tubing of the typical iron or brass bed; caned wood seat and back units and stretched canvas or leather are all approaches with a long history.

The word "modern" applies to this furniture for two reasons. It is free of decoration of an "applied" sort having any historic reference—in most cases it is actually devoid of any kind of decoration. It is also expressive of new ideas about the nature of furniture function and the importance of function as a controlling factor in determining design. Typically, the designer has started with basic questions about use: How do modern users move, sit, recline? Have their postures and habits changed from those of the Middle Ages or the intervening years? What objects do people own, store, and use? What arrangements are most suitable for these modern situations? Confronting these questions leads to shapes and sizes, even whole furniture unit types that are not part of furniture history. Also, the designer will usually consider, consciously or in the back of his mind, a setting, a kind of room and building in which he or she expects the furniture to be used. The many modern furniture design pioneers who were architects obviously had in mind their own buildings (e.g., the Barcelona chair for the Barcelona Pavilion, the Tugendhat chair for the Tugendhat house) or other familiar modern buildings (e.g., Breuer chairs for the Bauhaus itself). The ideas and forms of modern architecture thus become influences pressing for furniture of related character in visual qualities even when function remains totally conventional.

Where conventional materials are used, there may still be changes in ideas about *how* they can be used logically and economically. Metals that were rare and costly long ago are now commonplace and cheap. The hand labor of the skilled craftsperson that was once readily available and relatively cheap, is now rare and costly. Factory production, the current economic way to make furniture (and almost anything else), encourages methods that can be mechanized to a maximum degree and discourages operations that require handwork or individual control. These realities have an ideological counterpart. The modern designer is usually interested in designing in a way that will simplify factory production, but he or she is also interested in making designs show or "express" their industrial origins. Thus the idea of "machine art" that is so great a part of the origin of the modern movement becomes an influence encouraging smooth surfaces, rounded corners, gleaming finishes, and the presence of elements associated with mechanical things. The "machine look" has become a desirable thing for its own sake and is developed even in products that will, in fact, be individually handmade in a totally traditional fashion.

In recent years design literature has come to include gradually increasing protest against the "machine aesthetic" of modern architecture and design.

Recent design developments have become responsive to such protests leading to the twin themes of post-modern recall of historic forms and techniques in designs that make reference to earlier styles and the more radical approaches of Memphis and related design. These are directions that mix modern industrial materials and techniques with elements that reject the norms of modernism in an effort to break away from what might be called a "tradition of newness." In post-modernism, we see the return of moldings, inlays, strongly characterful veneers and construction techniques that make major demands on traditional hand craft methods of manufacture. The New Wave and Memphis related designers, in their eagerness to escape from the disciplines of function and the constraints of simple, logical, and economical criteria, also turn to materials and processes that are as often traditional as they are innovative even when the visual results are daring, adventurous and sometimes outrageous.

It is possible to categorize the furniture grouped here as traditional forms and types, modified to suit modern uses and production methods to some extent, but changed more drastically to generate forms that will seem related visually to the character of the industrialized modern world. When the designer is a master, this approach is clearly one that permits aesthetic success every bit as spectacular as anything ever achieved in preindustrial civilization.

The traditional Windsor chair in a modern adaptation by Paul McCobb.

Richard Riemerschmid chair, 1899. Some of the earliest truly "modern" furniture designs used wood and conventional craftsmen's techniques to produce "new" forms. (Courtesy of the Museum of Modern Art, New York. Gift of Liberty and Co., Ltd., London.)

Metals were the "new" materials of the 19th century. Once used only for special purposes, they became available for every kind of product. This adjustable chair with an iron frame was patented in 1876. It is an obvious ancestor of the modern "recliner," but more straight-forward in design than most current examples. (Photograph courtesy of the Metropolitan Museum of Art, New York; Mrs. Russel Sage Fund purchase.)

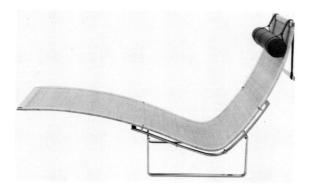

"Hammock chair" with stainless steel frame and cane seat by Poul Kjaerholm. (Photograph courtesy of Herman Miller, Inc.)

Aluminum castings supporting seat and back cushions in an office chair and in a seating unit for public spaces. Both designed by Morrison and Hannah. Photographs courtesy of Knoll International, Inc., New York.)

Aluminum castings supporting cushions in a chair from the "soft pad group" designed by Charles Eames. (Photograph courtesy of Charles and Ray Eames.)

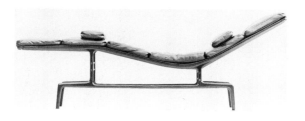

Chaise by Charles Eames. Cast metal frame supports a narrow contoured surface. (Photograph courtesy of Herman Miller, Inc.)

Office chair called "Ergon" by its designer, Bill Stumpf. (Photograph courtesy of Herman Miller, Inc.)

Conventional upholstery in a desk chair by Ward Bennett. (Photograph courtesy of Brickel Associates, Inc., New York.)

Rocking chair designed by Carlos Riart (1982) produced with wood frame of ebony (almost black) or holly (grey-white). (Photograph courtesy of Knoll International, New York.)

Office furniture designed by Andrew Morrison for Knoll—shown here with Mies van der Rohe "Brno" chairs in the foreground. (Photograph courtesy of Knoll International, New York.)

Sofa designed by Robert Venturi recalling "overstuffed" designs of the 1920s. (Photograph courtesy of Knoll International, New York.)

Maple framed, upholstered settee and chairs designed by Michael Graves for SunarHauserman. (Photograph courtesy of SunarHauserman.)

Drawing (half front, half rear elevation) of the chair illustrated above left right designed by Michael Graves. (Illustration courtesy of Sunar-Hauserman.)

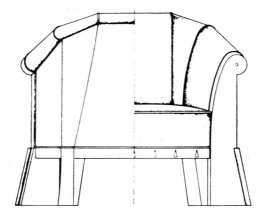

Tables cut from solid granite designed by Lucia Mercer for Knoll. (Photograph courtesy of Knoll International, New York.)

Arm chair designed by Richard Meier. The solid maple seat and frame parts are available in black lacquer or natural finish. (Photograph courtesy of Knoll International, New York.)

A large table and a small side table designed by Richard Meier shown with the Meier arm chair. (Photograph courtesy of Knoll International, New York.)

Upholstered seating on large-scale chrome steel tube support structure designed by Richard Schultz. (Photograph by Robert Levin, courtesy of Knoll International, Inc., New York.)

New Materials and Innovative Techniques

A key idea of the modern movement is that the scientific and technological revolutions of the modern world have made materials and techniques available that are often better than their traditional counterparts. We "owe it to ourselves" to explore these new possibilities and to put them to work wherever possible. Even if we do not accept this as a "duty," economic pressures urge new ways of making things whenever it becomes clear that a new way is cheaper and just as good, better and no more expensive or, best of all, both cheaper and better. Constructing a large building with steel and concrete is faster and cheaper than stone and the result can be just as good and may in some ways be better. The all-metal airplane is superior in many ways to its predecessor of wood and cloth; a suspension bridge is overwhelmingly more economical to construct than a stone viaduct in the same situation and may even look just as well or better.

Consciousness of these modern realities have made modern designers feel that it is essential to study new materials and methods and to experiment with them and use them when ever possible. Many designers seem to believe a product cannot be "truly modern" unless it incorporates some constructional innovation. Although this idea is debatable, new techniques have several other lures for the furniture designer. Thousands of years of furniture development and the restricted range of practical requirements for furniture has made this a field that has been explored with overwhelming thoroughness. As a result, the designer tends to find that every reasonable idea which comes to mind has been current and worked over for so long that almost every proposal turns out to have been discovered and exploited in the past. Thus the urge toward originality and innovation that every designer feels is frustrated repeatedly. The route to an escape from this trap is, reasonably enough, the realization that some new material or technique will make new forms possible and may even require new forms to make it usable.

The forms of bentwood furniture are, as at the time of their development, new and original, and we can see that development of this technique led to these new forms. Similarly bent and molded plywood as they became available, led designers into shapes that have no easily discoverable precedent. Chairs made entirely of thin wire may be similar in overall shape to earlier chairs, but the wire cage construction generated different details and new textures that are not part of previous history. Obviously, the materials that are almost totally new in the 20th century are the plastics, and the ways in which they can best be used in furniture are still being studied. It is certain that they have already led designers to solutions, perhaps thought of previously, but only now realizable, as well as to new forms suggested by the possibilities of these materials. New techniques can be similarly stimulating. A plastic material previously known for its uses when cast or molded, becomes something different when it is used with the foaming technique. Plastic foams have actually generated a whole new furniture vocabulary that is still being explored.

Plastic films or sheets, first used as a substitute for conventional upholstery coverings (such as leather), become entirely different when heat-sealed into bags and inflated with air or packed with some other filler. In this case and several others, an interesting new technique can lead to hasty and poorly thought out exploitation that can give a material or a process a bad name and retard its development for some time. Inflated furniture, a popular fad a few years ago, was quickly discredited because of the poor quality and careless design that was rushed into a "novelty" market. Yet the possibility of studying this concept seriously and developing high quality products that use it remains and will, no doubt, be explored successfully at some future time.

The widely voiced expectation of a few years ago that plastic would largely replace other, traditional materials has been sharply set back by the rise in the cost of the basic plastic resins that has resulted from the general increase in energy costs. (Most plastics are based on petroleum derivatives and so rise in cost is parallel with the cost of oil.) Nevertheless, plastics find increasing use in furniture, often in ways that have only limited impact on design, as in the use of plastic laminates in place of wood veneers or painted finishes where durability is important or in the plastic simulations of traditional wood components that are popular in cheap residential furniture designs that are generally repellant to design-sensitive critics. Plastic is now in frequent use, often in concealed locations, as a material providing flexibility that improves comfort in seating and it is not uncommon as a major material in the components of some of the office systems illustrated in the following section.

Technical innovation always involves some hazard. In the enthusiasm of discovering something new, it is easy to assume that the product offers advantages only. This is hardly what history suggests. As products go into use, unsuspected problems may surface, often only after an extended period of time. Furniture tends to be a long-lived product. We are ready to discard an automobile after 10 years of use, but we may well expect a piece of furniture to last a lifetime or longer. During such long time spans, slowly developing problems can become serious. Sunlight attacks some materials; pollution in the air can cause discoloration and damage. Flexing of some materials in use can cause fatigue and eventual breakdown. Unsuspected hazards (e.g., behavior in combustion) can surface when unusual accidents occur, usually only after an extended period of use during which the problem was unanticipated. Recent history of such problems suggests that designers and manufacturers have a larger responsibility than has been accepted in the past when using new materials and methods to explore every possible problem that can be imagined as emerging in a reasonable lifetime of use or in an unexpected and unusual eventuality.

In the past the rate of change in many aspects of human affairs has been so slow that it has been natural for designers to suppose that the status quo can be taken as a realistic context for design. What is practical, reasonable, and economic *now* tends to become the basis for what should be done, and there is an implicit assumption that such circumstances will probably last long enough to justify the development, commercialization, and use of whatever is designed on such a basis. Recent experience suggests that this is no longer a safe point of view. Plastic materials that were cheap a few years ago may now be expensive or in short supply. Labor and energy costs are in flux, and it is not possible to assume that a currently practical proposal will still be practical in five or ten years. The designer interested in innovative technique must confront a new need to predict, to whatever extent possible, what short range and longer range changes will do to alter the realities of the immediate present. An innovative proposal in today's context may be outmoded before it is fully accepted, not because of other innovation but only because of changing contextual circumstances.

The furniture designs illustrated here all derive from or depend on materials and techniques that are new to modern industrial technology. Some are obvious technical and commercial successes, and others have faced problems that have limited their acceptance but are included because of the interest of the innovations involved.

Molded plywood used in thin strips. Developed by the author with George Nelson and Company, Inc. (Photograph courtesy of Herman Miller, Inc. New York.)

Charles Eames plastic armchair. Fiberglass made it possible to produce the deeply curved shell that had proved difficult to mold in plywood, too costly to tool for steel stamping. (Photograph courtesy of Charles and Ray Eames.)

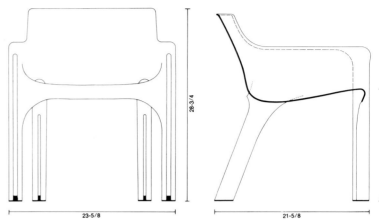

One-piece fiber glass chair designed by Vico Magistretti. (Photograph and elevations courtesy of Castelli Furniture, Inc., New York.)

Armchair designed by Gae Aulenti (1975) using frames of bent aluminum extrusions. Metal parts are offered in black, white, brown and a "bordeaux" (dark red) finish. (Photograph courtesy of Knoll International, New York.)

An Italian design of 1971 for a sofa convertible to a bed either with the back remaining as a head support or with the back flopped over to surround the sleeping area. In the latter position the unit resembles a life-raft justifying the name "Anfibio" (Amphibious) given it by its designer, Alessandro Becchi. (Photograph courtesy of I.C.F., New York.)

Arm and armless version of the Vignelli Design "Handkerchief" stacking chair using a molded plastic seat and back supported on a steel wire frame. (Photograph by Mikio Sekina courtesy of Knoll International, New York.)

Office chair designed by Richard Sapper. (Photograph courtesy of Knoll International, New York.)

"Handkerchief" stacking chair designed by Vignelli Design. (Photograph by Mario Carrieri courtesy of Knoll International, New York.)

"Penelope" stacking chair designed by Charles Pollock using seat and back surfaces of a woven steel mesh supported by a steel tube frame. (Photograph courtesy of Castelli, New York.)

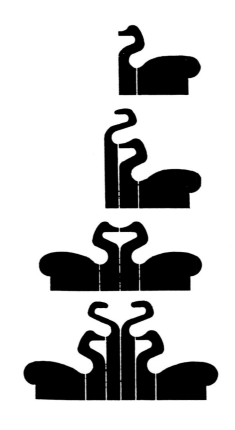

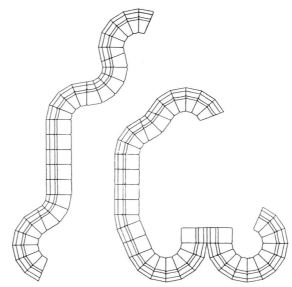

Flexible seating system of foam developed by Jørn Utzon in 1968.

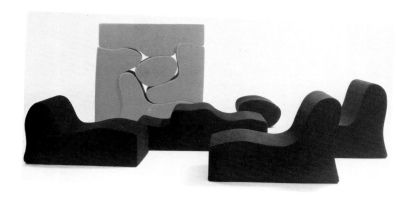

Foam blocks that assemble into a square and separate to provide various seating configurations. Designed by Sebastian Matta. (Photograph courtesy of Knoll International, Inc., New York.)

Systems Furniture

Conventional thinking about the physical realities of the human environment is based on concepts that may have their origin in language. Each thing has a name, and a name implies separate, complete wholeness. Just as each person tends to have a self-image as an isolated, self-contained being, each object is most easily understood as alone and disconnected. Traditional interior decoration involves placing in a space a certain number of separate units, each movable, removable, and replaceable. A *piece* of furniture always implies this concept of discrete units, each individually useful in its own way without connection to anything else.

Modern industrial society, when viewed in a more general way, cannot be understood in such unit terms. It exists in a world of systems where each thing depends on other things. Thus an electric lamp is useless without an active electric socket to which it can be connected. The socket implies a distant power plant with the distribution network in between to make it useful. A radio may seem to be an object, but it is worthless without broadcasting *systems* that make it functional. An automobile needs gasoline, tires, and roads to roll on. A factory depends on a flow of materials, energy, and a distribution system to carry off its products. Systems have always existed in human life to some degree, but the complexity of modern systems and the level of dependency on them that has arisen is unique to the developed civilizations of the 20th century.

The simplicity of the problems that furniture deals with has tended to retard the influx of systems concepts into this field. We still think of *a* chair and *a* table as isolated objects and design these objects in a disconnected way. The "suite" of matching furniture was never more than a superficial marketing concept and has tended to lose whatever attraction it may have had in the 1920s and 30s. It is probably natural enough that we need to look for systems furniture in its earliest forms in the office furniture and storage systems developed for office uses. The phrase "Globe-Wernecke bookcase" immediately identifies an early furniture system. It was not actually a bookcase but a system of units, each one shelf high, that stacked on a standard base and were capped by a standard top. Doors, special purpose inserts (such as desks), and other components made it possible for the user to plan a storage grouping of any size and any mixture of elements that might be required. In appearance this system belonged to the "mission style" or "golden oak" era of the turn of the century, but conceptually it introduced the idea of modularity as a basis for storage furniture. Doctors and dentists were enthusiastic users since books, pills, and drills could all be accommodated as required in a unified grouping. The same ideas entered the office furniture industry at about the same time through desks made up of separable and interchangeable drawer pedestals, top units, and file units. A manufacturer could make a small number of unit products and still offer a great variety of assembled "pieces" by putting together different combinations of standard parts.

The idea of modular grouping became best known and best accepted by the public in the quasi-furniture of steel kitchen cabinets—the "unit kitchen" of the 1930s, with its continuous and consistent counter and cabinet banks, demonstrated the effectiveness of modular storage units. Almost every modern storage furniture product group is based on a dimensional system and a unit assembly approach that permits modular groupings, but the units that make up the group are usually still isolated units. The true storage systems (sometimes called wall systems or pole systems, according to their details) were planned and discussed in the 1930s and 1940s, but only realized in the post-World War II era. They depend on a more or less complex, Erector-set like system of parts in which structure and utility inserts are assembled in place to make up groupings that can accommodate almost any imaginable utility complex. In addition, many such storage wall systems can substitute for conventional partition walls thus giving rise to the popular term "room dividers" for such assemblies.

Modularity in seating was hinted at in "sectional upholstery groups" and has finally become a well-accepted concept, especially in public spaces (lobbies and waiting rooms), where an assemblage of seat units can take the place of the more forbidding benches of earlier times.

Modularity is also the basis for the many seating systems that have appeared that permit curvature in arrangements which are simply convex or concave curves, combinations of straight runs and curves, or "serpentine" in varied, flowing curves. Most such systems call for a preplanned layout in which units are assembled after delivery into the desired curves, but some systems permit flexible contouring that can be moved and varied at any time as may be desired by users.

Most office furniture is now based on system concepts. Interchangeable frames, tops, storage units, and so on make up all but the most pretentious lines of desks and files. Office chairs also are usually assemblies of bases, seats, backs, chair bodies, and other components. The most fully system-oriented furniture now in production is probably the equipment that has developed to serve new concepts in office planning. By making offices totally open, large spaces without partitioning, great flexibility becomes possible, capable of response to the constantly changing organizational needs of modern business. The equipment that fills such "open offices" must provide for some level of visual privacy, for acoustical control, and for the distribution of telephone and electrical connections as well as the conventional functions of desks and files. Office systems of this type are becoming ever more complex and sophisticated.

An astonishing variety of office systems—more than 200 by some counts—are now in production. All too many seem to be near copies of other systems, but the leading manufacturers continue to introduce new systems that offer originality and special merits in relation to particular needs. The very rapid acceptance of computers in offices, the development of the so-called "electronic office," has created a demand for systems furniture particularly adapted to the world of computers. Desk-top terminals and tiny computers that fit on, over, and under desks have encouraged the development of components that are particularly suited to supporting and positioning keyboards, CRT units, actual computers and such auxiliary equipment as computer printers. The wiring to serve computers and complex computer network installations has led to systems with extensive provisions to house, conceal and provide access to the tangles of wiring and associated devices that are typical of the electronic office.

Another development in systems furniture relates to the gradual assimilation and modification of the concepts of "open office" or "office landscape" planning. While many office systems introduced in the 1960s and 1970s offered some level of privacy screening, the common assumption was that an open office would always be open to the extent that no full partitioning would be accepted. The gradually growing realization that many office activities require more visual and acoustic privacy than open office systems could provide has led to the introduction of systems that can offer floor to ceiling panels and even, in some systems, doors while retaining the flexibility of movable furniture. Some recent systems use panels that can be stacked vertically to permit partitioning of varied heights, with spaces left open where desired or glazed to permit varied degrees of visual privacy. Many systems are quite complex and the task of the planner has become complicated by the need to understand how a given system lays out dimensionally and how it fits together. Manufacturers now generally supply planning manuals and, in many instances, planning service as well to aid the planner or specifier working with a particular system.

Related ideas are frequently proposed as possibilities for residential furniture. System-based units could include electrical and electronic services, plumbing-related equipment, and the functions of conventional furniture as well, in some coordinated way. Many prototype designs for such units have appeared in recent years. These may combine the functions of a bathroom, closets, and bedroom furniture into a single unit, or tie together kitchen, dining, and living units into a system-based complex that has the effect of making furniture as isolated objects unnecessary. Such units, while seemingly logical in concept, still suffer from excessive cost and from a lack of flexibility and portability that has kept them (at least until now) interesting proposals rather than realistic products in production.

Perhaps the growth of system concepts has reached a plateau where the earlier enthusiasm for these approaches is beginning to meet some resistance, generated by a feeling that modern life in all its aspects is becoming too much a matter of systems, acting in ways that sometimes seem out of human control. Doubtless systems approaches in every area can achieve results and bring about economies, but being a part of "the system" now suggests to many people something not at all attractive in human terms. Furniture systems are characteristic of our time, but there is clearly resistance to the idea that *all* furniture in a given utility should be part of any one unified system.

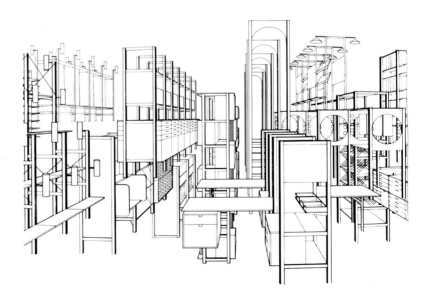

A storage system developed by the author with George Nelson and Company, Inc., using an aluminum extrusion pole as the basic support element. (Abstract drawings courtesy of Herman Miller, Inc.).

A modern office furniture system using steel as a primary material, organized into a variety of interchangeable components. (Photographs courtesy of Steelcase, Inc., Grand Rapids, Michigan.)

Office system developed by Otto Zapf. (Photograph courtesy of Knoll International, Inc., New York.)

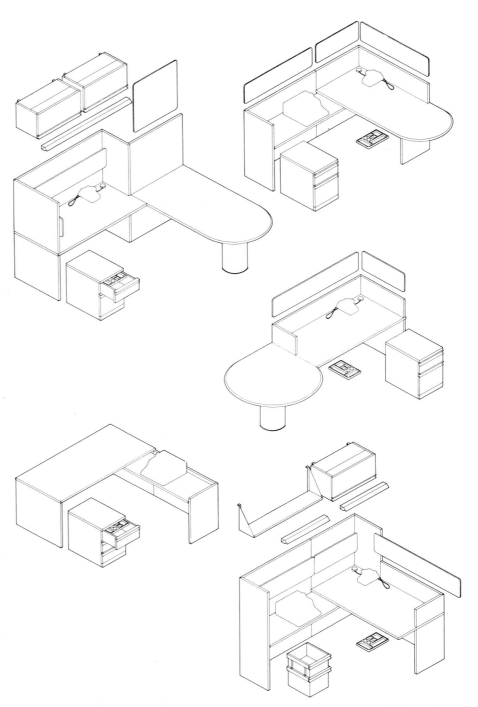

Office system designed by Mario Bellini under the name Marcatré. Typical work stations shown in diagramatic drawings. (Courtesy of Atelier International, Ltd., New York.)

Modulo 3, an office system developed by Bob Noorda and Franco Mirenzi. Flat panels are assembled with interlocking aluminum extrusions positioned diagonally at the upper corners of each unit. (Photograph courtesy of Modulo 3, Inc., Maryland Heights, Missouri.)

The Race office system designed by Douglas Ball for SunarHauserman. The name derives from the horizontal race or wireway which provides for power and communication wiring. (Photograph courtesy of SunarHauserman.)

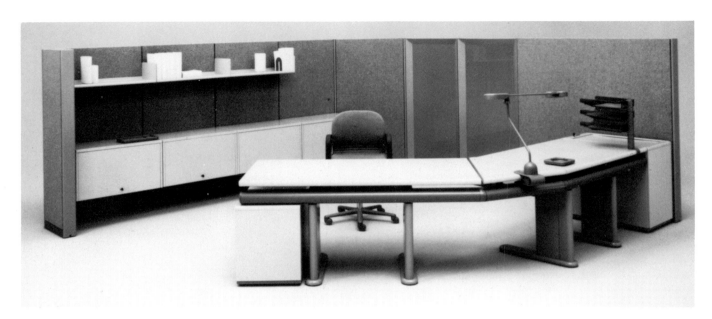

Harvey Probber ACM (Activity Center Module) office system. (Photograph courtesy of Harvey Probber, Inc.)

Steelcase 9000 system work stations placed between banks of lateral files. Sorting racks to aid paper handling are mounted on the work station panel above the desk. (Photograph courtesy of Steelcase, Inc.)

An office system installation using some solid panels and some glass panels to provide opening to light and view (Photograph courtesy of Steelcase, Inc.)

An office system installation using
the Steelcase 9000 system. (Photograph
courtesy of Steelcase, Inc.)

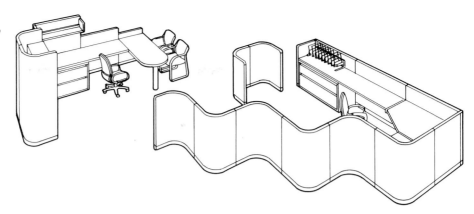

The office system illustrated in the photo left shown in line
drawing with additional work station area visible at right. (Illustration
courtesy of Steelcase, Inc.)

A cluster of Steelcase 9000 work stations in a typical open office installation.
(Photograph courtesy of Steelcase, Inc.)

*A work station using Herman Miller Action Office "Encore" system, an exten-
sion of the original Action Office system developed by Robert Propst in 1966.
(Photograph Earl Woods, courtesy of Herman Miller, Inc.)*

Knoll office system designed by Andrew Morrison. (Photograph courtesy of Knoll International, New York.)

Hannah office system with exceptionally extensive provision for power and communication wiring and many options for varied degrees of openness for communication between adjacent work stations. (Photograph courtesy of Knoll International, New York.)

Knoll Morrison system groupings (Photographs courtesy of Knoll International, New York.)

The Ethospace office system designed by Don Chadwick and Bill Stumpf for Herman Miller provides for wall panels made up from small modular units that can be arranged in varied vertical groupings to provide for desired degrees of privacy and permit development of a variety of visual patterns. (Photograph by Bill Sharpe Effective Images, courtesy of Herman Miller, Inc.)

Freestanding office furniture system designed by Tom Newhouse for Herman Miller to be compatible with the several wall systems produced by that firm. (Photograph courtesy of Herman Miller, Inc.)

Ethospace office system installation with compatible tall cabinets designed by Geoff Hollington and Jean Beirise. (Photograph courtesy of Herman Miller, Inc.)

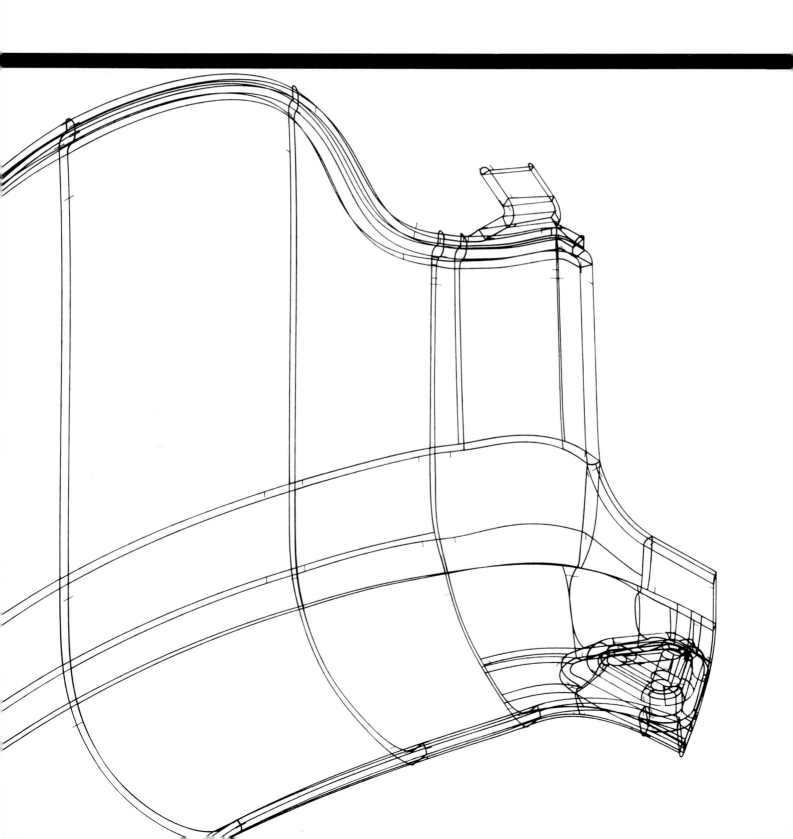

7

THE FUTURE

Future

It is always tempting to make some effort to predict the future directions that can be anticipated in any field under examination. The idea that "the future" is in some way a reality that exists and can be described is, of course, the basis for the many spurious skills that can be called "fortune-telling." Although most sophisticated and educated people understand that there is no way to "reveal" a future that has not taken shape, the urge to guess, to project, and to predict is still strong, and the new study of "futurism" has developed around the realization that, historically, very little serious effort has gone into even the roughest predictions of future probabilities.

One can speculate on the directions that a particular design field will take in the future, and designers are sometimes tempted to adopt an attitude in which "guessing" the future seems to promise heightened possibilities for success. This attitude says in effect, "If I can guess what will be successful in the near future, I will design those things now and so be first with a new success." Obviously, this attitude is related to the one that makes the superstitious believe in palmistry and tea-leaf readings; it assumes that the future is preestablished and that guessing it or "seeing" it is possible and constructive.

Actually the only productive future study must accept the truth that the future is uncertain because it has not yet taken form. This can lead to the more productive realization that what is done now can influence and mold the future, and that what is planned for the near future can guide and shape the more distant future. In this view, a designer no longer sees himself or herself as a passive traveler into the future who can only benefit by accurate guessing where it will lead, but rather as an active participant in forming that future. Thus the issue is not so much what the future will be, but rather what we want it to be.

Obviously, developments already in process will influence the future. Population already born will make up future population in part, and its character can be predicted with a fairly high degree of probability. Availability and cost of materials can be estimated on the basis of supplies on hand and what is known about how materials are produced. Processes already invented can be studied for their applicability to production problems of the near future. These aspects of predictability in future study are often ignored at great cost and certainly merit serious consideration. To design a product based on a material about to encounter short supply and rising cost can make the design obsolete almost before it is in production. No amount of study of the predictable aspects of the future can eliminate the unpredictable factors involved. New inventions, new materials, and changes in attitudes may develop in unforeseen ways, so that any future student must be tolerant of the near certainty that predictions will be, at least in part, quite wrong.

In fiction, Jules Verne predicted aircraft, submarines, and travel to the moon, and he was quite correct in his belief that each of these things would come to be. Anyone who rereads his stories will, however, be amused at how different these things are in actual detail from the images he envisioned. A modern submarine is very different from Captain Nemo's thoroughly Victorian overstuffed and upholstered *Nautilus*. The optimism of the builders of the great dirigibles has come to nothing, and yet we have giant aircraft different in form but far more effective in performance.

The modern movement in design is, by its very nature, concerned with molding the future, and modern designers tend to see their work as being more for the future than for the present. The furniture designs of the modern pioneers (e.g., Breuer, Le Corbusier, and Mies van der Rohe) achieved only a limited acceptance among a specially sophisticated group when they appeared in the 1920s but now have a far wider currency some 50 years later. We are probably correct if we assume that similar designs now being developed are, in a sense, 50 years late—that they will have a short life while other directions, less obvious and less acceptable at present, will survive and develop in the years ahead. If one searches for such future-oriented thinking in the present, it is not clear where it is to be found. In the 1920s the work of the modern pioneers was known and visible. A critic might have (mistakenly) predicted that it was merely a passing fad, or might have recognized it as an indication of a future direction. At present it is not easy to cite examples of work that is clearly and consciously future-oriented. The modern movement, having arrived and succeeded, remains with us with only minor progressive development. In spite of frequent announcements of its end,* its successor has not surfaced and all prediction of a lapse back into a previous era runs counter to knowledge of the movement of history and fails to materialize.

Our own particular moment in history is always hard to characterize because of our presence in it. We lack the perspective to see how "now" relates to "recently" and to "soon." Still, it is possible to notice that history tends to move in steps separated by pauses; an era of change is followed by an interval of consolidation before a new cycle of change begins. It is suggested here that the modern movement of the 1920s and 30s was, in the design world, a phase of change—virtually a revolution. We are now in an interval of consolidation, of proliferation and increasing acceptance of the changes that this movement initiated. It is premature to predict its end at this time and to look for the first traces of the next wave of change. Even the most advanced of contemporary design is actually only a working out of ideas that the modern movement announced but that required, for one reason or another, time for realization. An exhibit of Breuer furniture at the Bauhaus ended with the prediction, "in the end we shall sit on resilient cushions of air,"† and yet even now, in spite of a brief flurry of poorly realized inflated furniture a few years ago, this prediction awaits fulfillment.

The innovation that is dramatically altering the everyday working practice of designers is, obviously, the computer with its associated printers and plotters and CADD (computer-aided design and drafting) "software" systems. While architects and interior designers have rapidly accepted computer techniques, furniture design has only turned to computers in very limited ways. A reasonable future prediction will suggest that computer techniques will increase in usefulness, importance and popularity in the world of furniture design. The status quo reliance on precomputer design and drafting techniques has a number of causes. Furniture projects are, by their nature, limited in size and scope and relatively simple even at their most complex when compared to the design of vast architectural projects such as air terminals or health care facilities. One person can draw a chair or a cabinet in a few hours (even, sometimes, in

---

* See Brent C. Brolin, *The Failure of Modern Architecture*, (Van Nostrand Reinhold, 1976).

† See illustration in Gillian Naylor, *The Bauhaus*, Studio Vista/Dutton, 1968, p. 118.

A typical computer terminal work station. A computer-generated plan for a work station is visible on the center screen; a picture of a chair is displayed on the screen at left. (Photograph courtesy of Herman Miller, Inc.)

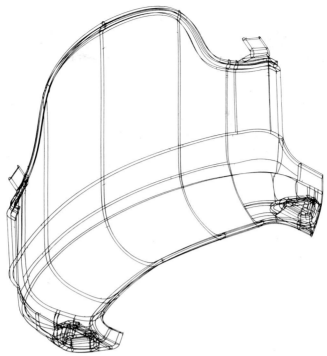

A computer-generated perspective view of a part, the rear outer shell of an office chair under development by its designer, Bruce Hannah. (Illustration courtesy of Bruce Hannah.)

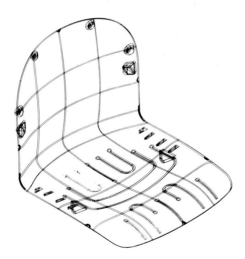

The inner shell part drawing for the office chair illustrated above in a computer-generated perspective. (Illustration courtesy of Bruce Hannah.)

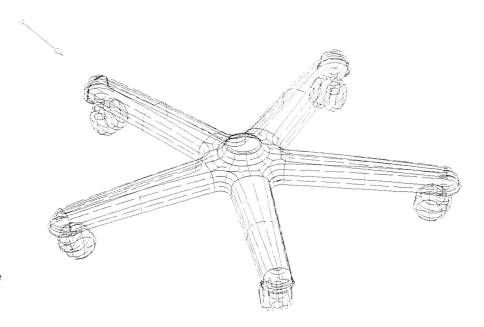

A Steelcase office chair base shown in a computer-generated perspective. (Illustration courtesy of Steelcase, Inc.)

minutes) and human memory can deal with most of the complexities of such a project without computer aid.

It is also often best to work, in furniture design, with models or prototypes made from real materials in three dimensions—techniques for which the computer offers little aid. Still, computer drafting is already in current use converting rough drawings (even ideas not yet drawn on paper) into neatly drafted orthographic projection views that, with keyboard or "slate," can be enlarged or reduced, revised, and modified with great ease and speed. Complex furniture projects that require many individual parts to be shown in engineering drawings can lead to a drawing set for a single chair, not to speak of an involved office system that may approach the drawings for an architectural project in complexity. Producing such drawings with CAD can be easy and rapid and the convenience of computer storage, print-out in desired format at any time and even conversion of dimensioning from English to metric system makes computer drafting worthwhile for many furniture design efforts. At present, it is usually furniture manufacturers rather than designers that find such computer applications worthwhile and economically justified. Equipment can be large and costly and it requires full utilization to justify automating of most traditional hand drafting techniques. A virtually certain future development will be the adoption of CAD by smaller design groups, even individual practitioners, as equipment continues its present trend toward becoming ever more compact and economical. At the same time, increasing familiarity is constantly converting computer resistance to computer devotion as equipment and techniques move from the exotic to the commonplace.

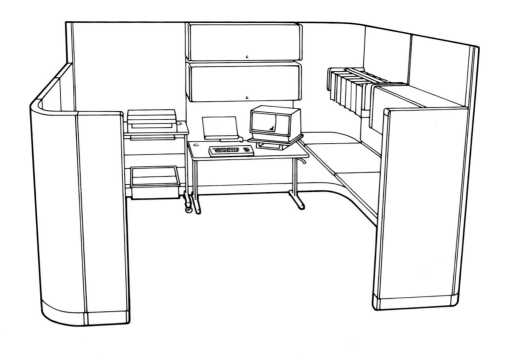

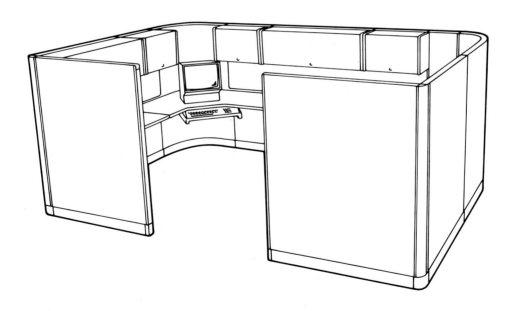

Computer perspective drawings showing Herman Miller office work stations in varied configurations. (Illustrations courtesy of Herman Miller, Inc.)

In the creative aspects of furniture design (as distinguished from the routines of draftsmanship), computer techniques offer valuable possibilities in the production of accurate perspective views generated almost instantaneoulsy once a "model" has been entered into computer memory in orthographic form. The traditional, hand-drawn perspective, whether sketched "by eye" or accurately constructed, takes some time to draw and shows only one view taken from a particular viewpoint at a particular viewing distance. A computer perspective can be produced in an instant from any distance and any viewpoint allowing the designer to see many views—even such unlikely ones as "worms-eye" views from below or extreme closeups of details and to move or "rotate" the designed object in a way that simulates walking around it or turning it about in reality. At the same time, design revisions can be made modifying the perspective as desired while retaining the original in memory for comparison. Revisions can be converted back to orthographic form as they are accepted. The techniques, programs, and software for doing such things are readily available and in wide use in any design fields. Their application in furniture design is certainly destined to increase as designers come to take "computer literacy" for granted and have ready access to the appropriate equipment and software.

Interior designers, space planners, and the manufacturers of furniture products used in larger interior projects (office and institutional buildings, for example) are already using computer techniques to aid planning and develop perspective visualization based on furniture already in production. It is only a short step for

A grouping of office work stations illustrated in a computer perspective. (Illustration courtesy of Herman Miller, Inc.)

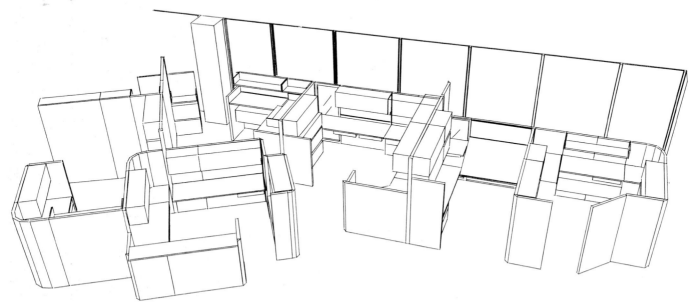

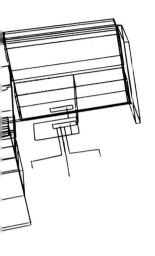

A computer-generated perspective with hidden lines remaining creating an X-ray or "skeleton" view. A grouping of Herman Miller Action Office furniture. (Illustration courtesy of Herman Miller, Inc.)

A Steelcase 9000 series office workstation shown in a computer-generated perspective drawing that uses varied grey tones rather than lines. (Illustration courtesy of Steelcase, Inc.)

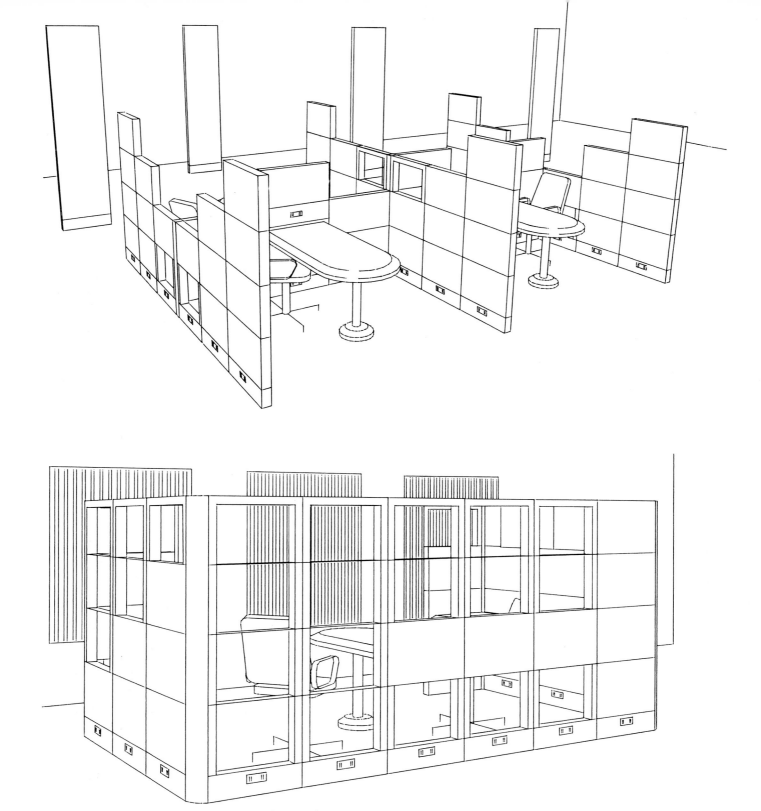

Computer perspectives showing various grouping of Herman Miller Ethospace system office groupings. Note the ease with which variations in arrangement of wall panels can be displayed for instantaneous comparison. (Illustration courtesy of Herman Miller, Inc.)

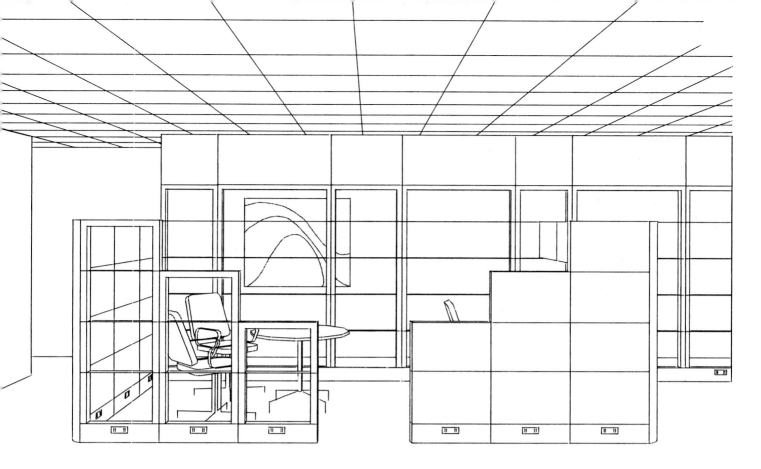

the furniture designer, once introduced to these techniques, to accept and adopt similar techniques for designing and visualizing new products in the process of development. The near future will make this commonplace routine.

There are further future possibilities related to computer use that have not yet surfaced—even as proposals—but which offer fascinating territory for exploration. The idea of *simulation* is central to many computer-based techniques. The use of a mathematical "model" makes it easy to test out possible alternatives in relation to various conceivable future events. A more direct type of simulation is in use for the training of aircraft pilots. A flight simulator is a complex device duplicating the cockpit, controls, and movements of an airplane in flight with a computer producing movement and instrument indications interactively with the student pilot's actions. Such equipment is elaborate and costly, but it suggests that much simpler devices could be developed to simulate proposed furniture designs. Drawings, entered into a computer along with data about materials and construction could control a device that would simulate the form and performance of a chair, bed, or any combination of furniture elements that are in direct contact with human users.

A kind of simulation has, of course, been used in many design efforts where mock-ups or test prototypes have been made for trials and testing before a commitment is made to actual production.

This kind of testing is, however, slow, laborious, and costly because each mock-up must be hand-built to demonstrate a particular design proposal. Any change requires reconstruction of the mock-up making it impossible to check the success of the change unless a totally new unit is built to permit side-by-side comparison. The idea of instant variability in a simulator, with each tested configuration stored in computer memory for instant recall suggests a vastly improved way of generating optimal results in the ergonomic aspects of furniture design. A selected optimum could readily be translated into construction drawings through the available CAD drafting techinques.

A further extension of the idea of computer controlled simulation in furniture would be the development of a simulator that would simultaneously simulate performance and *appearance* of a proposed design configuration. Managing this with a realistic prototype as the end-result calls for techniques that push into the territory of science fiction where actual objects can be physically transformed through computerized commands. A more modest simulation of physical reality in terms of performance along with visual images (on screen or in print-out form) only requires the combination of the available techniques for producing computer-generated perspective images with computer control of a simulation device far less complex than the flight simulators already in general use.

Searching for clues to a future cycle of change that has not yet begun to take form is probably less useful than some consideration of what the future of furniture *should* be. What do we now want and what may we soon want that will be different from what is now available and familiar? If we view matters in this way, it becomes natural to muster certain facts and probabilities that may influence present and future thinking. These might include the following observations, some perhaps less certain than others, but all worth serious thought:

1. Basic furniture materials are becoming increasingly scarce and/or increasingly costly. Hardwood trees take up to hundreds of years to grow, and we have been cutting them faster than they are planted for generations. Basic metals are not yet close to being mined out, but their costs must rise because of the cost of energy required in their production.
2. The belief in plastics as a solution to all problems of material shortages (a fashionable article of faith from the 1930s to the 1950s) has been undermined by the recent realization that plastics are largely produced from petrochemicals, the most threatened of all natural resources at present.
3. Materials that are produced biologically with a fairly short production time are least vulnerable to problems of shortage. Soft

woods and their by-products (paper pulp and plywood), cotton and linen fibers, and similar grown materials can be produced in quantities required as demand increases market prices to levels that encourage increased production.

Wool, leather, silk, and similar natural products may be similarly produced as needed on fairly short time cycles.

Even these materials must be expected to become more costly as energy costs rise.

4. Most furniture of good quality is already so costly as to discourage its ownership by a majority of the population, even in developed and wealthy countries.

5. Most furniture produced at prices regarded as acceptable to the majority of purchasers is so poor in quality, both in concept and in construction, as to make it nearly worthless and an even poorer investment than better (and more expensive) furniture would be.

6. Western developed countries have come to use an excess of furniture of questionable usefulness. Sleeping in beds, sitting in chairs, and storing objects in cabinets are, after all, customs known and accepted by only a small proportion of the world's population. While persuading the Third World to adopt Western furniture use habits may seem an attractive way to open markets, reducing the Western obsession with having a clutter of poor quality furniture might be more constructive in long-range terms.

The last of these observations is probably the most controversial. Certainly, it is hardly likely that the western world will give up its familiar clutter of furniture in exchange for a classic Japanese house, empty except for tatami mats, but a case can be made for a few steps in that direction. Anyone who has had occasion to move the contents of a house or apartment in the recent past will probably remember the revulsion connected with the experience of packing and paying to move the vast collection of largely unused goods that make up a modern, developed world household.

Ashley Montagu in an unpublished paper,* speaking of the "average chair," tells us that "it is an atrocity . . . in fact it could not be better designed than it is to produce simultaneous breakdown in several of the bodies sustaining systems." He goes on to detail the ways that constriction of the veins at the back of the knees contributes to varicosities, arteriosclerosis, and other cardiovascular problems. Chairs and soft beds both contribute to back problems. It is well known that sedentary occupations lead to health problems, but the connection between "sedentary" and the furniture it implies is

* Ashley Montagu, "The Human Frame and Furniture," paper read at an institute sponsored by The National Council on the Aging, New York, November 1962.

not often made specific. Third World people and the world of animals are free from many human diseases that trouble furniture users. The office worker, always seated in a chair, is vulnerable to physical problems that are much less likely to afflict the farmer, the ship's captain, or the symphony conductor whose work patterns are not chair-bound.

We can already observe a strong demand that the ergonomic qualities of furniture be improved. Particularly when furniture is intended for regular use for long periods of time, the impact of comfort on efficiency and satisfaction in work situations and recognition of the physiological impact of seating, working, and sleeping positions have led to increasing production of designs that offer carefully planned dimensions, adjustments, and flexibility or movement to promote both comfort and health. Improved ergonomic qualities often add to the designer's difficulties in harmonizing functional and visual qualities and tend to add to the cost of production. Recognition of the long-term gains in both human and economic terms can be expected to lead to a continuing demand for improvement of all furniture in these terms and in terms of the safety issues discussed in Appendix 3.

Storage furniture relates to possessions and the two interact. An inventory of a family's possessions—clothing, linens, dishes, utensils, books, papers, recreational gear, gadgets, and so on—is often astonishing, and if note is made of the "utilization factor" (the time the object is in actual use) for each item it becomes clear that storage is being provided for objects that are 80 to 100% unused. Availability of storage space tends to encourage the collection and retention of objects of questionable utility. Thus residence and office become largely warehouses, with only limited open space for actual activity.

It is unreasonable to suggest that modern populations can or will give up the habit of sitting or will abandon use of a wide variety of possessions, but some conscious effort at reduction of both kinds of furniture use is plausible. Standing, walking, "perching," leaning, and sitting briefly on stools and simple chairs is healthier and more comfortable than spending eight working hours in an "executive swivel-tilt chair" followed by six hours in a deeply padded lounge chair. Objects are, in many cases tending toward miniaturization. Radios and TV sets may be pocket sized, yet a gigantic console "entertainment center" continues to clutter most living rooms or "family rooms." In the 1920s Le Corbusier was already urging storage in rationalized closets and built-in cabinets, with a minimum of "pieces" that occupy visible space and attract unnecessary attention. His message has only been heard by a limited audience, but it is still valid. The advanced concept of office work and planning called "office landscape" calls for the elimination of desks and files and the substitution of open tables and rolling (open) file carts. Long-term filing needs to be centralized and, wherever possible converted to microfilm or other space-efficient forms.

The desire for furniture in *quantity,* as much for its value as a symbol of affluence as for any real utility, has generated the peculiar modern pattern in which the furniture offered to the "average family" in furniture and department stores is generally of poor quality in both design and construction, while "good furniture" is distributed through different channels to a small and special market. The furniture normally available in retail outlets is expected to have a short life in terms of both style and utility. It appears with the trash on city curbs and in town dumps, broken and not worth repair after 2 to 10 years of use along with appliances that have a similar life cycle. It has been bought because it is available and affordable and users have come to accept the idea that a broken chair, a collapsing sofa, or an obsolete "entertainment console" should simply be thrown away and replaced.

The economics of this pattern and its impact on our use of manpower and resources is rarely thought about. Consider the following comparison:

> A family household unit can be considered as having a probable lifespan as an entity of about 50 years. If its dining equipment is a table and four chairs (a "dinette set"), about $80 would be a reasonable minimum price for this furniture. It can be expected to have a lifespan of about 5 years, after which it will be junked as useless and without any residual economic value. Thus the family will (disregarding any fluctuations in the value of money) pay out about $800 to own 10 successive dinette sets over 50 years. Had $800 been invested initially in a table and four chairs of good quality, there is an excellent probability that the objects would have served the entire 50 years and would have retained that value or increased it during that time since well-designed furniture from the 1920s is worth more now than it was when new. Good furniture from the 18th century or earlier has developed enormous market value. The materials and labor invested in high quality furniture are, as its lifespan extends, a small fraction of what is wastefully consumed in shoddy equivalents.

The obvious objection that the average family may not be able to afford better furniture comes into question if one checks the investment made in other products with short lifespans, such as appliances, automobiles, and recreational equipment. The idea that furniture can be an investment with a life of many generations, delivering both aesthetic and utilitarian satisfactions over that long period, has simply been lost sight of. It is time to recover that sense.

The mobility and variability of modern life also suggests a genuine need for furniture planned for easy transport, economy of materials and workmanship and, possibly, for some level of disposability. Hints of this direction have appeared in some porch and garden furniture, in proposals for paper furniture and units of inflated plastic, and in camping equipment. Some products in these areas have been well designed and are of good quality, but it is all too easy to drift in the direction of "novelty" furniture that is even poorer in quality and even more wasteful than the standard, shoddy retail product. Both designers and consumers need to think more clearly about categories of furniture quality. Valid needs might include:

1. Light, portable, inexpensive furniture, possibly (but not necessarily) of limited lifespan, made with minimal use of scarce materials and with minimal input of energy and labor.
2. High quality furniture made of high quality materials and with quality workmanship leading to a lifespan of at least several human generations. Paradoxically, in long-range terms, this furniture is less costly than the "temporary" furniture of item 1 above.

It is not difficult to think of examples of furniture products now in production in each of these categories, but the list is not as long as it might be in either. Actually, it is a very short list when compared to the in-production roster of furniture of the third type—of shoddy quality, bad design, and wasteful of materials, energy, and human labor.

A popular evasion on the part of both manufacturers and designers of bad furniture insists that they are only responding to "public taste." This tired argument has been advanced to support the making of class-B movies, the production of worthless television "entertainment," the design of tail-finned automobiles, and dozens of similar activities of the wasteful and brainless 1950s and 60s. Within recent years it has been possible to watch the increasing success of fine quality photographic and audio equipment, the gradual retreat of the tail fin under threats from more rational European and Japanese imports, and any number of comparable instances in which reasonable design and good quality are pushing aside shoddy products that are supposedly aimed at the level of public taste. In the furniture field, bentwood chairs, folding director's and campaign chairs, utility shelving, and similar simple products have a record of continuing success over many years. It is the "styled" furniture developed in terms of the market imagined by the editors of consumer home-furnishings magazines that has a short life of hit or flop and that then disappears into a handful of houses and apartments for a brief life, which ends in the town dump a few years later. The cliché that "we must educate public taste" is in reality misleading. Public taste is far more informed and discerning than stylists, buyers, editors, and other self-appointed taste merchants imagine. The real need is to produce products that match public taste and to make those products available through the distribution channels that reach a large public. There is a public response that is responsive to good design and to quality. The real need in the immediate future is to make design, production, and distribution responsive to that public.

DIMENSIONAL STANDARDS FOR TYPICAL FURNITURE FUNCTIONS

The work of the furniture designer would be greatly simplified if it were possible to establish ideal standard dimensions and profiles for every furniture type. This can be done most successfully where the functions involved are simple and the things to be accommodated are well standardized. File cabinets are such a case. As a furniture use involves more variables, standards become more difficult to establish. The most difficult of all problems, the chair, continues to defeat all efforts to arrive at one, or even several, ideal forms. The comments and data offered in this section should serve as a starting point for the designer and may help to avoid obvious errors, but cannot take the place of careful measurement of existing related examples and experimentation with prototypes.

Seating

Innumerable experiments have been undertaken in an effort to arrive at "ideal" profiles and dimensions for chairs and other seating, leading in many cases to published recommendations. The results are by no means consistent, and users have varied reactions to examples based on such recommendations. Chairs of widely differing forms are found satisfactory by some users and for some uses. The difficulty in arriving at standardized ideal forms results from several issues that deserve some detailed discussion.

1. **Objectives.** A seat is intended to provide an alternative to standing or lying down. Human desire for this possibility comes from a number of sources, and a particular seating unit may be intended to provide for one or several of the following:

   Comfort. Standing or walking about may become tiresome after a period of time, or inconvenient for certain activities. Sitting rests some muscles and makes it easier to remain still without discomfort. What will be considered "comfortable" by a user depends very much on the way a seat is used and on how long it is used. A hard stool is fully satisfactory for a short rest, and is often useful for longer times for certain kinds of activity involving considerable body motion (e.g., drafting, laboratory work, or playing drums). As the degree of motion involved in an activity decreases, the need for back rests, padded surfaces, and so on increases, so that a theater or lecture room chair, an automobile or airplane seat, or a dining chair must offer more than a simple stool. Desire for additional relaxation indicates changed profiles and surfaces to provide postures offering some of the restfulness of lying down while permitting activities such as conversation, reading, television watching, and brief rest. A reclining chair found comfortable for a nap will not be suitable for dining. A classroom chair will not (and should not) encourage sleep. Comfort can, in the end, only be judged in relation to intended use.

   Physiological Considerations. In addition to providing comfort, a seat is expected to be "healthful" in the sense of encouraging satisfactory sitting postures and avoiding physiological stress. Everyone has experienced a foot "asleep," a leg cramp, or some variety of stiffness or other physical discomfort after using a chair for some time (which may have seemed comfortable initially). Such minor discomforts give notice of problems that can, over a period of time develop into serious physiological problems. Dr. Ashley Montagu, in an unpublished paper,* has suggested that badly formed chairs are a major contributing cause in the increase in cardiovascular ail-

---

* Ashley Montagu, "The Human Frame and Furniture" paper read at institute on furniture for the elderly sponsored by the National Council on the Aging, New York, 1962.

ments and such diseases as varicosity and phlebitis as well as various back ailments. Seeming comfort is no assurance that such problems are not present although a physiologically satisfactory seat will almost inevitably be comfortable.

Secondary Function. In addition to the basic function of providing bodily comfort, most seating must satisfy other requirements—some established by the user and others imposed by outside considerations. Seating for work must not impede whatever bodily motion the work involves. This may include turning or moving of the entire chair (e.g., the typical office chair on casters). Some seating must accommodate the user in minimum space (e.g., transportation or theater seats), others must discourage long occupancy (e.g., in quick-food restaurants), still others must offer maximum durability and ease of maintenance (e.g., in public lobbies or waiting rooms), and some must also offer a sense of dignity or status through visual form and the postures induced in users. Obviously no one seating form can deal with all of these differing needs and, in many cases, one or another of these secondary needs will lead to compromise with desired standards of comfort and physiologically sound form.

2. **Body Dimensions and Mechanics.** Seating furniture must be related in form and dimensions to the body of the user. If human beings were made in a standard size and shape, this might be an easy problem. No one would expect to satisfy all users with one size of suit or shoe, yet a chair is normally made in only one size, often without any capacity for adjustment. "Normal" adults range from very tall to very short and from very thin to obese. Among all the possible combinations there are such variations as long legs and short trunk, or the reverse. In addition, we expect seating to be useful to children, to the aged, and to users with various physical handicaps. No set of dimensions or profiles can be optimum for this vast range of users. In an effort to satisfy as large a proportion of possible users as possible to some degree, it has become customary to design for "average" bodily proportions, noting that extreme departures from the average represent only a small percentage of the total population. That small percentage must seek out special furniture, adjustable or of unusual proportions, or must make do with regular furniture with whatever degree of discomfort may result. Average body dimensions are given in various publications,* and a cut-out articulated figure profile made in the same scale as the

---

* A particularly good reference is *Human scale 1/2/3* by Diffrient, Tilley and Bardagjy, MIT Press, 1974.

designer's drawings will prove very useful in developing forms that relate to body forms.

Some dimensions will cause minimum problems when kept to a minimum while others can be kept closer to a maximum. For example, a chair seat that is too deep will be uncomfortable to shorter users and users with short legs, while a chair seat that is short will serve these users without causing any problems to users who are tall or have long legs. A reclining chair intended to give head support will not serve a tall user unless the head support surface extends far enough, while an extended head support area will not cause any discomfort to the short user. Cut-out figures representing a very short and a very tall user (at about the 95th percentile dimensions) are useful in checking the way that different dimensions will relate to users who depart from average size.

The aim in establishing seating dimensions and profiles is not, as is often supposed, achievement of a contoured fit with body profiles. While contours that attempt this may achieve good comfort, they cannot actually arrive at a fit with more than a few users because of the wide variation in body form. In a seated or reclining position, body weight is actually transferred to the supporting surface at a few points where bone structure comes close to the supporting surface. If these points are supported to place the body in a position that can be held without strain, good comfort will result. Surfaces between these support points do not require support, and an effort to fit to them can result in discomfort to users who do not conform to average body size and shape.

In chairs, the primary area for weight transfer is obviously the seat, where a concentration of pressure will occur at the ischia where the body is particularly insensitive to feel. The relative comfort of bicycle and tractor seats shows that only a small area provides adequate body support. When upright seating is desired (as in desk or dining chairs), back support is required only intermittently, and only minor pressure is placed on the support. Back support must be at the right height to contact the lumbar region at the point of maximum forward curvature—a support set too high or too low is almost worse than no support at all. If a chair is intended to provide for more relaxed seating positions, back support becomes more important since more body weight is transferred to the chair through its back. In addition, the back slanted upper part of the body tends to produce forward thrust, which will, if the seat surface is horizontal (and particularly if it is also slippery), lead to the all too familiar slump in which the back is left arching between the seat and a high point of contact with the back in an uncomfortable curvature. This kind of discomfort is common in all seating that is low and combines a slanting back with a horizontal seat. Comfort requires that the seat slant down

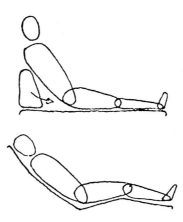

Sitting on a flat surface such as a bed (above) is certain to cause uncomfortable "slump." Contoured surface (below) avoids the problem, but dictates a particular posture.

toward the rear so that gravity will pull the body back into the chair against the forward slump that the slanting back will otherwise generate. The more the back slants to the rear, the more important it is that the seat slant downward to the rear.

When the trunk is sloped back in a semireclining position, the head is normally held upright. To reduce the muscular effort this requires, the seat back may rise high enough to give head support. This becomes essential when the back slant is very great. A small point of contact behind the head is all that is required, but this point must be placed at the right height for the particular user—a difficult requirement unless some adjustability is provided because of the great difference in body trunk height from minimum to maximum.

Padding and springing can contribute to comfort to some extent by reducing pressure at the points of weight transfer by spreading the area in which that transfer takes place. They also assist, in some degree, in mediating between the fixed form of the seat unit and the varied forms of different users' bodies and differing body positions. Too much softness can, however, do more harm than good by distributing weight too widely, away from the areas suited to weight transfer and, in effect, pinching flesh between the bone structure of the body and the soft surfaces of cushioning. This accounts for the fact that many extra-soft ("overstuffed") chairs seem very comfortable when first tried, but quickly become tiring with extended use. Springs contribute to a sense of comfort when get-

Chair with level and overly deep seat causes a combination of "slump" and pressure behind the knees (left). Down-slanted seat of proper depth reduces the problem, but may still cause uncomfortable pressure behind the knees (center). Adjustable leg rest (right) provides maximum comfort.

ting into a seat, and provide for a limited continuing adjustment to changes in position; of course they are also important in vehicle seats to help to absorb vibration and the effects of motion.

Only mechanical adjustability can make seating suitable to a wide range of body sizes or accommodate to changes of body position that become necessary when a seat is occupied for a long time. Adjustability involves mechanical parts that can be troublesome and costly and also requires that the user make intelligent use of the adjustments provided (the adjustable office chair is constantly used badly misadjusted because the user is unaware of how to position it suitably). Where the nature of the seat function or some other considerations rule out adjustability, any seat design will be at best a set of compromises that approach comfort for a reasonably large proportion of users.

Several techniques are available to the designer to aid in arriving at satisfactory forms for seating providing reasonable comfort to most users of seating having a particular function. An obvious approach involves finding an existing example that offers good comfort, taking key measurements and using these as a basis for a new design. When this is done, it is important to remember that materials and construction influence the relationship of dimensions to comfort so that, for example, a seat with deep and soft cushioning of given dimensions cannot be simply translated into a hard seat of the same dimensions with an expectation of comparable results. An example used as a guide must be similar in construction to the new design if it is to be a useful prototype. It is also, of course, possible to use an existing dimensional example with some dimensional modifications—a change of height, seat slant, or depth, for example, to introduce a desired change or improvement in the new design under development.

The group of charts provided here show dimensions taken from available examples drawn on graph paper to facilitate easy enlargement or transfer. The profiles include those of commonplace "average" products along with those of some historic, modern, and specially admired designs. Comparison of these profiles suggests the wide variation in ideas of comfort. In practice, such diagrams are only useful as a starting point with the idea that combination, modification, and creative invention will surely be needed in order to arrive at a "best" dimensional set up for a new design.

Another aid to seating design that can be extremely valuable, is the use of an accurately drawn human figure profile showing a seated figure in the position (or positions) that the new design is intended to accommodate. Such a diagram can even include indication of internal bodily structure, particularly skeletal structure, aiding in providing support at appropriate locations and avoidance of undesirable pressure points. With a human figure diagram in seated position as a starting point, design sketches and drawings can be

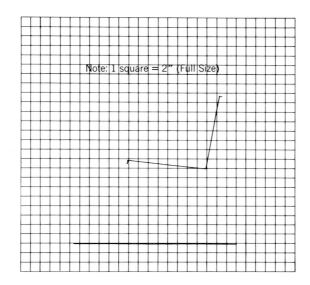

Note: 1 square = 2" (Full Size)

A typical "straight" chair.

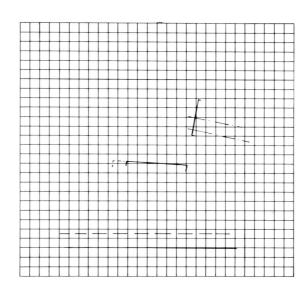

An adjustable "work" chair with height adjustment and adjustable back.

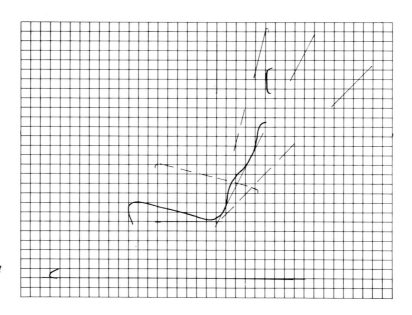

Lounge seating with a range of back angles. Arm location shown by dotted outline; outermost toe position indicated at left.

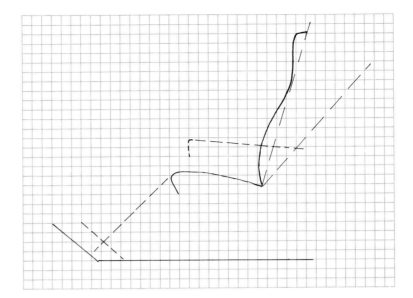

Adjustable upright to lounge seating, typical of transportation seating. Leg support (dotted outline) can increase comfort, but is rarely provided in vehicles where space is at a premium.

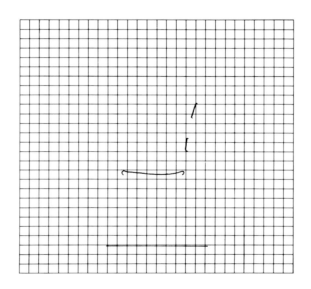

A simple ladderback chair of unusually good comfort (probably early 19th century). The seat is taped, and back support slats are shaped wood.

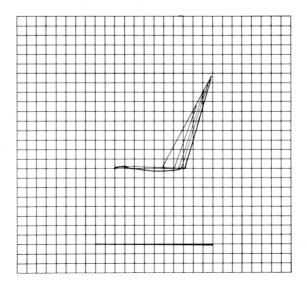

An American Windsor chair of the late 18th century. The wood seat is scooped out, and the back consists of spindles connected to curved rim.

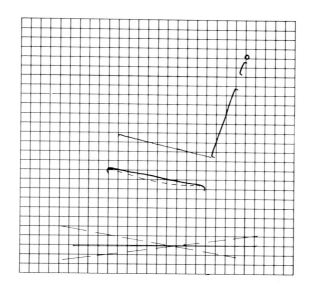

Shaker No. 7 rocking chair. Seat and lower back panel are tape-webbed. Normal range of rocking oscillation is indicated by dotted floor lines.

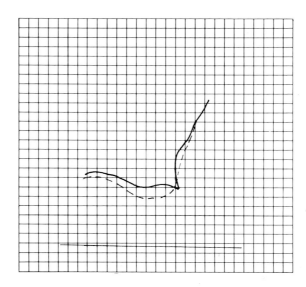

Profile of a German automobile seat regarded as exhibiting exceptional comfort.

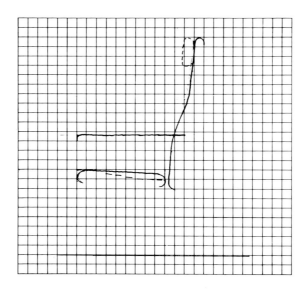

A Danish chair developed to provide ideal physiological and comfort characteristics, particularly for the use of the elderly.

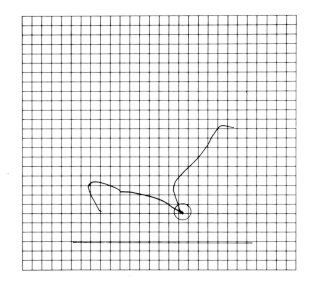

Volvo automobile seat. Back stiffness can be adjusted by varying tension on rubber webbing support straps; back angle and seat height are individually adjustable.

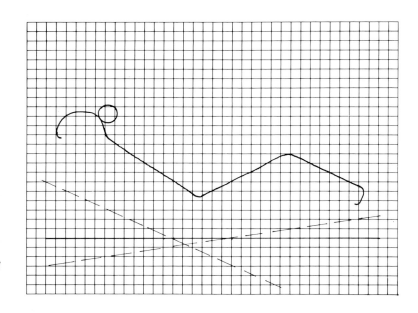

Le Corbusier chaise. The base permits movement through a range from moderately upright to extreme reclining with legs elevated (indicated by dotted floor lines). Neck rest is movable.

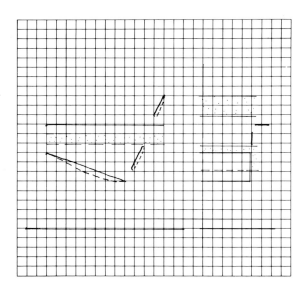

Profile and half-front elevation of the Breuer Wassily chair. Seat, back, and arm surfaces are leather or canvas and deflect to some degree under load.

developed as discussed in Chapter 5, with some confidence that the resulting designs will conform to physiological needs. Working in this way requires a satisfactory figure diagram, truly representative of the anticipated user population. Usual practice is to obtain a profile of an "average" person at a convenient scale such as 3″ = 1′-0″ (¼ full size) in cut-out form with the many body parts pivoted together at joint points so that the profile becomes "articulated" in a way that matches human bodily articulation.

Various sources provide human dimensions as a basis for making up such a profile figure and some offer an "average" figure ready for tracing and cutting out. It must be remembered that human dimensions vary widely with age groups, sex, and geographical distribution of populations so that there is no one "average" applicable to every user group. The complex charts provided by the publications *Humanscale 1, 2, 3, 4, 5, 6,* and *7, 8, 9,* give very complete dimensional data on almost any imaginable user population group, but may leave the designer with difficult choices resulting from the profusion of information provided. They are particularly useful when designing for groups that differ widely from any general average, such as children (for school furniture) or elderly users. Since most seating is intended for use by an unselected general population such as office workers, transport passengers or household furniture purchasers, it is most often best to accept a figure that illustrates an "average" made up of a large general population. The figure provided with Henry Dreyfuss' publication *The Measure of Man* is in wide use as a starting point, although it must be remembered that it is a male figure and therefore not representative of a population mix of both sexes.

A chart is provided here that is the result of combining and modifying a number of "average" figure diagrams. With the parts cut out of cardboard or plastic sheet and pivoted together, it is a useful design aid. It should be noted that the pivoted joints permit "double-jointed" movements that the human body cannot achieve, but if used with reasonable care, it will serve as a starting point in developing seating profiles and it is a useful device for checking any proposed design. Note that some dimensions should favor users *larger* than average while some should favor *smaller* users. In particular, seat height and depth need to favor the smaller user since a low and shallow seat will not inconvenience a large user while a high and/or deep seat many leave the small user with feet hanging in the air and the backs of the knees constricted by the seat's front edge. Head support, when it is provided, must be carefully considered to serve users both larger and smaller than the average. A checklist of the key dimensions for checking is as follows:

1. Height of seat front edge from floor (to allow foot to rest on floor or foot rest).

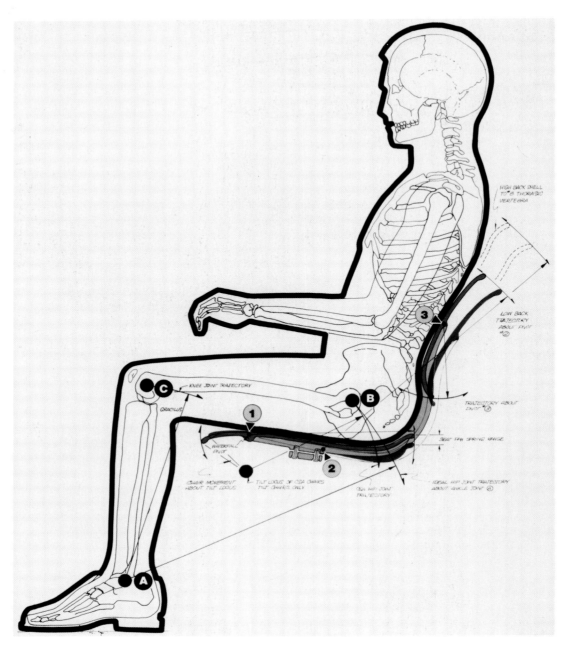

A carefully drawn human figure with "X-ray" indication of the skeleton developed by designer Bill Stumpf and shown placed on the profile section of the Stumpf Equa chair as it was in design development. (Illustration courtesy of Herman Miller, Inc.)

An average male figure in scale cut-out form. This chart can be reproduced in exact size, cut out and assembled with paper fasteners (passing through holes punched where black dots appear) to create an articulated figure suitable for use in preliminary design of seating furniture. The scale is ¼ full size (3" = 1'0").

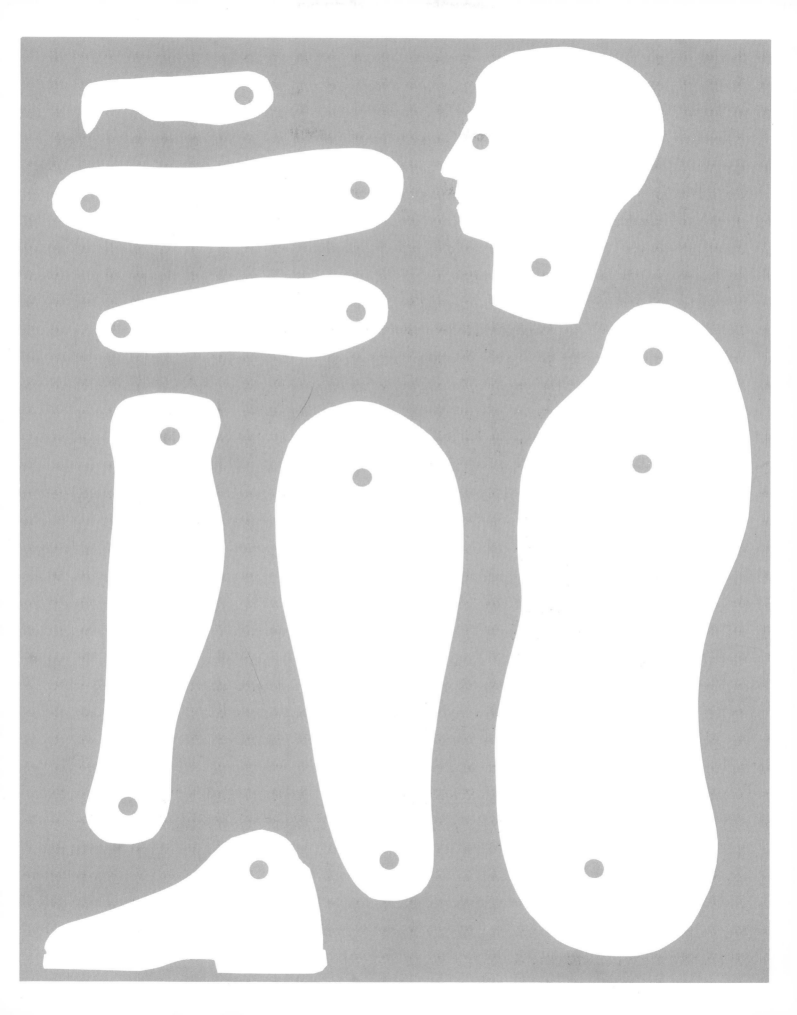

2. Depth of seat to avoid pressure to back of knees.
3. Correct position for lumbar support for back.
4. Clearance at base of back to avoid larger user being pushed forward (away from lumbar support).
5. Appropriate position of upper back support (when provided) to avoid pushing shoulders forward or pressure on shoulder blades.
6. Position of head support (when provided) to suit both larger and smaller users and to avoid pressing head forward.
7. Arm height (where arm is provided) set high enough to be useful to all users but low enough to avoid pushing up on arms and shoulders of users with long arms.

Compromising the demands of these various criteria and fully satisfying criteria 6 and 7 can be difficult or almost impossible, but an effort should be made to approach these ideals.

An articulated human figure cut-out in use placed on a furniture design drawing under development.

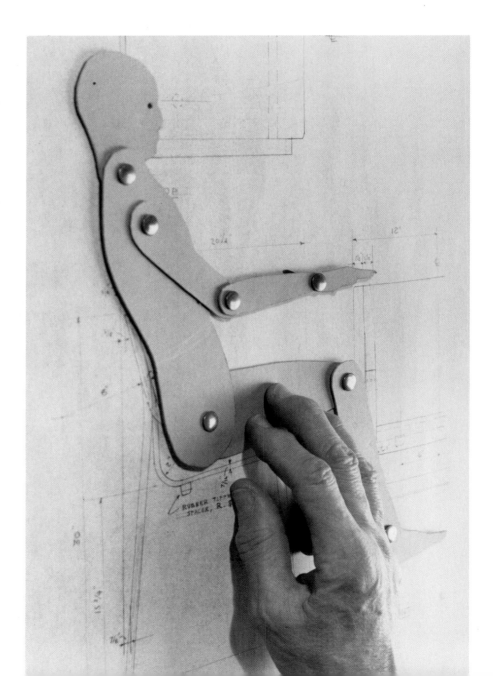

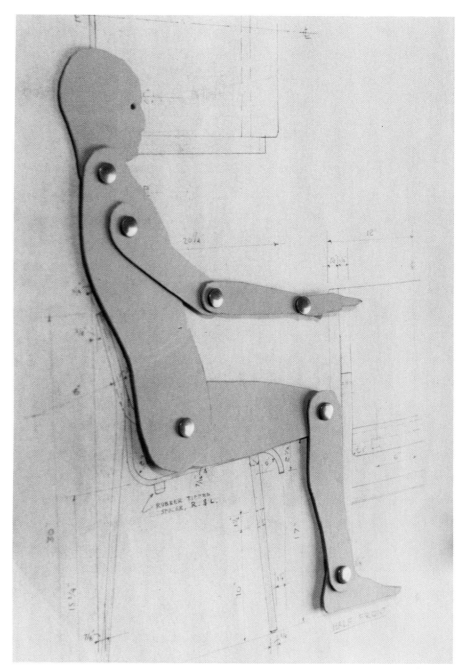

The relationship of the figure to the scale profile drawing is a useful aid in predicting seating comfort.

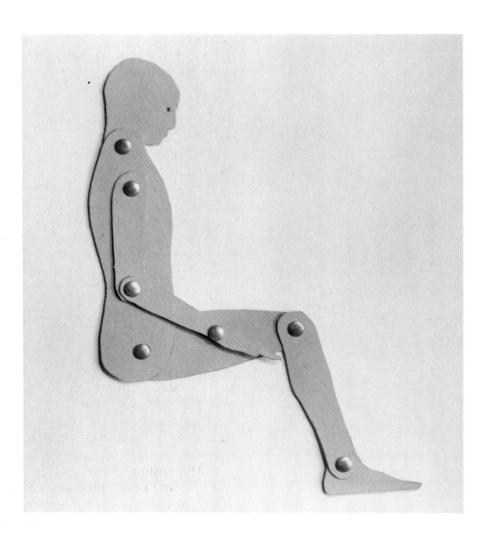

Upright seating position (above) and reclined position (below) can be studied and compared as design studies are developed.

A three-dimensional articulated figure can also be used as a design aid, but is not so easily obtained. A figure offered in art supply shops as an aid to students of drawing and sculpture is an available possibility, but it is not based on carefully selected anthropometric data, and so is not altogether trustworthy. In practice, since profile is the key element in developing seating comfort, the flat articulated figure is generally satisfactory in most design work.

Width dimensions for seating are much less critical than profile dimensions and usually require no more than checking to be sure that adequate width is provided between arms (where included) and sufficient width for adjacent bodies in multiple seating. Where lateral support is desired, as in transportation seating to avoid unpleasant sideways movement generated by vehicle motion, or to encourage separation between adjacent users, suitable curvature to give side support for the thighs and back and can be developed quite easily without resort to anatomical dimensional charts.

Tables and Desks

As compared to seating, tables and desks pose very simple problems. A table is merely an elevated flat surface to make various activities more convenient, especially when the user is seated in a chair. A desk is a table intended for writing and related work and often provides additional, sometimes rather specialized storage.

1. **Dimensional Considerations.** Height is the most sensitive of table and desk dimensions. A widely accepted standard height for tables and desks is 30 inches, although this may be higher than ideal for average users. A height of 29 inches has become a secondary standard in many modern furniture systems. Typewriters and other office machines are usually 27 inches high although there is no indication that this is preferable to the 29 or 30 inch height for any specific reason. Under a desk or tabletop, clearance below any structure or obstruction must provide leg room. This requires a distance of 25 inches from the floor level. Leg and knee clearance in a horizontal dimension requires 16 to 18 inches to any base, leg structure, or other obstruction. A width of 20 to 24 inches is required for leg and knee space.

   The articulated figure diagram discussed above can also be used as an aid in setting table or desk heights if it is placed in the seating position generated by an intended chair. Checking elbow height and arm positions will confirm suitability of proposed height. The special problems proposed by CRT terminal (keyboard and screen) use can also be studied with the aid of the articulated figure. Head position and tilt to provide good vision of keyboard and CRT screen can be checked in relation to the positions determined by the proposed desk, table, or work-station dimensions.

Top surface space relates to anticipated use. A primary work area is defined by the space swept by arm reach, a quarter circle swung by each arm with a radius of about 18 inches, 12 inches for easiest access, plus a zone of about 10 inches additional radius reachable with some stretching. A dining place setting occupies space 12 to 18 inches deep and 18 to 24 inches wide. Increasing formality and luxury of dining arrangements demand increasing space. A typewriter requires space about 16 to 18 inches deep and 24 to 30 inches wide (including carriage travel).

Desk storage arrangements may include space for paper and envelopes, pencils and other incidentals, and some provision for filing. Typical dimensions for these uses are covered under *storage,* below.

Special purpose tables of various top dimensions are in general use. Heights are more closely standardized according to the type of use. Typical dimensions are shown in the following table.

Use	Height (in.)	Top Size (in.)
Coffee table	15	15 × 30–30 × 60
End table	20–24	15 × 24–30 × 30
Corner table	15–20	24 × 24–36 × 36
Bedside table	15–30	12 × 18–20 × 24
Serving table or cart	24–28	16 × 24–22 × 36
Stool-table	16–22	12–22 round
Drafting and art work table	30–42	24 × 30–36 × 72
Informal conference and dining table	25*	30 × 30–36 × 72

* This low table is frequently used in Europe with chairs having seats lower than standard dining height. It has never had wide acceptance in the United States.

2. **Special Functional Provisions.** Certain uses can be facilitated by special table or desk forms. Adjustable height is useful for art and drafting use. A slanted top aids many types of work, but may cause objects to slide or roll. An adjustable slope top is a favorite provision for drafting. Some drafting (particularly on large sheets) can best be done on a vertical or near-vertical surface. A second top surface above the primary top set back 16 to 24 inches is often useful in providing an extra work surface. A second top below the primary one may be useful for storage. Unusual top shapes (angled or cut out to increase area swept by

arm reach, for example) may have advantages for special purposes. Tables for home use often attempt to provide for multiple uses (coffee table to dining table conversion, for example) and for adjustable size. Dining tables with dropleaves or extension leaves are the best known and most useful of the latter type. In planning extendable dining tables, each degree of extension should relate to a particular number of place settings logically, and no uncomfortable interferences with legs or bases should occur in any typical seating arrangement.

Storage

Shelf storage, open or behind doors, or in drawers is most often provided for general, non-differentiated use and is not very critical in its dimensions. Small spaces will only accommodate items smaller than the controlling dimensions involved, and spaces too high or too deep may be wasteful or inconvenient to use. Some designers have attempted to make careful inventories of objects to be stored in order to plan highly specific and highly efficient storage arrangements. The difficulty of this approach is that the exact storage needs of the end user are usually unknown and will probably change over a period of years. A nonspecific approach is therefore usually more reasonable, especially if some degree of adjustability can be provided for shelf spacing. Some specific uses (e.g., filing or record storage) make more precise dimensional planning desirable and possible.

1. **Dimensions for General Storage**. Bookshelves require a depth of 8 to 16 inches, with greater depths desirable as shelf spacing is increased. A 12 inch depth is satisfactory for more than 90% of books. Shelf spacing is best made adjustable in 1 to 2 inch increments. If shelves are to be fixed, spacing should range from 8 to 13 inches. Wide, closely spaced (3 to 6 in.) shelves are sometimes provided for large books, laid flat.

    Dishes and glassware require shelves 9 to 12 inches deep, spaced 8 to 12 inches apart. Liquor and similar bottles require 13 inches of clear height. Wines, if stored horizontally, fit in 3½ inch square openings in traditional wine racks. Silver and related utensils are often stored in compartmented spaces about 2 inches deep, 3 to 5 inches wide, and 6, 8 and 10 inches long (corresponding to tea spoons, forks, and knives). A longer space, 15 to 18 inches, is useful for carving and serving implements.

    Clothing storage requires drawers ranging in depth from 3 to 10 inches, in front-to-back dimension from 14 to 18 inches, and in width from 18 to 36 inches. A wrapped shirt measures under

10 × 15 in. Most clothing, linens, and blankets are foldable in so many ways that exact dimensioning to suit is futile. Efficient use of available space usually requires refolding.

Miscellaneous objects such as sports and photo equipment sewing machines, and similar household gear are also too variable in size to guide dimensioning. Larger objects are likely to find space in closets rather than in furniture.

High fidelity and tape-recording equipment is also variable in dimension and subject to constant change. Records are consistent in size at present. The following dimensions (in.) are a current guide.

Tuner, amplifier or receiver	24 W × 6 H × 12–15 D
Record changer or turntable	20 × 20 × 12 H, including top access clearance
Speaker (shelf type) in enclosure	12 × 12 × 24
12 in. LP records	12½ D × 13 H
12 in. records in albums	14 D × 13 H
7 in. tape in boxes	7½ D × 8 H
Tape cassettes	3½ × 4½

2. **Dimensions for Office Storage.** General storage in offices (pencils, pads, boxed supplies, etc.) like home general storage can best be provided for with adjustable shelves in .a fairly large open space with or without door closure. Shelf or drawer depth of 15 to 18 inches is desirable. Paper and envelope sizes, as well as those of file folders and file cards, are well standardized although European standards are slightly different. Storage space for office stationery and for filing can be based on the following standards (in.):

Letter paper	8½ × 11
Legal paper	8 × 12½
Legal pad	8 × 13
Business envelope	4 × 9½
File cards	3 × 5, 4 × 6, 5 × 8
IBM (punch) card	3¼ × 7⅜
Letter file folder	11½ × 9
Legal file folder	9½ × 15

These dimensions do *not* include clearances for handling, divider index tabs, and so on.

Beds

Of all furniture types, beds have become most highly standardized. A flat, soft sleeping surface has become almost universally accepted, and dimensions have settled into a small number of standards. While unusual sizes and shapes are possible, the availability of standard mattresses, springs, linens, and blankets make standard sizes highly convenient. In fact, furniture designers and manufacturers rarely concern themselves with any parts of beds except head- and footboards, which are primarily decorative. The functional parts of beds are produced by a specialized bedding industry whose production is so efficient that efforts to approach the bed in a different way hardly seem worthwhile. If there is any reason to depart from this norm, a mattress of any size may be made to order, and a support platform, solid or sprung, is simple to produce. The following are current U.S. dimensional standards:

LENGTH AND WIDTH (in.)

Single bed	30–36 × 75
Twin bed	39 × 75
Full size (double) bed	54 × 75
"Queen" size bed	60 × 80
"King" size bed	76 × 80
Crib	30 × 53 ("full size")

Height. This is the dimension that usually varies. "On-the-floor" beds only 4 to 8 inches high are possible, but are usually considered inconvenient to get in and out of and to make up. A range from 11 to 16 inches to the sleeping surface is normal, and 18 inch height not unusual.

PROBLEMS OF DESIGN PROTECTION AND DESIGN CREDIT

The field of modern furniture design, particularly in the United States, is overshadowed by several disturbing problems that do not usually come to the attention of the furniture buyer or user. They are also problems for the furniture designer and should perturb the furniture industry. These problems are as follows:

1. Original furniture designs cannot be easily protected through patents or copyright. As a result any successful design can be freely imitated ("knock-off" in trade slang).
2. As a result of this situation most furniture manufacturers make no effort to commission original designs, but prefer to "pirate" or "knock-off" other manufacturers' designs, possibly with a few minor changes to suggest originality.
3. As a result of these two interacting situations, furniture design hardly exists as a viable profession. The designer who has developed or wants to develop new designs finds that they have no market. This helps to explain why so many furniture designers

have had to become their own manufacturers and/or distributors (e.g., Jens Rison, Ward Bennett).

4. Where manufacturers by chance, good luck, or by retaining competent designers actually introduce good quality furniture products (in a design sense as well as functionally), the designer is usually not credited. Thus it is impossible to discover who actually designed most of the furniture currently available. Neither credit nor blame can be fixed on the people involved. This makes it difficult for the skilled designer to build a reputation and encourages resort to knock-off design.

5. A small number of manufacturers *have* supported good design over the years, firms who view interior designers, architects, and other professionals as their primary customers at least insofar as they are the decision makers in some kinds of furniture purchase. These firms have usually identified their products with a designer's name, often the name of a well-known, even famous designer. Unfortunately, the designers identified in this way are often only marginally involved or not involved at all in the production of the designs that carry their names. This comes about because of the very American reality that most successful designers become the chiefs of large organizations in which all actual creative work is done by a staff—often a large staff. In this situation the actual designer turns is not only anonymous but must also tolerate the indignity of seeing his or her work attributed to his employer, who is assumed to be the actual designer by the consuming public. Ironically, the designer who *has* actually designed the furniture attributed to him finds that the authenticity of that attribution becomes a matter of doubt and uncertainty.

The situation described above is reminiscent of the status of publishing in the 17th or 18th centuries, before copyright protection established the situation we now take for granted—any written work, any piece of music, any work of art has a known author who has certain rights resulting from authorship. Duplication of another's work is plagiarism and leads to legal consequences. In the design fields, no such strictures have been established and the equivalents of plagiarism are tolerated as norms. Patent protection is only available when a truly original, mechanical invention is involved, an unusual circumstance in most furniture design. "Design patents," while more easily available, have a poor record for sustaining protection when tested in court and are generally considered to be worthless. As a result, copying any successful design must be expected and is not currently subject to any effective legal restraint.

The unwillingness of manufacturers to support original design and to give credit to designers might diminish if the consumer public were more concerned with such matters. Support for original design through publicly visible expression and through the most effective of all supports, commercial acceptance, and a corresponding rejection of poor quality design of anonymous origin might encourage greater support of identified work of good quality.

The problem of inaccurate and false attribution of design work is more difficult and calls for more concern, within the design professions, with standards that will assure accurate and complete credit given in some publicly visible way to those actually responsible for the creative work involved in the design of any product. We take it for granted that the author of a book is, in fact, its writer; that the composer of a piece of music was, in reality, the person who composed it. It will require both legal pressures and changes in custom to ensure that a similar confidence can be felt in attributing design work to a particular designer.

The following steps are needed to bring about a more reasonable, honest, and ethical situation:

1. Availability of some form of design registration, comparable to copyright, that will establish the rights of a designer in relation to a particular design and will forbid unauthorized copy.

2. Establishment of an obligation on the part of every manufacturer and distributor to provide identification of the design or designer responsible for every product in production. No book appears without an authors name. Why should objects almost always be anonymous?

3. Establishment within the design professions of a more equitable code of ethics that makes it obligatory for design organizations to give full credit to individuals who are responsible for the specific, creative work involved in the product design. Such credit is given, for example, to every individual involved in the production of a film. Comparable credits should be given to those who design any product.

For many years various forms of design registration or patent have been available to designers in Europe. The generally superior quality of European design, and the recognition offered to European designers is, in large measure, connected with this reality. In the United States, product design of all kinds, and furniture design in particular, fail to give proper recognition and protection to design creativity.

SAFETY CONSIDERATIONS

Furniture is so commonplace in life and seems, on the face of it, so much less threatening than firearms, bicycles, or automobiles, that it is natural to assume it does not involve any significant safety issues. Actually, after stairways and bathroom fixtures, furniture is one of the most significant factors in household accidents. Since we are all in contact with furniture so much of the time, and because it is a significant part of the environment for the aged and the very young (who may be less able to deal with hazards), even minor risks that furniture may present can become significant. There is a new awareness of safety problems with all sorts of modern products, and it is reasonable to give more serious consideration to these issues in relation to furniture than might have seemed necessary even a few years ago.

It is probably impossible to ensure totally safe furniture. Bumps and falls, in no way the fault of furniture, can still produce injuries, and insistence on extremes of "foolproof" construction are probably unrealistic. Still, it is reasonable to expect every furniture designer to give some thought to avoiding obvious and less obvious hazards. The use of new materials in so much modern furniture also generates an obligation to be sure that no new threats are introduced to users who may be unaware of surprising characteristics of certain materials.

The following is simply a checklist of the furniture characteristics most likely to relate to safety considerations. In every case, it is suggested that the issue be considered not only in relation to average users but also in regard to the special problems of users who may be aged, handicapped, or very young. Furniture designed specifically for infants, children, the aged, or the handicapped should meet particularly rigorous safety standards.

Stability. Overturning furniture is a significant cause of accidents. The stability issues discussed earlier (p. 51) are basic. Most overturning accidents occur in unexpected types of use. Tables and chairs are used to climb on and stand on; chairs are tipped back for comfort or relaxation; tall objects are leaned against. Special care should be taken in connection with:

An object with long cantilever beyond its base area.

Any tall, thin object.

Any wall-hung or floor-to-ceiling supported unit. Shelf systems are particularly vulnerable to overturning or collapse.

Any drawer units where several heavy drawers may be opened at once. File cabinets are a well-known hazard, usually provided with drawer interlock to prevent overturning when several drawers are opened at once.

Three-legged chairs and tables.

Furniture on casters or rollers.

Mobility. Any furniture that can be moved about presents special risks. It may roll away from a user unexpectedly, roll down an incline or stair, or show an unexpected inclination to overturn as a result of stability problems.

Dimensions. Low furniture is easier to trip or fall over than furniture of standard height, particularly for older and handicapped users. On the other hand, high beds are a risk to both the very young and the aged. Double-deck beds with an upper bunk, with or without a ladder, are a major hazard to children and a cause of a surprising number of major injuries and deaths. Narrow spaces between rails or bars that may permit a head to be caught are also a risk to infants and young children and are a major issue in the design of cribs and children's beds.

Shapes. Sharp edges and sharp corners also present a hazard. It is hardly reasonable to expect all furniture to have all corners rounded, but there is no question that rounding and softening of corners will minimize injuries and such inconveniences as torn clothing. Sharp corners on lower faces of table and desk tops are a particular hazard to infants and young children.

Materials. Hard and sharp materials (metals and glass are obvious examples) make sharp edges and corners particularly dangerous. Wood and plastics, although they seem less threatening, can also present hazards when corners and edges are sharp and placed in locations that make accidents possible. Glass is a particular hazard because of the possibility of breakage with resulting sharp, cutting edges. Consider shatterproof glass or clear plastic as an alternative to glass shelves and table or desk tops. If glass is to be used, consider rounded corners or construction that surrounds the glass with protective framing. Avoid glass elements that may easily slip out of place and fall.

Fire Safety. This special characteristic of materials deserves special consideration. Most fires in buildings start in furniture or are supported, at an early stage, by furniture and other furnishings (e.g., rugs). Metals will not support combustion, but most other furniture materials will, and upholstery and bedding materials are major contributors to many fires. It is hardly practical to expect all furniture to be totally fireproof, but there is an increasing tendency to expect fire-resistance in furniture for use in specially hazardous situations such as theaters and auditoriums, hotel and motel rooms, offices in high buildings, and in transportation equipment (aircraft in particular). Wood and most traditional upholstery materials (e.g., hair and natural fiber textiles) might be called "slow-burning" because they do not ignite easily and tend to smolder rather than to burst into flames. Many new materials, particularly certain plastics, are less benign and may either flare up easily or, if they smolder, produce lethal gasses and fumes. Legal restrictions on the characteristics of furniture materials are becoming increasingly common, but there is a clear need to check on the fire safety characteristics of any unfamiliar material being considered for use in furniture. Upholstery and bedding materials are particularly worthy of concern, but all plastic parts, especially foams—whether soft, semi-rigid, or rigid—should be checked for fire safety characteristics.

BIBLIOGRAPHY

The vast literature concerned with furniture design is heavily concentrated in books on historical furniture of the various "periods" organized for the use of antiquarians and collectors. Such books are not included in this bibliography, although a few works on premodern furniture history are mentioned where they offer insights into the development of modern furniture. Manufacturers' catalogs are also omitted except for the few cases where they are of sufficient quality to be considered worthy of serious study. Magazine and journal articles are not listed, but a short list of periodicals that carry frequent articles and news reports on modern furniture is provided.

    Publications lacking an identified author or editor are given at the end of the main listing, which is alphabetical by author.

Adam, Peter, *Eileen Gray*, Harry N. Abrams, 1987.

Amaya, Mario. *Art Nouveau,* Dutton Vista, 1960.

Ambasz, Emilio (Ed.). *Italy, the New Domestic Landscape,* Museum of Modern Art, 1972.

Andrews, Edward Deming and Faith. *Shaker Furniture,* Yale University Press, 1937 (reprint, Dover, 1950).

Barilli, Renato. *Art Nouveau,* Hamlyn, 1966.

Barnes, H. Jefferson. *Some Examples of Furniture by Charles Rennie Mackintosh in the Glasgow School of Art Collection*, Glasgow School of Art, 1969.

Blake, Peter. *Marcel Breuer,* Museum of Modern Art, 1949.

Boesiger, W. and Le Corbusier, *Le Corbusier 1929–1934*, Girsberger, 1935.

Boger, Louise Ada. *Furniture, Past and Present,* Doubleday, 1966.

Boyce, Charles. *Dictionary of Furniture*, Roundtable Press, 1985.

Bradford, Peter and Prete, Barbara, eds. *Chair*, Peter Bradford and Thos. Y. Crowell, 1978.

Caplan, Ralph. *The Design of Herman Miller*, Whitney, 1976.

Cathers, David M. *Furniture of the American Arts and Crafts Movement*, New American Library, 1981.

Chippendale, Thomas. *The Gentleman and Cabinet-Maker's Director*, 3rd ed., 1762 (reprint, Dover, 1966).

Le Corbusier. *1929 Sitzmöbel*, Heidi Weber, 1959.

Dal Fabbro, Mario. *How to Build Modern Furniture*, 2nd ed., McGraw-Hill, 1957.

Dal Fabbro, Mario. *Modern Furniture*, Reinhold, 1949.

Dal Fabbro, Mario. *Upholstered Furniture Design and Construction*, McGraw-Hill, 1957.

De Fusco, Renato, *Le Corbusier, Designer: Furniture 1929*, Barron's, 1977.

Diffrient, N., Tilley, A., Bardagjy, J. *Humanscale 1/2/3, 4/5/6, 7/8/9*, M.I.T. Press, 1967, 1974, 1981.

Ditzel, Nanna and Jørgen. *Danish Chairs*, Høst & Søns Verlag, 1954.

Ditzel and Juhl (with others). *Møbeltegninger*, Frederiksberg Tekniske Skole, 1950.

Drexler, Arthur. *Charles Eames, Furniture from the Design Collection*, Museum of Modern Art, 1973.

Dreyfuss, Henry. *Measure of Man*, Whitney, 1967.

Emery, Marc. *Furniture by Architects*, Harry N. Abrams, 1983.

Faber, Tobias. *Arne Jacobsen*, Praeger, 1966.

Fastnedge, Ralph. *English Furniture Styles from 1500 to 1830*, Pelican, 1955.

Ferebee, Ann. *History of Design from the Victorian Era to the Present*, Van Nostrand Reinhold, 1970.

Fleig, Karl (Co-editor). *Alvar Aalto*, Verlag für Architektur, 1963.

Gandolfi, Vittorio. *Gli Studi Nella Casa*, Editoriale Domus, 1945.

Gandy, Charles D. and Zimermann-Stidham, Susan. *Contemporary Classics: Furniture of the Masters*, McGraw-Hill, 1981.

Garner, Philippe. *Twentieth-Century Furniture*, Van Nostrand Reinhold, 1980.

Giedion, Sigfried. *Mechanization Takes Command*, Oxford University Press, 1948 (reprint, W. W. Norton, 1969).

Glaeser, Ludwig. *Ludwig Mies van der Rohe, Furniture and Furniture Drawings*, Museum of Modern Art, 1977.

Goldfinger, Erno. *British Furniture Today*, Alec Tiranti, 1951.

Graham, F. Lanier. *Hector Guimard*, Museum of Modern Art, 1970.

Guyer, H. and Meyer, P. (Eds.). *Möbel und Wohnraum*, Verlag für Architektur, 1946.

Hanks, David A. *Innovative Furniture in America from 1800 to the Present*, Horizon Press, 1981.

Hathaway, M. and Foard, E. *Heights and Weights of Adults in the United States*, U. S. Department of Agriculture, 1960.

Hatje, Gerd (Ed.). *New Furniture*, Verlag Hatje, Vol. I, 1952 (issued annually thereafter).

Hennessey, J., and Papanek, V. *Nomadic Furniture*, Random House, 1973; Vol. 2, 1974.

Jaffé, Hans L. C. *De Stijl*, Abrams, 1967.

Johnson, Philip C. *Mies Van der Rohe*, Museum of Modern Art, 1947.

Kaufmann, Edgar, Jr. *Prize Designs for Modern Furniture,* Museum of Modern Art, 1950.

Kaufmann, Edgar, Jr. *What is Modern Design?,* Museum of Modern Art and Simon and Schuster, 1950.

Kepes, Gyorgy. *The Man-Made Object,* Braziller, 1966.

Kettell, Russell Hawes. *Pine Furniture of Early New England,* Doubleday, Doran, 1929 (reprint, Dover, 19XX).

Larrabee, Eric and Vignelli, Massimo. *Knoll Design,* Harry N. Abrams, 1981.

Leoni, Pietro. *La Costruzione del Mobile Moderno,* Editore Hoepli, 1954.

Logie, Gordon. *Furniture from Machines,* Allen and Unwin, 1947.

Lucie-Smith, Edward. *Furniture: A Concise History*, Thames and Hudson, 1985.

Madsen, S. Tschudi. *Art Nouveau,* McGraw-Hill, 1967.

Mang, Karl. *History of Modern Furniture,* Harry N. Abrams, 1979.

Massobrio, G. and Portoghesi, P. *La Seggiola di Vienna,* Martano Editore, undated.

Meadmore, Clement. *The Chair,* Van Nostrand Reinhold, 1900.

Meilash, Dana Z. *Creating Modern Furniture,* Crown, 1975.

Moody, Ella. *Modern Furniture,* Dutton Vista, 1966.

Naylor, Gillian. *The Bauhaus,* Studio Vista Dutton, 1968.

Nelson, George (Ed.). *Chairs,* Whitney, 1953.

Nelson, George (Ed.). *Storage,* Whitney, 1954.

Neuhart, John; Neuhart, Marilyn; and Eames, Ray. *Eames Design: The Work of the Office of Charles and Ray Eames, 1941–1978,* Harry N. Abrams, 1989.

Nielsen, Johan Møller. *Wegner, Sitting Pretty,* Gyldendal, 1965.

Noyes, Eliot F. *Organic Design in Home Furnishings,* Museum of Modern Art, 1941 (reprint, Arno, 1969).

Page, Marian. *Furniture Designed by Architects*, Whitney Library of Design, 1980.

Panero, Julius. *Anatomy for Interior Designers,* 3rd ed., Whitney, 1962.

Panero, Julius and Zelnick, Martin, *Human Dimensions and Interior Space,* Whitney Library of Design, 1979.

Pevsner, Nikolaus. *High Victorian Design,* Architectural Press, 1951.

Pevsner, Nikolaus. *Sources of Modern Architecture and Design,* Thames and Hudson; Praeger, 1968.

Radice, Barbara. *Memphis,* Rizzoli International, 1984.

Raymond, Antonin. *Architectural Details,* Architectural Book Publishing, 1937 (2nd ed., 1947).

Read, Herbert. *Art and Industry,* Faber and Faber, 1934.

Rheims, Maurice. *The Flowering of Art Nouveau,* Abrams, 1966.

Russell, Gordon. *The Things We See: No. 3, Furniture,* Penguin, 1947.

Russell, Frank; Garner, Philippe; and Read, John. *A Century of Chair Design,* Rizzoli International, 1980.

Schaefer, Herwin. *Nineteenth Century Modern,* Praeger, 1970.

Schwartz, Marvin D. *Please Be Seated,* American Federation of Arts, 1968.

Selz, P. and Constantine, M. *Art Nouveau,* Museum of Modern Art, 1959.

Sembach, Klaus-Jurgen. *Contemporary Furniture,* Architectural Book Publishing Co., 1982.

Shapira, Nathan H. *The Expression of Gio Ponti* (Design Quarterly 69–70), Walker Art Center, 1967.

Shea, John G. *American Shakers and their Furniture,* Van Nostrand Reinhold, 1971.

Sheraton, Thomas. *Cabinet-Maker's and Upholsterer's Drawing Book 1791– 94* (edited and with preface by Ralph Edwards), John Tiranti, 1945.

Stamberg, Peter S. *Instant Furniture,* Van Nostrand Reinhold, 1976.

Symonds, R. W. *Veneered Walnut Furniture,* John Tiranti, 1947.

Wanscher, Ole. *Art of Furniture,* Wittenborn, 1967.

Wilk, Christopher, Marcel Breuer, *Furniture and Interiors,* Museum of Modern Art, 1981.

Wingler, Hans M. *The Bauhaus,* M.I.T. Press, 1969.

Architectural Woodwork Quality Standards Illustrated, Architectural Woodwork Institute, 1963.

Eames Celebration, reprint from Architectural Design magazine, September 1966.

50 Years Bauhaus, exhibition catalog, Royal Academy of Arts, 1968.

Furniture by Charles Rennie Mackintosh, Glasgow School of Art, 1968.

The Herman Miller Collection, Herman Miller Furniture Co., 1948, 2nd ed., 1952.

Knoll au Louvre, Knoll International, Inc., 1971.

Modern Chairs 1918–70, exhibition catalog, Whitechapel Art Gallery, 1970.

Nelson, Eames, Girard, Propst; The Design Process at Herman Miller, Design Quarterly 98/99, Walker Art Center, 1975.

Thonet: 150 Years of Furniture, Barron's, 1980.

Periodicals

Contract, Gralia Publications, New York.

Design Quarterly, Walker Art Center, Minneapolis.

Domus, Editoriale Domus, Milan.

Furniture Forum, Furniture Forum, Inc., Los Angeles (discontinued).

Industrial Design, Design Publications, Inc. New York.

Interior Design, Whitney Communications, New York.

Interiors, Billboard Publications, New York.

Mobilia, Mobila Publications, Snekkersten, Denmark.

INDEX

Rotational molding, 148
Router, 166–167
Rubber (Pirelli) webbing, 159

Saarinen, Eero, 71, 72, 73–74
Safety considerations, 22, 299–301. *See also*
　　Environmental considerations and hazards
Salginatobel bridge (Switzerland), 15
Sanders (machines), 169
Sapper, Richard, 234
Saws, 165
Scale, *see* Dimensional standards
Scale drawings, 190
Scale model construction, 96
Scale sketches, 183–184
Schultz, Richard, 228
Screws, 154–155
Seating dimensional standards, 273–289
Seconda chair, 79
Senses, *see* Human senses
Sezession movement, 59
Shaker style, 53–54, 281
Shaper (machine), 166
Shear stresses, 98
Sheet metal, 132, 139
Shelf supports, 157
Sheraton, Thomas, 49
Sheraton Venturi chair, 38, 211, 212,
　　213
Side stresses, 104
Side thrust, 89–90, 94
Signature chair, 214
Sketches, 179–184
Sketch models, 184–185
Slenderness ratio, 103–104
Sliding door, 171
Sliding door hardware, 157
Social class, 49, 52, 269
Sottsass, Ettore, 78
Stability, 300
　　axis analysis, 95–96
　　center of gravity and, 90–91
　　defined, 85
Stains, 130
Stam, Mart, 66
Standards (design), 13–16
Staple, 154
Static loads, 86
Steelcase system, 244, 246–247, 260,
　　263
Steelframe storage system, 32–33
Stern, Robert A. M., 214–215
Stickley, Gustav, 59
Stone, 100, 152
Storage, dimensional standards, 291–
　　292
Storage furniture, 71, 238, 240, 268
Streamlining, 69
Strength:
　　analysis of, 98–99
　　defined, 85
　　loads and, 96–98
Stresses, 96–98
　　design considerations and, 99, 101–107

materials and, 100–101
Structural geometry, *see* Geometry
Structure, 23–24
Stumpf, William, 198, 222, 251, 284
Styrene, 144
Sullivan, Louis, 14, 57
Symbolism, 43
Systems furniture, 236–253

Table, dimensional standards, 289–291
Table hardware, 158
Tacks, 154
Taste, *see also* Aesthetics
　　aesthetics and, 19
　　design and, 13, 16–18, 54
Technical considerations, 15–16
Technology, 83–173
　　construction details, 170–173
　　design and, 10–11, 52, 60
　　engineering perspective and, 83–109
　　factory processes/equipment, 163–
　　　164
　　production machinery, 164–170
Tensile stresses, 96–97, 104
Testing, 84
Thermoforming, 148–149
Thermoplastics, 142–143
Thermoset plastics, 144–145
Thonet, Michael, 60–61, 62, 66
Tools, *see* Production machinery
Torsion stresses, 98
Transfer molding, 149
Triangulation, 104, 106–107
Tryglyph table, 215
Tubing (metal), 131–132
Tugendhat chair, 196, 197, 218

Upholstery, 159–163, 169
Upholstery hardware, 158, 160–161
Upholstery nail (tack), 154
Urethane, 145
Utzon, Jørn, 192, 236

Vacuum forming, 149
Van de Velde, Henri, 54, 55
Veneer, 52, 114–115
Venturi, Robert, 38–39, 75, 76, 77, 78, 208–213,
　　224
Verne, Jules, 256
Victorian style, 2, 17, 18, 27–28, 51, 52, 53, 54,
　　77
Vignelli, Massimo, 80, 233, 235
Vinyls, 144
Vitruvius, 18–19

Wagner, Otto, 59
Wassily chair, 28–30, 282
Wegner, Hans, 75
Weights, 87–90
Welding equipment, 169
Windsor chair, 4, 25–27, 49, 50, 219,
　　280